The Poverty of Radical Orthodoxy

POSTMODERN ETHICS SERIES

Postmodernism and deconstruction are usually associated with a destruction of ethical values. The volumes in the Postmodern Ethics series demonstrate that such views are mistaken because they ignore the religious element that is at the heart of existential-postmodern philosophy. This series aims to provide a space for thinking about questions of ethics in our times. When many voices are speaking together from unlimited perspectives within the postmodern labyrinth, what sort of ethics can there be for those who believe there is a way through the dark night of technology and nihilism beyond exclusively humanistic offerings? The series invites any careful exploration of the postmodern and the ethical.

Series Editors:
Marko Zlomislić (Conestoga College)
David Goicoechea (Brock University)

Other Volumes in the Series:

Cross and Khôra: Deconstruction and Christianity in the Work of John D. Caputo edited by Neal DeRoo and Marko Zlomislić

Agape *and Personhood with Kierkegaard, Mother, and Paul (A Logic of Reconciliation from the Shamans to Today)* by David Goicoechea

The Poverty of Radical Orthodoxy

Edited by
Lisa Isherwood and Marko Zlomislić

CONTRIBUTORS:

Marko Zlomislić, Lisa Isherwood, Michael J. Todd,
Katie Terezakis, Leo Stan, Jenny Daggers, Paul Hedges,
Angus Paddison, Sigridur Gudmarsdottir,
Christopher Newell, Marcus Pound

POSTMODERN ETHICS SERIES
3

☞PICKWICK *Publications* • Eugene, Oregon

THE POVERTY OF RADICAL ORTHODOXY

Postmodern Ethics Series 3

Copyright © 2012 Wipf and Stock Publishers. All rights reserved. Except for brief quotations in critical publications or reviews, no part of this book may be reproduced in any manner without prior written permission from the publisher. Write: Permissions, Wipf and Stock Publishers, 199 W. 8th Ave., Suite 3, Eugene, OR 97401.

Pickwick Publications
An Imprint of Wipf and Stock Publishers
199 W. 8th Ave., Suite 3
Eugene, OR 97401

www.wipfandstock.com

ISBN 13: 978–71-60899–937-8

Cataloguing-in-Publication data:

> The poverty of radical orthodoxy / Edited by Lisa Isherwood and Marko Zlomislić.
>
> xiv + 236 ; 23 cm. Includes bibliographical references.
>
> Postmodern Ethics Series 3
>
> ISBN 13: 978–71-60899–937-8
>
> 1. Philosophical theology. I. Title. II. Series.

BT40 P65 2012

Manufactured in the U.S.A.

Contents

List of Contributors | vii

Introduction | xi
Marko Zlomislić *and* Lisa Isherwood

1 **Impoverished Desire** | 1
Lisa Isherwood

2 **Evidential Theology, an Antidote to Orthodoxy:** *An Example* | 13
Michael J. Todd

3 **J. G. Hamann and the Self-Refutation of Radical Orthodoxy** | 32
Katie Terezakis

4 **The Less Sublime Allure of the Paradox:** *Some Kierkegaardian Provocations to John Milbank* | 58
Leo Stan

5 **Girls and Boys Come Out to Play:** *Feminist Theology and Radical Orthodoxy in Ludic Encounter* | 97
Jenny Daggers

6 **Radical Orthodoxy and the Closed Western Theological Mind:** *The Poverty of Radical Orthodoxy in Intercultural and Interreligious Perspective* | 119
Paul Hedges

Contents

7 Reading Yoder against Milbank: *A Yoderian Critique of Radical Orthodoxy* | 144
Angus Paddison

8 Touch, Flux, Relation: *Feminist Critique of Graham Ward's "The Schizoid Christ"* | 164
Sigridur Gudmarsdottir

9 Communities of Faith, Desire, and Resistance: *A Response to Radical Orthodoxy's Ecclesia* | 178
Christopher Newell

10 Paper Cut-outs of Christ in Plato's Cave: *Casting Aside Radical Orthodoxy* | 196
Marko Zlomislić

11 Eucharist *Is* Drive | 213
Marcus Pound

Contributors

Dr Jenny Daggers is Senior lecturer in Theology and Philosophy at Liverpool Hope University, England. Her interests lie in feminist theology and philosophy and their intersection with the Christian tradition. Her books include *The British Christian Women's Movement: The Rehabilitation of Eve*; and *Gendering Christian Ethics*.

Rev Dr Sigridur Gudmarsdottir obtained her PhD from Drew University in the USA. She is a Lutheran minister working in Iceland. Her academic interest lies in the area of ecofeminist theology and she is part of the polydoxy group working on new ways of thinking about the cosmos and theology.

Dr Paul Hedges is Senior lecturer in Theology and Religious Studies at the University of Winchester. His recent publications include *Controversies in Interreligious Dialogue and the Theology of Religions* (2010); *Christian Approaches to Other Faiths: A Reader* (2009, co-edited with Alan Race); and *Christian Approaches to Other Faiths: An Introduction* (2008, co-edited with Alan Race).

Professor Lisa Isherwood FRSA is director of the Institute for Theological Partnerships, University of Winchester. She is a liberation theologian who believes theology to be a communal project fuelled by notions of radical equality and empowered by divine companionship. Her work explores the nature of incarnation within a contemporary context and includes such areas as the body, gender, sexuality, and eco-theology. She has written, co-authored, or edited 19 books such as *The Power of Erotic Celibacy* (2006); *The Fat Jesus: Feminist Explorations in Boundaries and Transgressions* (2007); *Introducing Feminist Christologies* (2001); *Liberating Christ* (1999); and *Patriarchs, Prophets and Other Villains* (editor, 2007).

Contributors

She has been series editor of five international series: Introductions in Feminist Theology; Queer Theology (co-edited with Marcella Althaus-Reid); Theology, Gender & Spirituality; Religion & Violence; and Controversies in Contextual Theology (co-edited with Marcella Althaus-Reid).

Professor Isherwood is an Executive Editor and founding editor of the international journal *Feminist Theology*. From 2007–2009 she was Vice President of the European Society of Women in Theological Research.

Rev Chris Newell is an Anglican priest and mental health chaplain in Cornwall England. He is studying for a doctorate in the area of feminist liberation theology and mental health.

Dr Angus Paddison is a senior lecturer in Theology and Religious Studies at the University of Winchester. His publication include *Scripture: A Very Theological Proposal* (2009); *Paul, Grace and Freedom: Essays in Honour of John K. Riches* (2009, co-edited with Paul Middleton and Karen Wenell); *The Pope and Jesus of Nazareth* (2009, co-edited with Adrian Pabst); and *Christology and Scripture: Inter-disciplinary Perspectives* (2007, co-edited with Andrew Lincoln).

Dr Marcus Pound is Catholic Research Fellow in the Department of Theology and Religion at Durham University. His interests are found at the intersection of continental philosophy and psychoanalysis. In particular, his work is framed in terms of an ongoing engagement with the French psychoanalyst Jacques Lacan and the Slovenian Slavoj Žižek. He has published, *Theology, Psychoanalysis, and Theology* (2007); and *Žižek: A (Very) Critical Introduction* (2008). The former work takes the psychoanalytic metaphor of trauma to rework our understanding of the Eucharist, as well as arguing that psychoanalysis finds its completion in doxology. The latter work takes a critical approach to Slavoj Žižek's social reworking of Lacanian analysis as the basis for rethinking theology.

Dr Leo Stan is a Kierkegaard-existentialism scholar, trained in Judeo-Christianity, with an interest in the phenomenology of religion. He is currently an assistant professor of philosophy at York University in Toronto. He has published numerous articles and book chapters such as "Slavoj Žižek. Mirroring the Absent God," and "Mircea Eliade. On Religion, Cosmos, and Agony," in *Kierkegaard's Influence on the Social Sciences* (2011); "Michel Henry. The Goodness of Living affectivity," in *Kierkegaard and*

Existentialism (2011); and "The Hidden Ethics of Soteriology: A Reconsideration of Kierkegaard's Understanding of the Human Other," *Journal of Religious Ethics* 38.2 (2010).

Dr Katie Terezakis received her Ph.D. in Philosophy in 2004 from the New School for Social Research. Her research interests include German Idealism, Critical Theory, Aesthetics, and the Philosophy of Language. She has published numerous articles and book chapters and is the author of *The Immanent Word: The Turn to Language in German Philosophy, 1759–1801* (2007); the editor of *Engaging Agnes Heller: A Critical Companion* (2009); and the co-editor, with Jack Sanders, of *Lukács's Soul and Form* (2010).

Dr Mike Todd is a retired research scientist who has recently completed a second doctorate at the University of Winchester in the area of theology of marriage.

Dr Marko Zlomislic is professor of philosophy at Conestoga College in Kitchener, Canada. His research interests include Critical Theory, Continental Philosophy and its intersection with Ethics and Theology. He has published *Jacques Derrida's Aporetic Ethics* (2007); and *The Sorrowful Mysteries: A Postmodern Poethics* (2000). He is currently completing a manuscript entitled, *Crossing out the Crucifix*.

Introduction

MARKO ZLOMISLIĆ *and* LISA ISHERWOOD

This is a project that began with an e-mail exchange between two people who had never met—and at the time of publishing still have not! If nothing else, this highlights what community has now come to mean in our hi-tech world of virtual communication. What we share is a concern that Radical Orthodoxy does not go far enough to be radical and sits on the assumption that there is and was an orthodoxy, a claim we do not accept in the light of readings of church history.

Radical Orthodoxy, whose founding father is John Milbank, claims that God has been pushed to the margins in modernity and a false and misleading neo-theology has taken hold, which needs to be revisited and contested. Further, how this happened needs to be investigated and the root causes removed by a return to pre-modern theology. It is this return to the pre-modern which often leads theologians to have reservations about Radical Orthodoxy when they might otherwise have some sympathy for many of its positions. After all, not many people would dispute that God is not a high priority in much of western thinking, let alone seen as the ground of all that is, but not all would see a return to Augustinian or Thomist theology as the way to make God relevant in contemporary society.

Theologians such as Catherine Keller,[1] Diarmuid O'Murchu, and others may prefer to engage with a new cosmology, and in some cases, reflect on how Nicolas Cusa may look through that lens, while yet others may see the way to remove hierarchical dualism as the way God speaks to the modern and even postmodern world. These theologians would not under-

---

1. Catherine Keller, *Face of the Deep: a Theology of Becoming*; Diarmuid O'Murchu, *Quantum Theology: Spiritual Implications of the New Physics*.

Introduction

stand their work as handing God over to a competing power struggle of truth claims, the theological being one among many.[2] Rather, they see it as a renewed engagement with God in the world, but, as said before, to understand this they look ahead, incorporating the newness of God's revelation rather than always looking back; and in so doing, they at times tie themselves to some errors in the old ways of thinking. Errors because no one would claim these days that even Christian theology has a blemishless past, or that it never in its history incorporated into its methods and outcomes beliefs and practices that were oppressive as well as liberating. There will always be error in any kind of thinking, even that which claims to be based on revelation; the key seems to be to be able to see it and move from it, even if this involves dismantling some of the tight-knit theological world that has been created. The lives of people, as the incarnation so clearly shows, are more important than any system of thought.

Perhaps one of the hierarchical assumptions, which many find difficult in Radical Orthodoxy, is that it is really only theology that has truth. In the introduction to *Radical Orthodoxy*, the editors state "in the face of the secular demise of truth, it seeks to reconfigure theological truth."[3] For the liberation theologians amongst us, this is a backward step on two fronts. Firstly, because the working out of the divine in the so-called secular world is seen as being in the realm of orthopraxis, the kinds of actions all can be part of without having a shared theological starting point, the working out of justice being the shared goal. Secondly, from this lived experience what may be known as the divine will become clear. So, there is no rigid set of theological truths that begin the process and determine its moves, but there is an unshakable belief in the love and liberating power of God, who works through the created order and unfolds in that process.

These different starting points also, of course, illustrate where these theological movements sit in relation to power. Radical Orthodoxy, like most traditional theology, claims the power of God is in all creation and God sits everywhere for all to partake of. What they seem to fail to see is that church and theology do not set in place systems that live out this basic assumption. This is where, in this case, Liberation Theology—which shares much of the same assumption that God is everywhere and to be shared—also engages a critique of the structures claiming to facilitate this vision, and it finds them wanting. From here then, liberation theologians

2. Milbank and Oliver, *The Radical Orthodoxy Reader*.
3. Milbank et al., *Radical Orthodoxy*.

attempt to refigure our understanding of shared power in order to broaden the vision, while it may be argued that Radical Orthodoxy simply restates the assumption with little political critique of the issues. Perhaps this point shows why this book is named *The Poverty of Radical Orthodoxy* rather than Radical Error!

Bibliography

Keller, Catherine. *Face of the Deep: A Theology of Becoming*. London: Routledge, 2003.

Milbank, John, and Simon Oliver. *The Radical Orthodoxy Reader*. London: Routledge, 2009.

Milbank, John, et al. *Radical Orthodoxy*. London: Routledge, 1999.

O'Murchu, Diarmuid. *Quantum Theology: Spiritual Implications of the New Physics*. New York: Crossroad, 1999.

1

Impoverished Desire

Lisa Isherwood

Desire has always been a tricky issue for dualistic Christian theology: on the one hand, Christians should have it and it should fuel their pursuit of God, but on the other, it has to be strictly controlled as it is commonly held to be a treacherous emotion that can lead to ruin. Female desire, of course, has been considered the most dangerous, as women have been thought incapable of the spiritual will necessary to control and direct desire toward the right goal. In addition, the Fathers, in this case Augustine, tell us that once we come to God, then desire itself will cease, since its home is in God and the end of all desire is God. We will be restless with desire until we rest in God. This has usually been understood as a final stage, since the living, it is assumed, cannot find union with God necessary for desire to cease. In this scenario, we come to understand desire as a rather troubling aspect of what it means to be human, an emotion that should be directed to God, but one that is unsettling, problematic, and easily misled. In short, it is an emotion that should make us on edge with ourselves—a blessing and a curse. While this may work well within Christian theology, and it is a position most would recognize, it perhaps leads to lives cautiously lived in fear for ourselves; thus, perhaps this is not celebrated in quite the way the incarnational strand of Christian theology could and should lend itself to. We fail to see ourselves as the original blessings Matthew Fox urges us to be, and we have half an eye to the ever-lurking possibility of rampant desire leading to disaster.

The Poverty of Radical Orthodoxy

It would, of course, be quite unfair to suggest Christian theology alone has placed us in this tense and in the "on guard" position with ourselves. Deleuze and Guattari believe the troubling nature of desire entered our consciousness when Plato associated it with acquisition. This association made it, they claim, a dualistic concept with, on the one hand acquisition, and on the other lack.[1] It also meant desire, by its very nature, must always go unsatisfied, as according to this scheme when desired object is present desire will cease. Of course, the desired object must also be thought of and created in the mind's eye, or else there would be no trigger for desire in the face of lack. Fantasy therefore plays a large part in this formation of desire. Perhaps we can then begin to understand why Christianity has sat easily with this view of desire, since it has at its center a God it cannot see but desires to know and be in the presence of. The being with God will not only bring about the end of desire, but in some sense it will lead to the revelation of the true self, who has, for some theologians, been only partially known when desiring God. By implication, if there is to remain a self, then there must also remain desire; it must always be unsatisfied.

The idea of losing one's self once desire is satisfied sits very uneasily with me and other feminist theologians, since we have observed and experienced the suppression of female desire and the limiting and, at times, destructive results of such a move. To be fair to the tradition, it does have within it one or two who have a more positive outlook on desire, for example, Pseudo-Dionysius, who credited God's creative power to God's other directed desire. Pseudo-Dionysius could imagine a God who lacks nothing but desires everything, and who in the act of creation also creates desire. Although this is part of the tradition, it is not a part that is usually highlighted. However, in Carter Heyward we find something of an echo when she says:

> In the beginning was God
> In the beginning was the source of all that is
> God yearning
> God moaning
> God labouring
> God giving birth
> God rejoicing
> And God loved what She had made
> And God said
> "It is good"

---

1. MacKendrick, *Word Made Flesh*, 12.

> And God knowing that all that is good is shared
> Held the Earth tenderly in Her arms
> God yearned for relationship
> God longed to share the good Earth,
> And humanity was born in the yearning of God
> We were born to share the Earth.[2]

Here we see that if God loves us, indeed, desires our very creation, then we are needed, since: "A lover needs relation—if for no other reason, in order to love."[3] And further, we too are required to love, to desire in response to the desire that brought us into existence. This is a rather different starting point in the consideration of desire from many orthodox theologians. For Heyward, God's creative power is the power to love and to be loved, to desire and be desired. Heyward declares it was this incarnate, loving, dynamic, relating God that Jesus declared through the incarnation. For it was here that God could be touched, held, and desired. It was in flesh that the desire, of which both Pseudo-Dionysius and Heyward refer to, could be fully lived out as the relationality of the ever-desiring God became possible as a mutually relating and desiring relationship. Heyward suggests Jesus saw no difference between our love for our God and our love for our neighbor [Mark 12:28–31]. Therefore, we are laboring to create a new life based on mutual love, one in which "we are dealing with a real love for man for his own sake and not for the love of God."[4] There can be no passive observance if we are to be in mutual relation. Heyward is not alone, of course, in talking about the love of God, but for her it is a love that is passionate, erotic, and desiring, not a sanitized form of love that Christianity has been able to handle once it is stripped of any passion or desire.

Heyward sees this as quite contrary to what the life of Jesus was meant to highlight and not in line with what the gospels proclaim. She asserts that humans must dare to acknowledge their divine nature through *dunamis*, which is the gospel term for our raw, dynamic, erotic power, a power that draws us out to each other in vulnerable mutuality. This is the power she claims Jesus lived by and left as our heritage; it is radical love through the skin and in the world, pulsating with desire and transforming potential. She claims radical love incarnates the kingdom because intimacy is the deepest quality of relation. Heyward says to be intimate is to be assured we are

---

2. Heyward, *Our Passion For Justice*, 49–50.
3. Heyward, *The Redemption of God*, 7.
4. Ibid., 16.

known in such a way that the mutuality of our relation is real, creative, and cooperative. It is possible to see Jesus's ministry as based on intimacy, since he knew people intuitively, insightfully, and spontaneously. Most of all, Heyward's Christology is fully embodied, sensuous, and erotic, seeking vulnerable commitment, alive with expectancy and power. This is not a Christology that could ever imagine our desiring should or could cease, since it is in the very nature of God to desire eternally, as made incarnate and demonstrated in the life of Jesus. Further, it is an idea of God which requires us to be fully human, to embody a self, and to touch others through that enfleshed self in order to learn how to increase the transforming power of radical love in the world. This view may seem a very great distance from what we have understood as traditional theology, but there appears to be echoes of Pseudo-Dionysius here, as well as a solid gospel base for what Heyward claims. It might be this kind of theology, then, we could expect to see in any movement with "radical" in the title, and this level of engagement with both biblical and traditional questions, as well as questions of humanity and who we may be.

Radical Orthodoxy, of course addresses the issue of desire, but to a large extent it simply dresses up the long-standing orthodox position in order to appeal to more radical audiences.[5] For the most part, the realities of being human are largely placed within a pre-existing theological frame, thus drowning any authentic voice of enfleshed humanity. The end result then, is still very much the same: desire is seen as a mixed blessing that only finds its end in God. However, when we turn to Daniel Bell's book *Liberation Theology and the End of History*, we find that a large part of his argument deals with desire and the fact that it has been captured by the forces of capitalism, which sounds as though it may actually get to grips with people and the systems they struggle under. Any initial hopes are soon dampened when Bell tells us what we need is a "therapy of desire," which he believes lies in forgiveness.[6] Through returning God's gift of forgiveness of us to others, we are liberated from the hold of capitalism. God did not demand what was due to him, rather he forgave us and gave up on the terror of justice as Bell sees it. Bell states, "the claim that forgiveness more faithfully characterizes the way God overcomes sin than does the liberationists' account of justice rests upon an interpretation of the atonement."[7]

---

5. Hanby, "Desire: Augustine Beyond Western Subjectivity," 109–26.
6. Bell, *Liberation Theology and the End of History*, 143.
7. Ibid., 146.

This interpretation is, of course, that of substitution atonement, which has certain problems attached to it. We may not have paid, but an innocent did, an interpretation that sits well with savage capitalism, since Christ's sacrifice is interpreted as belonging to an economy of credit and exchange, which is reimaged as a gift of love, a point Bell seems to entirely overlook. Bell understands those events as Jesus returning the gift of love and obedience to God[8]—the fact is, there was a crucifixion and this should not be overlooked, even in the light of a resurrection, in the world in which we live today. Bell, in fact, does not overlook it, but he states that crucified people are bearers of salvation in the world—that is, of course, as long as they do not complain about their crucifixion, and their communities remain open and hospitable to those who have oppressed and crucified their compatriots.[9] Bell finds it amazing that, despite the fact that the blood and tears of the poor make capitalism grind on, they do not lash out. They forgive. They open their doors and share what they have. This is a very sentimentalized view, the kind that allows us to place the blood and pain within a greater scheme that has the effect of neutralizing it through an argument about greater goods. It is not based in much reality either, since in the countries Bell speaks of, there has historically been resistance, which has been met with U.S. backed defeat. America has not been slow to bomb countries that do not fall into line, train torturers of regimes that hold people in bondage, and provide money to governments that fulfill its global aspirations. We see if we transfer his argument to the Middle East, there are outcomes other than forgiveness. Bell is, however, insistent that forgiveness is the first step and once people receive grace they will change their ways. He boldly states that capitalism can't handle forgiveness. This is the male theology feminists have been critiquing for decades. It is the kind that valorizes suffering, seeing it as a way to ontologically change reality. Children continue to die and women continue to sell their bodies to feed their dying children (a reality which is now in Iraq as well as many other parts of the world), but if aligned with the suffering and obedience of Christ, all will be ultimately well. This seems to me to be a green light for savage capitalism, which does not have to worry about suffering, but can console itself because it gives people the opportunity to be noble, heroic, and salvific for themselves and others under its crushing weight. As feminist liberation theologians have endlessly pointed out, this is a narrative that only works in theory. When

---

8. Ibid., 150.
9. Ibid., 168.

placed against the lived experience of women and men, new stories emerge that are less reassuring to the supporters of this slightly warped theology. Suffering and oppression take their toll in the lives of people who do not necessarily become ennobled by it—they simply become reduced and worn down, dehumanised, and marginalized.

Bell, however, is relentless. He says reparation is never possible, and for Liberation Theology to look for it is futile. Unjust suffering is not overcome by looking for justice but by being borne, just as Christ bore his own unjust suffering—it is the refusal to cease suffering, which is the great act of hope in God; and this is the only solution to savage capitalism. It may be an act of hope, but it flies in the face of the God who left the heavens in order that all may have life in abundance! At the heart of this theology is crucified power where the community of the crucified gather together, and where God empowers them and delivers them from being disempowered victims.[10] These are extraordinary claims from an author who early in his work called for religion and politics to be closer bedfellows and criticized even Liberation Theology for not being radical enough. It illustrates the way in which many of those who claim to espouse radical theology can double back on themselves. This happens when they wish to be radical in the application of their theology without being radical with the core beliefs of their theology. I do not wish to suggest there is no theological mileage in forgiveness, but my own feeling is it works best on the individual level, where people look each other in the eye when there is equality in the way in which reconciliation will be worked for. I also feel when we are considering multinationals, other means may be necessary.

To his credit, Bell does wonder if forgiveness makes people more vulnerable, which for him is a weakness. However, for Carter Heyward, our response to fear and uncertainty should be an embrace of vulnerability. Vulnerability, for her, is Christic in nature, is one that truly opens us to mutuality in relation and offers redemptive possibilities. Vulnerability, in her theological scheme, also involves engaging with social and economic injustice,[11] not simply "feeling" vulnerable in order to have some inner experience that moves us on. For Heyward, as for many feminist theologians, the very nature of Christ is relational and ethical; therefore, any statement or suggested way of living to be considered Christian must have justice and openness at the heart. There seems to be little that can be exchanged here

---

10. Ibid., 192.
11. Heyward, *Our Passion for Justice*, 79.

with Bell and his fellow theologians when he is still moving from the place of the God who overcomes it all, in whom vulnerability has no place. This may indeed be orthodox, but it is not very radical.

Bell argues for the urgent recovery of desire, understanding as he does Deleuze's claim that capitalism does not only exert power by extracting labor and production, but by capturing and distorting the fundamental human power of desire. Mary Grey has reminded us that this reclaiming of desire is also a language game because the language of desire, once the domain of theologians, has been taken over by the High Priests of the market. While we continue to long and yearn for the new car, the new house, and all the goods that shine so brightly, we silence God. She is right, but I would also wish to point out that the traditional language of theology also sounds like that of the market. In other words, the market did not totally distort it, there were traces there of capitalist exchange in the beginning! Grey engages with the work of Tim Gorringe in order to come to a fuller understanding of what this process of recovering desire may involve. For Gorringe, there is a need to develop a renewed theology of the senses, which he understands as possible through a wider notion of sacramentality.[12] He argues that a revaluation of the place of *eros* will enliven Christians to find alternatives in a world of bland sameness. However, for him this *eros* is best situated within a Eucharistic understanding and best celebrated within the same context. The obvious drawback here is that not all people attend church and not all find the liturgy to be a place for renewing and reviving the senses. Gorringe attempts to confine the *eros* Heyward has re-released in the Christian tradition, the raw power of dynamic connection, which in her theology underpins and propels us to the vulnerability in mutual relation she advocates as the way to wage peace. Although I am sure it was not his intension, his portrayal of *eros* tends to build boundaries and create us-and-them, rather than releasing us into a dance of erotic connection, which I understand as redemptive praxis.

We have to acknowledge that the Christian God and the salvation he offers has always had hints of an exchange economy. This exchange economy is evident in some of the more bloody notions of substitution atonement, where the exchange is seen as fair and the sacrifice sufficient in order that the gift of salvation may be bestowed—the price has been paid and the wages of sin satisfied. It is no accident, therefore, that it tends to be fundamentalist

---

12. Tim Gorringe, *The Education of Desire*, 194.

Protestants who make links between financial prosperity and salvation, totally encompassing the suffering of others into their blessed life.

Bell overlooks this glaring problem and prefers to profess that our desire is restless in consumerism, which consumerism encourages, because its true end is found in God. What Bell, like so many others in Radical Orthodoxy, is doing here is asserting, along with Francis Fukuyama,[13] that we are at the end of history and nothing new is possible. All we have before us is repetition and the spread of one ideology. Ironically, while wishing to challenge this view in relation to advanced capitalism and its hold on the soul, he uses the same theological repetitions in order to attempt to advance the cause. While his suggestion that we are restless until we find rest in God is not a new suggestion, it has a new twist when Bell suggests to achieve this fulfillment of desire we should examine the world of the twelfth century monastery. Bell asserts we are constituted by desire for God, a desire that has been corrupted through sin, which bends desire towards unnatural ends. Capitalism is one such sin that disciplines and enslaves desire, and Christianity "is a therapy, a way of life that releases desire from its bondage"[14] in order that desire may flow again.

Relying heavily on Deleuze and Foucault, Bell argues the subject is an assemblage of desires in varying intensities captured as it is by particular regimes. The state and capitalism include a host of what Foucault calls technologies of the self,[15] but, says Bell, so is Christianity; it works with technologies of desire and this is its great strength in overcoming capitalism.[16] Liberation theology, with its appeal to justice, has failed precisely because it does not work on this level of desires; it does not have a therapy for desire. Of course, the big assumption Bell makes here, which I wish to challenge, is desire for justice is itself misguided, and so not real and correctly aimed desire. Bell seems unable to understand God as justice, a concept biblical in origin, and so he is able to relegate the desire for justice to some second-rate position. It is also necessary to understand human desire as distorted if he is to do this. Feminist liberation theologies certainly have what Bell would wish to call a therapy for desire, and it is Christological in nature, understanding our very passions and desires, our *dunamis*, to be the stuff of Christ. The therapy for desire is, in this case, being able to embrace and

13. See Fukuyama, *The End of History and the Last Man*.
14. Bell, *Liberation Theology and the End of History*, 3.
15. Ibid., 19.
16. Ibid., 2.

develop the passion that draws us into mutuality with one another and not just with an abstract God. What is called for is an engagement with all that makes us human—passion, desire, and relationality—in order to be grounded more fully in who we are, rather than uprooted still further through a "therapy" that assumes some innate dysfunction, which can only be put right through rooting in an external divine.

We may be alarmed to know that it is through a re-evaluation of Cistercian monasticism that Bell believes we can rehabilitate desire, understanding it as something that springs from God and in its true form is full of God. Within the monastery, distorted impulses "were sublimated, redirected or re-channelled into a spiritual engagement: doing battle and winning glory for the sake of divine love and the Divine Lover."[17] At first glance, Bell appears to be reassessing desire, which he says has had poor press in Christian theology. But here lurks the same basic assumption that desire, even if it was good once, is not so anymore due to the fall; it needs monastic discipline to rehabilitate it through battle, and the winning of glory for the divine who is clearly imaged as external to our being. He still places at the center of our being alienation, competition, and overcoming/subduing, all of which deliver us into the system he speaks so vehemently against. The notion that life is unfolding, drawn out by desire and fueled by erotic energy that is the raw stuff of the divine, seems to have passed him by.

Bell's valorization of military discipline when considering desire does nothing but continue the alienation from self, which is destructive to our desires and passions and allows us to destroy others in the name of this alienation from self. I wish to suggest most traditional Christian theology, with its insistence on dualism, encourages us to do necessary damage to ourselves through a fundamental removal of ourselves from our passion, and by extension, enables us to create enemies and learn to hate through that same fundamental distrust that dualistic thinking fosters. What is needed in my opinion is engagement with raw/radical incarnation, the vulnerability and bravery to feel and to touch—after all incarnational theology is a skin trade. Dualistic theology rips us from ourselves and cauterizes us, enfeebling our judgment, our heart, and our passion. When we look at savage capitalism and what it leads to, that is the violence and alienation between peoples we have to create theology that makes such ways of being "unfeelable" within our skins. I think we have to take incarnation much more seriously, to take

---

17. Ibid., 93.

the flesh as the place where the utopian vision of heaven is felt and lived—we have to enflesh the Christ in whom we are baptized and profess to believe in.

I understand Jesus to be a comrade who invites us into transgressive praxis, not a "school of charity." I understand Jesus as one who made a hole—created a space, read the gaps—in what was hitherto understood as reality, then invited others to join the justice-seeking transformation that becomes possible when we understand reality differently. The full living out of *dunamis* through transgressive praxis is the incarnational reality we are asked to embrace; it is Christ. I have argued in the past[18] for an understanding of incarnation as the flesh becoming word, which is the drawing out through engaged praxis—skin on skin—of our Christic natures, and the living of what it is we prefer to project into the realm of metaphysics. The flesh made word enables us to find a voice and to make our desires known—we do not have to conform to agreed absolutes, but rather discover where *dunamis* leads us. Further, our bodies and the bodies of others, far from being aliens to us through the basis disassociation much Christian doctrine has required, become sites of moral imperatives. We can no longer witness the genocides of advanced capitalism when we understand the incarnation to be in your skin and in mine. I do not wish to do away with the utopian vision that the distance of metaphysics has traditionally supplied; rather I wish to see it incarnated here and now, amongst us—I wish to see it enfleshed, because in that way the nuts and bolts of what it means have to be worked out on the skin of people. We have to enflesh incarnation deep in the marrow of who we are, stripped of the trappings of false and created identities, be they commercial or theological. In my view, this entails desire and lots of it if we are to truly connect with others and ourselves in a way that leads to passionate counter-cultural living. Such living is not achieved by those who have given up a sense of self in the greater abundance of God, or constrained their desire in order to fit patterns of living in a discreet manner.

In claiming to be radical, Radical Orthodoxy does not in my view go far enough. It seems to require of itself that what it understands as the basic doctrine of Christianity remain static—something that it actually has never done—and that this static nature somehow makes it orthodox, again a very contentious claim when looking at the history of Christianity. In the example above, it seems more than human for those who suffer to desire to be free of it, rather than to have to discipline their desire and find it within

---

18. Isherwood, *Liberating Christ*.

themselves to forgive. Desire, it seems, always seeks to break limits and so most certainly has its place at the heart of struggles against the limiting of humanity that is the result of advanced capitalism. Of course, a realist would have to admit that the victories, if any, that liberation theologies have achieved when facing up to capitalism have been few and limited, but this is no reason to claim desire, both for freedom and as a fuel for the fight, has in itself been found wanting. Forgiveness does not seem to be the way ahead within a system which is itself unforgiving and relentless. Such a suggestion even points to collusion in the oppression in some ways.

The suggestion that desire is a lack—and with that understanding it can be used in the way it has been by Radical Orthodoxy—is really to miss something fundamental about its very nature. Desire, when understood as the nature of God, can easily be seen as something that can be satisfied but insatiable; as the Christian God is seen as infinite then too can desire be infinite. Once more for the Christian who is invited to join the dance of incarnation that form of desire is what we are called to experience. The place of satisfaction then becomes one that does not signal anything lacking, but rather it helps fuel the striving of humans who may otherwise be rather downcast if no satisfaction without extinction were not possible. After all, God created and saw it was good, was satisfied with creation, but went on desiring that very creation and the loving exchange that creation enabled.

Perhaps another oversight that is often made is to acknowledge that desire is also intellectual, not simply somatic,[19] but further that it does have the ability to give a language to things that are often hard to know. In this way then it is invaluable in the process of incarnation to which we are all called. The notion that the self who is able to have any intellectual insight should somehow cease to be because desire will cease in God seems to be a counter-intuitive argument, since the God who is the author of desire also needs to continue to know and engage through the created order so dearly loved. Certainly, from the perspective of a feminist liberation theologian it seems that Radical Orthodoxy overlooks much of the theology which has gone on in recent years, seeing it as not grounded sufficiently in what has come before. This is not a correct assumption and one that does not give enough credit to those attempting to tackle current problems from a solid theological base. In this case of the question of desire there is an impoverishment desire which limits the full incarnational potential of the created

---

19. McKendrick, *Word Made Flesh*, 45.

order and to some degree the infinity of God through the suggestion that desire ceases.

Bibliography

Bell, Daniel. *Liberation Theology and the End of History*. London: Routledge, 2001.

Fukuyama, Francis. *The End of History and the Last Man*. New York: Free Press, 1992.

Gorringe, Tim. *The Education of Desire*. London: SCM, 2002.

Hanby, Michael. "Desire: Augustine Beyond Western Subjectivity." In *Radical Orthodoxy*, edited by John Milbank et al, 109–116. London: Routledge, 1999.

Heyward, Carter. *Our Passion for Justice: Images of Power and Sexuality and Liberation*. New York: Pilgrim Press, 1984.

———. *The Redemption of God: A Theology of Mutual Relation*. Lanham: University Press of America, 1982.

Isherwood, Lisa. *Liberating Christ*. Cleveland: Pilgrim Press, 1999.

MacKendrick, Karmen. *Word Made Flesh: Figuring Language on the Surface of the Flesh*. New York: Fordham University Press, 2004.

2

Evidential Theology, an Antidote to Orthodoxy: An Example

Michael J. Todd

Introduction

My doctoral thesis[1] set out to establish a fresh approach to marriage theology, using three situations with little or no history in order to address perceived weaknesses in current orthodoxy. In order to undertake that work, a methodology was created which was named *Evidential Theology* (ET), together with a further development called *Uncertain Theology* (UT). This essay is written from the particular perspective of seeking a theology of marriage and the aim here is to see to what extent Radical Orthodoxy (RO) may provide an alternative basis. It is not intended to be a detailed critique of RO across the board, in the terms in which RO sets itself.

It appears to be a constant fact of human nature to seek new ideas and wider understanding of the world around us, and yet also to cling to the comfort of the familiar, the traditional. The one excites us and gives hope that the future will not be as hard as the past whilst the other reassures us that the future can be understood on the basis of the past.

Innovation is the means by which we seek to escape from the demonstrable short-comings of what we already know or have. Orthodoxy is the litmus test which every new idea has to pass: that whatever successes it may

1. Todd, "Marriage at the Edges."

have in addressing past difficulties, it must be at least as good as what went before. On the other hand, orthodoxy finds innovation a challenge and can easily resort to defenses which ignore the benefits that can be sought in moving forward. It is also easy for those who espouse tradition to forget that the orthodox was once an innovation, but an innovation that stood the test of time and experience.

ET and RO are reactions to both modernism and postmodernism. To caricature: modernism seeks to use the knowledge of science to prove—on an agenda set by scientific method—things about God, such as his existence and his nature. Postmodernism finds that no observation of the world is objective or absolute and therefore all views are equally valid. Whilst postmodernism can be congratulated on the way in which it gives value to experiences wherever they are found—not restricting them to an elite—it leaves us with the often impossible task of having to re-invent solutions at great cost when a perfectly serviceable solution is already at hand. The law of gravity may only be an approximate description of how things behave, but it is good enough for most practical, everyday purposes, and we rely on it to avoid having to deduce its conclusions every time we drop a cup on the floor. (Whilst some writers—e.g., Smith[2]—claim RO to be postmodern, in reality it is better described as post-secular or even, in some criticism, pre-secular.)

Whilst RO seeks to address the limitations of modernism by setting aside secular thought processes, ET provides a means of using them effectively to guide theological conclusions. Evidence is the antidote to orthodoxy.

Evidential Theology

ET is based firmly on the belief that God not only reveals himself and his intentions through the world, but is incarnate in that world. Furthermore, incarnation is not a fixed matter: God continues to be incarnate in the world and that world is the only means we have by which we can gain some degree of comprehension of what God is and what he intends, in the past, in the present, and in the future. This fundamental assertion means that our knowledge of God is not only limited by how much we have been able to learn about the world, but also by our point in time within that incarnation. Conclusions which it may have been reasonable to draw at one point may be overtaken by greater knowledge and experience at a later time. This

2. Smith, *Introducing Radical Orthodoxy*.

does not invalidate those earlier conclusions—which in any case are mere approximations—but serves to highlight the fact that we cannot know all that there is to know about something that is infinite in time as much as in any other sense.

ET adopts a classical approach to scientific method, one predominantly of seeking to disprove a counter hypothesis, allowing us to hold to an *a priori* assumption. The method recognizes that it can never prove—in the sense asserted by modernists—but can prevent error. (This approach is fundamental in the mathematics of statistical significance: correlation cannot prove X is related to Y and certainly not that X *causes* Y, but can potentially refute the possibility.)

Of course, some aspects of the incarnate world may tell us more, and be more specific, than others. Christian churches place particular regard on the role of scripture as a form of revelation, but we do well to keep in mind that any human process, even if we believe it to be God acting in and through it, is inherently finite and can therefore only be an approximation. Yet, we have nothing else to go on: we know nothing other than what we have taken in through our senses. Without looking at the world around us we can know nothing of God. A world of utter isolation is inherently God-less.

But this is not a modernist view: it does not suggest that simply by looking at the world we will inevitably conclude that not only does God exist, but we can read off a script of what it is God intends for humankind (see Moore[3] for a critique of this approach). Nevertheless, we have to recognize the damage modernism has done in that there are still large numbers of people who instinctively assume either that it is a valid method or that Christian theology necessarily embraces it. This is the root of the vulnerability of critics such as Dawkins, who rail against Christian theology by taking advantage that most people who believe the church broadly subscribes to the modernist agenda.

More recently, Hawking has suggested in *The Grand Design* that the laws of physics will provide all that is needed to "describe" how the big bang created our universe—he also posits the existence of other universes of which we cannot have any direct awareness. That much presents no problem for theology, but when he transforms "describe" into "causes" there are significant issues. Of course, science cannot prove—or disprove—the existence of God, and to suggest so is a category error.

---

3. Moore, *The Body In Context*.

Even worse is the notion that God exists because the church exists. The failings of the church, both collectively and as individuals, suggest that even if such a God did exist he is not one to be admired, let alone worshipped and adored. As if humanity's assessment of God's qualities could make him disappear! ET is driven more by a classical scientific agenda and refuses to buy into its perversion by late modernist atheists.

If we accept that incarnation is a continuous and continuing process—one in which God maintains a relationship with the world as something which is alive and growing—then we more easily come to terms with the fact that we cannot know all there is to know about God and his intentions for us, not just because we do not have infinite capabilities, but because it has yet to happen. This is not to say God is circumscribed or defined by time as a dimension, any more than by any other dimension, geometric or otherwise. But it does say past observations are true only insofar as they describe the collective experience up to that point. Human wisdom *is* constrained by dimensionality as much as by context and experience.

This recognition is a healthy counterweight to the tendency to want to believe that we already own the truth and it remains only a matter of evangelism to communicate that wisdom to the unbelievers. Down this route lies arrogance, as encapsulated in the story of Babel, that a single message is all that is needed or justified. To suggest everything we do, feel, experience, think, or say can be expressed in a single language makes huge assumptions about our ability—or at least that of the collective ability of tradition to encompass all there is to know, especially about God and his intentions. Language, and by this we include the different ways of thinking, which are expressed in terms such as theology and scientific method, is only able to contain that which we have already experienced, collated and understood. If, however, as we have asserted above, the incarnation of God in the world is continuous and continuing on an unending basis, then we have to accept that any particular language will only be able to capture some specific perspective on that infinity. Words rarely have a static meaning and a literal text today may have to be heavily interpreted tomorrow in order to recover its original intent. Theology, specifically Christian theology, has to have the humility to accept input from wherever it may come, as evidence, not to be driven by it, but rather to be tested by it. Dissonance between different languages may, as in Babel, be inevitable, but we have to learn from those points of difference. We may well continue to need many languages in order to encapsulate even our finite experience of God's infinite incarnation.

A theology that depends too closely on one language, fixed in time, runs into difficulties sooner or later. Despite the expectations of twentieth century linguistic investigation, the existence of a Deep Structure (Chomsky) that gives a single, consistent meaning to expressions from different languages has proved elusive. We have to come to terms with the fact that translations are only ever approximate. If we are not careful, this can lead to a situation in which what we assert about God is different, based on language and the associated cultures. Problems also arise in the context of learning disability: ecclesiology and liturgy have become increasingly cerebral and dependent on language, without giving particular concern about what this does for people with limitations on using or understanding words.

In ET we assert that what we glean from our study and experience of the world we inhabit must moderate what it is reasonable to assert within our theology. A critical example is that of Galileo and the sentence attributed to him in Brecht's dramatization of the conflict between science and the church in relation to astronomical observations: "But it moves." In saying this, Galileo recognizes how his observations of planetary motion make it unreasonable for theology to assert a contrary view that the sun revolves around the earth. The observations, like any scientific "law," do not dictate either to God or to theology, but we would have to have some very good explanation why we would wish to continue to believe, for example, in a flat earth rather than a round one.

In the same way, ET allows us to take into account conclusions from other discourses such as that which arises from Rights Languages: if there is a consensus view that certain human rights exist, and perhaps are inalienable, then we have to have a very good explanation in order to assert theologically that they are to be denied.

Uncertain Theology

A further development of ET is that of Uncertain Theology (UT), based on drawing parallels with the changes in physics during the earlier part of the 20C, that the world cannot be wholly described in the deterministic manner which Newtonian Mechanics claimed to be able to do.

UT allows for the possibility that there may not be a single and univocal response to specific theological, and more especially, ethical issues. It asserts that there are situations in which the more we attempt to be precise about a certain matter, the less certain we become about counterbalancing factors.

Milbank appears to misrepresent modern physics.[4] The uncertainty of physics is very different from the postmodern rejection of certainty. In fact, what quantum mechanics establishes is that certainty in one dimension *can* be obtained, but only at the expense of complete uncertainty in another. This is very different from claiming nothing is certain; in the sense of modern physics, some things are most definitely certain, not "everything is always somewhat partial and uncertain, veiled, fragmentary and never foreclosed."[5] The ongoing incarnation on which ET is built does not require an instantaneous uncertainty. Rather, it accepts that what may reasonably be concluded as definite at this time can change into something else, either at a different time or different place.

In some ways, this builds on Jesus's dictum: Give to Caesar what is Caesar's, and to God what is God's (Matt 22:21). In saying this, it is recognized that different expressions of truth may appear in different domains, neither of which can be wholly asserted over the other. The more precisely we seek to define a particular ethic, the less we will know about God.

Radical Orthodoxy

It is not the place of this chapter to provide a comprehensive or unified criticism of RO. Our aim is to identify points at which it is at variance with our ET in order to establish whether the latter is able to provide either the antidote or control the way RO reaches its conclusions, or whether RO is a better basis, giving improved solutions to the problems of marriage theology we seek to address, where tradition has held too strong a stranglehold over evidence.

Milbank continues to accept it is a valid description of RO that it is primarily about rejection: rejection of everything that has happened since Scotus made—for Milbank and others—the first erroneous steps towards secularism and modernism. That RO rejects both secularism and modernism is not surprising in that both depend on a belief in the physical world as an ultimate authority, in and of itself. By contrast, ET relies on the evidence it takes from the physical world only because of its relationship with incarnation and its means of communication with God.

Almost all of the arguments advanced by RO writers return to Augustine and Aquinas, with a touch of Plato thrown in, without ever identifying

---

4. Milbank and Oliver, *The Radical Orthodoxy Reader*, 31.
5. Ibid.

why that particular point in the evolution of theology and philosophy should be so authoritative. There is very little recourse to Scripture, other than moderated through the views of Augustine and Aquinas. Everything since then is rejected—sometimes for little more than that it is inconsistent with their chosen baseline.

The Consultant's Nostrum goes like this: "You have a system/idea/product/method (X) which has a problem or deficiency. I have a solution for you," and indeed, the consultant's proposal does solve those defects. However, the question that then has to be asked is how well does the proposal stand up against all the ways in which the existing X is entirely successful. All too often, the consultant's idea fails in many more ways than it succeeds, but is often adopted because it is much easier to focus on the failings of the past X rather than to identify its successes.

Evolution acts as a filter to the Consultant's Nostrum allowing valuable new ideas to progress whilst leaving behind those which are less effective overall than what was already in place. One of the questions which RO has yet to answer is what does a return to a much earlier position say about the issues which newer thinking sought to address. Developments such as liberalism, modernism, postmodernism, secularism, and statism all took root and survived for considerable time exactly because they correctly identified weaknesses in what went before and found better ways. The fact that, eventually, such solutions themselves are found to have fault lines is not itself a reason for going backwards.

Look at sub-atomic physics. Just because the electron model of the atom was not found to be perfect was no excuse for seeking a return to Newtonian mechanics. Rather, we always need to build on what has been successful and seek to be more successful, not less. As we shall see later in the case of Marriage Theology, the "orthodox" position is failing just because there are now situations which did not exist in the times when that orthodoxy was formulated. There simply is no earlier, more orthodox position worth reclaiming.

RO clearly rejects statism—the over-riding role of the state in regulating human behavior, seeing it as a failed consequence of liberalism. In its place it constructs an alternative authority: the church. Although wanting to see something that does not repeat the worst excess of church-dominated societies of the past, nevertheless RO espouses an ultimate autocracy. It does so on the basis that, expressed "properly," Christian theology should lead to an inherently peaceful and benign community. RO appears to say very little about the nature of humanity (other than referring everything back to Augustine and Aquinas) and so does not accept unredeemed humankind—Original Sin, perhaps. In a practical context, we have to accept that this world, and any community within it, is imperfect and that we need some degree of authority to guarantee the safety of individual citizens. Increasingly, societies across the world have encapsulated their concept of what it means to be human in a set of Rights which states have the duty to maintain. The evidence in front of us is clearly that, in the absence of such codes and their guarantors, society (and that includes the church) does not act in the interests of individuals—something that has been the case across a wide variety of periods in time, liberal, modern, postmodern, and, yes, pre-modern. There does not appear to have been a period (certainly post-lapsarian) when this has not been the case. But the expression of Rights is not necessarily always consonant with Christian principles and a method must be found for accommodating these differences—Uncertain Theology seeks to recognize this, without falling into the trap of wanting a deterministic or univocal answer.

Some aspects of RO seem to echo the ET emphasis on seeking God incarnate by observing the world about us: ". . . at the heart of Radical Orthodoxy's vision is participation. All creation shares in the nature of God."[6] However, the obvious consequence of this observation—that which exists must be considered to be of God, even if it does not easily fit into the patterns which our (orthodox) theology constrains our response. Nevertheless, Milbank remains adamant, "I think there is a fundamental conviction among all people who inaugurated the movement that there's something unreal about a lot of sincere religious belief and practice at the moment, that too many people are looking at nature and society in a basically secular way, with spirituality tacked on."[7] This, we insist, is—as is explored further below—to confuse science with engineering: exploration with intent.

One of the points at which ET and RO diverge is in the assumption that God's creation must be orderly and inherently "beautiful"—notwithstanding the problem that beauty is culturally dependent. Even with the benefit of Occam's Razor to guide us, the created order displays endless untidiness, which is neither simple nor necessarily beautiful. We must find God in the ugly just as much as we find him in the good looking.

---

6. Shakespeare, *Radical Orthodoxy*, 30.
7. Milbank and Oliver, *The Radical Orthodoxy Reader*, 29.

Montag (Milbank et al. 1999) comes closer to ET in asserting that "revelation . . . concerns pieces of information which God has decided to impart."[8] What is not clear is whether he accepts the idea that God continues—by way of on-going incarnation—to make that "decision to impart" in a way that makes our perception of him an infinitely evolving process.

The views of the Church equally diverge. RO sets a high ideal for the Church, as an extension of the incarnation,[9] such that it can become the ultimate authority, the determinant of what is ethically right and what is wrong. As such, it seems to lose the Servant role, key to both Old Testament and New Testament theologies. ET seeks to put the church at the service of humanity, determining its role and action on the basis of evidence: client-led care, as it were.

Evidential Theology as an Antidote

Whilst RO seeks to find truth primarily in and through the church, pre-eminently in the Eucharist, ET places a high value on seeking God where he put himself first and foremost: in the reality of the created universe. But we do not have a simple, almost bucolic view of creation and nature: rather, what humankind has done with the world is as much part of creation as Adam and Eve in the first place, a practical outworking of God's creation plan, as it were. If we seek God in this way then we have to admit into our evidence all human constructs and behavior, just as much as any other part of the universe. This universe is not something static or even fixed at some (past) point of creation, but continues to evolve in a way that requires us to accept God is making a continuous input—incarnation—which is a very different view from the mechanistic idea that God sat down one day and created all there is ever to be. One consequence of this is that we can never expect to be able to predict the future effectively (which is arguably the goal of science, although it is better seen as having a descriptive rather than predictive intent: the ability of science to predict is wholly based on its ability to describe), for that would imply that all there is to know is out there, simply waiting for us to find it, document it, and encapsulate it into descriptions we sometimes call scientific laws. ET is neither fideist nor secular.

---

8. Milbank et al., *Radical Orthodoxy*, 5.
9. Shakespeare, *Radical Orthodoxy*, 84.

Marriage: An Example

In my study of marriage theology, three specific areas were considered:

- marriage where one or both partners has a learning disability
- post-menopausal (and childless) marriage
- changes in the parenting role

The purpose behind this selection was to take areas where there is much less overloading from history, where situations dramatically different from those our predecessors had to assimilate into their marriage theology, necessarily have to be faced.

It may also be the case that this selection is also a challenge to a RO version of marriage theology which seems primarily to seek solutions in the past—but we know our particular concerns are very unlikely, other than by mind-blowing adaptation, to find meaningful consideration hitherto. For example, learning disability marriage was just not considered and, for the most part, was not even an option. Eiesland's approach[10] to physical disability blew a fatal hole in any theology based on perceiving God entirely in terms of perfection.

MARRIAGE AND EVIDENTIAL THEOLOGY

In my doctoral thesis these three areas are considered in some detail and here it will have to suffice to draw out some of the conclusions without presenting the evidence.

Recourse to Human Rights (let alone the NT message that the gospel is for everyone, Jew and Gentile alike) leads to the conclusion that no human being should be excluded from marriage on the basis of their human characteristics—such as disability. However, it is generally accepted that people with a learning disability may not be able to conclude contractual (legal) agreements. For marriage, theologically, to be described in contractual terms would exclude some people. We therefore need to find an alternative, which can be found in adopting a covenant approach. Whilst, in the past, marriage liturgies have conflated contract and covenant, there are important and inherent differences between the two concepts, each of which leads to a very different idea of marriage (as a sub-class of enduring relationships).

Historical reviews of how marriage has culturally evolved lead me to reject marriage as a paradigm for the God-human relationship, especially

---

10. Eiesland, *The Disabled God*.

when marriage is viewed as contract. Marriage-as-covenant takes us into a more helpful place, but we still have to be careful with the use as paradigm—otherwise we end up either viewing the nature of God as being culturally-dependent or we constrain marriage from any form of evolution, something society has so far proved unable to resist.

The impact of medical practice on increasing life expectancy well beyond a reasonable child-rearing age means that marriage may be formed without any element of procreation. Marriage theologies which have procreation as a *sine qua non* then run into difficulty. Equally, the traditional view of marriage relationships—as, in sequence: a) virginity; b) marriage; c) procreation; d) child rearing; e) old age dependency—is seriously undermined by the widespread acceptance of serial, procreative, relationships. Church weddings today often involve pre-existing children, not necessarily having the new couple as both parents. Widespread evidence indicates that parent-child relationships well outlast any failure of the relationship between the parents. Consequently, we need to establish more clearly the covenant undertaking between adults and children made as part of a marriage as something that is not dissolved when the contractual relationship is closed—a permanence that outlives finite contracts.

Medicine also creates the opportunity for intervention, not only to prevent conception, but to enable it in situations where it does not occur naturally. Although 20C debate focussed on the prevention, theological considerations of fertility treatments have largely looked at the ethical aspects of its methodology, rather than its consequences for marriage theology. However, it is difficult to sustain the view that there is either a duty and a right to procreate—if there were one, then there also ought to be the other. Orthodox marriage theology was not constructed with this context in mind.

Until quite recent history, child dependency was a short period: children started to become economically contributive from as young as nine. Today, the dependency may actively continue for up to three times that length—and some of that change has occurred since the parents were married. What does that say about the notion of the contract into which they entered? Should they be bound by undertakings made in very different circumstances with altogether different liabilities—and benefits?

All of this leads us to the conclusion that we need to do something more than merely recover past solutions. Thatcher[11] attempted to solve the problem this way—especially in the area of betrothal—but, with hindsight,

---

11. Thatcher, *Marriage after Modernity*.

this does not appear to have been successful, not because the ideas have not yet been acted upon, but because it fails to address the presenting issues.

The conclusion of our analysis is to propose that a marriage theology, constructed in a way that can encompass a much wider notion of enduring relationships, should no longer have any contractual element, one which encourages a postmodern focus on self (what do *I* get out of this relationship)—to be replaced by a covenant basis—one which encourages a focus on what I can do for the other, or others, in this relationship, one which does not immediately insist that as soon as the benefit *I* get out of the arrangement falls below what I put into it, then it is justifiably terminated.

A contractual framework may well be generally needed, in the context of Rights language, to protect the property rights of both partners. This is properly the role of the state and not the church, despite RO's rejection of such a nakedly statist approach!

A practical consequence for the church is that it should withdraw from the legal registration process—one which is primarily concerned about exit conditions. As a result, by focusing on a covenant approach (and here we must be careful to distinguish what we mean from the special Covenant Marriage movement in North America, which is almost diametrically opposite to what we propose) the church can be more flexible, responding better to cultural changes and accommodating the consequences also of UT, namely that what might be prescribed in one context is different from others. The church would also be freed from secular demands to register marriages in circumstances with which it is less than happy—on the grounds of human rights.

MARRIAGE AND RADICAL ORTHODOXY

In its intent to avoid secularism, RO seems to find it hard to identify how the church should engage with meeting the needs of those whom it encounters in the real world. Perhaps this has two causes: firstly, the underlying emotional pull is to see the role of the church in the past through rose-tinted glasses (seeking to re-establish an idealized church), a time in which the church was actively involved in social policy and the direct alleviation of suffering. Of course, seen from our present-day standpoint, much of what the church wanted to do lacked the means to achieve its aims with the result that it was often so palliative it gave credence to claims that it was in cahoots with state powers, a criticism that was only ever partially true. However, the extent to which it was valid has clouded the wider debate.

A second cause for the ambivalence of RO towards social action is perhaps its fundamental rejection of secularism and the views of society that states have established, such as human rights. (Milbank rejects Rights language as being irredeemably modern liberalism, depending as it does on the existence of a state as authority and power).

In present day society, it is no longer feasible to consider the church acting wholly independently of secular society when engaging in social action, not least because in most countries—and the UK is a prime example—the state has created a regulatory framework which the church cannot, nor should not, avoid. It is likely that had the church been as vigilant in pursuing similar protective ends then some of the more widespread abuse scandals would not have arisen. It may well be that Blond's "Red Toryism" is a political cover for the belief that, not only is Christian theology the only valid method for discussing any aspect of the world, but society would be better served by returning to a time when "good works" were the province of the church, where it could seek to enforce its ethical standpoint through control of service delivery. In the U.S., opposition to President Obama's reform of heath care for those with low income has come from the "Religious Right," who see it as a reduction of their influence as they cease to be providers of charity care. More recently, a similar reaction to the government's Big Society has been voiced as an opportunity (e.g., Thornton[12]).

Society as a whole accepts the need for some degree of statism, and much progress has been made by balancing rights and responsibilities: the rights of individuals to certain ends, with the state (and others) taking responsibility for ensuring that these rights can be accessed. There are, of course, tensions in popular opinions between the principles of various rights and the way in which these sometimes play out in practice. For example, does there exist a right to *have* a child (as distinct from the right to *try* to have a child? That is, is there a right, which the state is obliged to enable, for each person to have a child regardless of whether it involves more than natural processes?

One way forward is to draw a clear distinction between the covenant and contractual views of marriage. Furthermore, the latter, principally concerned with property, ownership, and exit conditions, is better seen as the role of the state, whilst the church's role is to encourage and nurture a covenant view, primarily concerned about the quality of the relationship whilst it still exists, less about what happens when it comes to an end.

12. Thornton, "Caveats and Fears."

It is not obvious, but a more detailed consideration may well show that there are some parallels between this distinction and that which RO has talked about in terms of "gifts" and contracts.

RO writers have largely ignored marriage—a little more has been said about gender and sexuality. However, the relevant of Milbank's 24 Theses says, "Old sexual puritanism and recent commodification of sex are both opposed: indeed opposed as the same thing. Modernity is viewed as increasingly de-eroticizing; childbirth and sexual love must not be pried apart in the interest of a commodification of the human subject itself. Nevertheless, gay civil partnerships should be acknowledged by the churches, though not gay marriage." This last phrase —"though not gay marriage"—is interjected without recognizing how inconsistent it is with what precedes. On the one hand, it is not surprising, given the close relationship between RO and Rowan Williams's struggles to relate his own instincts to the realities of international politics between different parts of the worldwide Anglican Church, which have resurfaced during his tenure as Archbishop.

Our interest here is not in gay marriage specifically, but the way in which the above thesis shows how RO has not established a basis on which a comprehensive theology of marriage can be based, which reflects the reality of current society—or societies, given the almost unbridgeable gulfs which divide. On the one hand, there is a closet liberal tendency to be inclusive whilst at the same time wanting to return to past orthodox teachings and practices. This inevitably creates problems when faced with the "marriage paradigm" problem noted earlier. If marriage is to be a paradigm for the God-mankind relationship, then we have to agree on what version of marriage we are to keep as the one—out of all of those which have been adopted over past history—which represents a true understanding of God. RO too easily, it seems, is prepared to buy into a particular past version of this paradigm, just because it is a previous orthodoxy, rather than being ready to establish an understanding which recognizes that what has gone before cannot possibly contain all which there is to know about the God-mankind relationship. As Shakespeare says, "Milbank's desire to have some structure to human identity betrays him into the hands of a traditional sexist stereotype."[13]

In his rejection of human rights, Milbank is squirming when he relies on the untestified assertion that European gays are content with civil partnerships, even preferring the idea, in order to avoid having to create

---

13. Shakespeare, *Radical Orthodoxy*, 139.

an equal right to marriage. Similar equivocation leads to insurmountable difficulties when addressing the three situations we considered above.

Whilst Milbank accuses the *state of aspiring both scientifically to control reproduction and to keep its citizens "drugged" with dreams of sex* he ignores the fact that, through its long involvement in regulating marriage and marriage laws, the church has done exactly the same and, through its use of the marriage paradigm, has justified itself in doing so.

Radical Orthodoxy Assessed

The purpose of this final section of the essay is to assess RO in the light of the discussion regarding marriage theology. These comments may or may not hold in other or wider contexts—that option is simply not considered here.

Histories of marriage through many different cultural contexts establish that it has never remained a constant for very long. The fact that enduring, sexual and procreative relationships have been so important to humanity inevitably leads to the creation of an orthodoxy at each stage—usually a distillation of what has just disappeared back over the horizon of historical experience. The evidence of on-going change: "A tradition that is itself revolutionary cannot preserve itself by remaining static."[14] Equally, he makes clear that maintaining continuity with tradition does not mean being bound by it.

No theology of marriage, let alone the practice of pastoral care, can hope to be effective if it is continually looking backwards. Yes, it must build on the collective experience and wisdom from the past (tradition), but always temper that with a proper use of the never-ending challenge of fresh evidence of God incarnate in humanity in ways which lead us forward, seeking always to be closer to that unattainable relationship with God we saw in the pre-resurrected Jesus.

Regardless of its intent, RO leaves us with a sense that at some point in the past (for most RO writers that point is characterized as pre-Scotus) there was a rightness about our understanding of God and its implications for the organization of human society. Whatever may be right about Augustine and Aquinas—and the period of society they represent—it can hardly be advanced as showing much understanding of marriage, sexual or enduring relationships, and gender, as understood in the light of subsequent evidence. We may yet want to accept the principles on which they sought to explain—but more often control—sexuality, whilst necessarily coming to

14. Plank, "Radical Orthodoxy of Rowan Williams."

different conclusions. It is at the very least tempting to conclude—even accepting to do so is logically weak—that the need to reach such dramatically different conclusions implies inherent weaknesses in the fundamentals of the RO approach.

RO also appears to seek deterministic-univocal solutions, a criticism raised by Shakespeare.[15] The consequences are unresolved conflicts between social aims and a specific orthodoxy or tradition. Not only does RO not give us anything better than to say any conclusion inconsistent with the specified tradition must be wrong; but worse, it leaves us with no methodology to resolve matters for ourselves. In the specific context of marriage theology, we are left floating. The deterministic imperative denies access to the goals of UT, namely to reflect the fact that differing experiences of the evidence of God in and through the created universe may lead to different conclusions about specific ethical matters. These differences should be seen not as pointing to inherent flaws in one or the other, needing a univocal resolution, but rather an endorsement of the ongoing incarnation of God and our inability to perceive the totality.

The rejection by RO of all things secular leads Smith[16] to seek something distinctive. Like many incoming governments, there is a move to replace what went before with something different, just for the sake of being different, lest there is a suspicion of being associated with what is seen to have failed. In this case, Smith seeks a distinctly Christian theoretical framework, which is clearly neither secular nor liberal. This means that RO is unable to examine critically what secular experts have discovered—for example about relationships and sexuality—and to take that evidence as guiding the theological framework away from ideas that are inconsistent with the evidence.

There is a sense Smith[17] confuses, or at least conflates, science and engineering. True, much "social science" is more like "social engineering," but it is unhelpful to ignore the inherent distinction. Science is solely about examining and describing the natural world in ways that are helpful in predicting future behavior. Laws of science do not themselves control the way in which things behave—after all they behaved that way long before the laws were first enunciated. Engineering is, however, purpose-driven. Based on an understanding of the world established by science, engineering seeks

---

15. Shakespeare, *Radical Orthodoxy*, 71.
16. Smith, *Introducing Radical Orthodoxy*, 42.
17. Ibid., 144ff.

to create artifacts that achieve a given, selected purpose. Sometimes, the pursuit of engineering goals (which includes economic and business, as well as ethical criteria) leads into areas where the lack of established knowledge becomes apparent. On several occasions in the 20C, bridge design pushed at the boundaries of existing knowledge[18] to the point at which designs failed, sometimes spectacularly. Each time, this led to a renewed scientific investigation to determine better ways of describing and analyzing the behavior of artifacts under newly-created circumstances. Similarly, the rapid expansion of the need to carry large quantities of crude oil around the globe, led shipbuilders to go beyond existing knowledge in the late 1960s to the point of failure.

There are clear parallels for ET here: the pursuit of scientific investigation matches our determination to discover God's ongoing incarnation in the world. As with Galileo, we can only respond to uncomfortable discoveries by stating the evidence. No amount of wishing it were otherwise, nor revisiting the inaccurate understandings of past generations, can alter the discovery. What we do about it from there on is engineering: we have to use that knowledge in the context of a wider ethical, economic—or in our case theological—purpose. In that sense, RO is correct to reject a purely secular formulation for theological engineering, but is equally wrong in rejecting scientific evidence as giving us a better understanding of God. To use a critique of all post-Scotus ideas as a reason for reverting to an earlier position is insufficient, if that critique is based on an "engineering" analysis of whether the philosophies have succeeded or failed in meeting independently established goals.

Smith[19] seeks to establish a *vocation* for all things—something in which each created entity has a purpose that, in some unidentified but anthropomorphic way, constrains it to what it wants and ought to be doing. It would appear that, yet again, we find a fundamentally invalid understanding of scientific laws, which has often been used elsewhere to justify excluding certain behaviors as unethical on the basis of what is *not natural*. Human nature has never been constrained by a fixed, given, universe: both individuals and societies have used their abilities to create things which are not natural—humans with their current life-expectancy are but one important example. In instinctively looking backwards all the time, RO fails to come to terms with the fact that advances in engineering (social, mechanical, political) are

18. Todd, "The Finite Element."
19. Smith, *Introducing Radical Orthodoxy*, 191.

necessarily linked with ethical and theological changes—it simply is not possible to have one sort of advance without the other.

From 1945 onwards, a large part of world society has been driven by Rights and various legal formulations in general and specific contexts, whether for adults, children, disabled, minorities, and so on. RO broadly rejects this development on the basis that it is part of the liberal agenda and, perhaps it is correct in this part of its analysis, a focus on the individual—rights rather than duties to society. This imbalance leads RO to prefer the establishment of the rights of the church rather than the individual. At the very least, such an agenda needs to establish a means of preventing a return to church autocracy, more concerned with its own survival than the welfare of individuals.

Oliver[20] assesses "attribution"—the process of seeking to describe God by analogy with human behavior—and concludes that it presents potential problems. In so doing, he seems to be agreeing with our rejection of marriage as a paradigm, although perhaps for slightly different reasons. Hopefully, the formulation of ET as exploring the evidence of God incarnate in the world avoids his criticism of pantheism: to assert God is incarnate in the world does not necessarily imply God is nothing without that incarnation. Nothing in ET suggests God is other than something independent of humanity. Rather, incarnation—especially an ongoing incarnation—is at the heart of the relationship between God and humanity, both of which has a distinct existence. Incarnation is the means of revelation, not the essence of God.

Conclusion

RO has been considered from the point of view of Marriage Theology, seeking to discover whether it can provide a methodology for an approach that addresses problems and shortcomings with various traditions. Although there are some useful aspects—such as the notion of gift which bears on the construction of covenant—we have found RO is unable to reflect adequately the evidence gathered from a study of how marriage (and the wider notion of enduring relationships) has culturally evolved over millennia, especially in coping with phenomena, which simply did not exist until now.

As in other matters, RO is left with a disjunction between its radical, forward-looking, aspirations and its dependency on orthodoxy, an assumption that all that is needed to be known about God and his relationship with

20. Milbank and Oliver, *The Radical Orthodoxy Reader*.

humankind can be found by reverting back to a particular baseline, one set by cultural conditions in the time of Augustine and Aquinas. As a means of resolving modern ethical/theological conundrums, RO seems to be ineffective, whatever success it might have in dealing with those of yesterday.

Separate from the use of Evidential Theology as a methodology, I came to the conclusion that it is important for Marriage Theology to separate the aspects of contract (exit conditions) from covenant (what happens within marriage). For this to happen, the church needs there to be a State which can establish and supervise the rights of parties to a marriage contract. Without the State, the church becomes fatally compromised. If RO continues to be so adamant in rejecting the role of the State, in association with the church, then I suspect that RO will be of limited assistance in seeking a fresh expression of marriage theology.

To summarize the differences, it would seem RO believes that (a fixed) God reveals himself *through* the world, whilst ET asserts God *is* and continues to be incarnate *in* the world, which is where we have to encounter him. Rather than *creation is nothing*[21] we assert *creation is everything*.

Bibliography

Eiesland, Nancy L. *The Disabled God: Toward a Liberatory Theology of Disability*. Nashville: Abingdon, 1994.
Milbank, John, et al. *Radical Orthodoxy: A New Theology*. London: Routledge, 1999.
Milbank, John, and Simon Oliver. *The Radical Orthodoxy Reader*. London: Routledge, 2009.
Moore, Gareth. *The Body In Context: Sex and Catholicism*. London: Continuum, 1992.
Plank, Karl A. "The Radical Orthodoxy of Rowan Williams: The Discourse on Sexuality, Religious Pluralism and the Recent Crisis." No pages. Online: http://www.davidson.edu/academic/religion/PLANK/Rowan_Williams.pdf
Shakespeare, Steven. *Radical Orthodoxy: A Critical Introduction*. London: SPCK, 2007.
Smith, James K. A. *Introducing Radical Orthodoxy: Mapping a Post-Secular Theology*. Grand Rapids: Baker Academic, 2004.
Thatcher, Adrian. *Marriage after Modernity: Christian Marriage in Postmodern Times*. Sheffield: Sheffield Academic, 1999.
Thornton, Ed. "Caveats and Fears in Christian Welcome for the Big Society." In *Church Times* (2010). No pages. Online: http://www.churchtimes.co.uk/articles/2010/23-july/news/caveats-in-christian-welcome-for-the-big-society.
Todd, M. J. "The Finite Element Method Applied to Thin Shells and Box Structures." PhD diss., Loughborough University, 1970.
———. "Marriage at the Edges—From the Margins to the Centre." PhD diss., Winchester University, 2010.

21. Smith, *Introducing Radical Orthodoxy*, 102.

3

J. G. Hamann and the Self-Refutation of Radical Orthodoxy

Katie Terezakis

Commentators on Radical Orthodoxy to date tend either to express bewildered admiration for the range of historical figures its theorists address, or take up those figures in turn, arguing that Radical Orthodoxy's lineal self-portrayal and the theological program that extends from it amount to misappropriation of the history of ideas.[1] The question of Radical Ortho-

1. *Deconstructing Radical Orthodoxy* by Hankey and Hedley is devoted to showing how Radical Orthodoxy relies on mis-readings of thinkers from Plato through Derrida. Max Stackhouse's succinct review of John Milbank's *The Word Made Strange* for *The Journal of Religion* is discriminating as regards Milbank's historical appropriations. Robin Lovin's review of Milbank's *Theology and Social Theory* for that same journal seems instead so enthralled by the "vast body of material" covered in Milbank's text that no critical evaluation of it is undertaken. Again, Douglas Hedley's exceptional article, "Should Divinity Overcome Metaphysics?" advances a number of arguments which effectively debar Milbank's utilization of a set of historical thinkers and themes. "Radical Orthodoxy and the New Culture of Obscurantism" by Paul D. Janz forcefully exposes the historical and scholarly sciolism of the movement. Wayne J. Hankey's "Radical Orthodoxy's *Poiesis*" calls Radical Orthodoxy's "falsification of the past" "compulsive" and gives good reason to reject its readings of the pre-Socratics, Plato, Aristotle, Kant, and others. In a review of Hankey and Hedley's *Deconstructing Radical Orthodoxy* for *Ars Disputandi*, Maarten Wisse objects to recurring criticisms of Radical Orthodoxy's use of different historical figures, arguing that critics should focus instead on developing an alternative to the movement. Anthony Paul Smith and Daniel Whistler provide a forceful account of the theological and philosophical scene within which Radical Orthodoxy has worked over the last two decades. See their editor's introduction for *After the Postsecular and the Postmodern*.

doxy's construal of the canon tends to be central, for the ethos of the movement, as well as its theological and political imperatives, are drawn from its theorists' delineation of historical developments which, they claim, open the space inadvertently (or more wickedly) for secular theory and practice from within classical and enlightenment thought. The theorists of Radical Orthodoxy read the historical dissociation of religious faith and human reason, and the illegitimate granting of epistemic and political authority to the latter, as a consequence of both unintended and imprudent theoretical initiatives, which they spend the bulk of their writing exposing. Yet given the contingency of history, they suggest, things might have gone another way, and the heroes of the movement's historical reconstruction are those who fought against the rationally hubristic, scientistic, secularizing tide of their time. These thinkers held fast to a theological vision responsible for exerting the hidden influence behind key enterprises in modern thinking, and they are our guides in challenging the failures of the contemporary world with a genuinely Christian alternative.

Johann Georg Hamann (1730–1788) is such a hero for John Milbank. Milbank takes Hamann to be the paradigmatic anti-enlightenment "radical conservative," as such, he is the epitome of the "redescription of Christianity" and the value of "Christian difference" Milbank means to articulate; likewise, the communication of Hamann's enigmatic but stealthily influential ideas offers a prime illustration of the significance of Milbank's revealing historical inquiries. For according to Milbank, Hamann is the covert agent whose work causes Kantianism to be so quickly abandoned, and which likewise provokes the rapid rise and fall of the critical projects of Fichte, Hegel, and Schelling; Hamann is the initiator of an approach to language which seismically shifts the course of later modern philosophy; and Hamann's is the animus which subverts the myth of givenness installed by German idealism and replaces it with uncompromising insistence on our "faithful reception of the divine gift."[2]

Their portrayal of Radical Orthodoxy's approach to the "postsecular" provides a context for understanding Radical Orthodoxy's response to recent intellectual movements and their historical sources.

2. As I will assert in this chapter and have shown elsewhere, Hamann is indeed the initiator of a "metacritical" approach to the study of language that is of profound consequence for later modern philosophy. The truth of this claim helps to explain why it would be helpful for Milbank's case if Hamann also shared Milbank's theological position, though I will argue that he does not. Milbank writes of the abandonment of Kantianism and of the rapid rise and fall of subsequent critical philosophies in his contribution to *Radical Orthodoxy*, 22–23 (Hereafter, "*RO*"). It is here that he makes the case Hamann

Still, in light of recent efforts to contextualize or repudiate the way in which Radical Orthodoxy reads its historical champions and villains (and the fact that it does so split the world: into good Christians and bad nihilists), the reader would be justified in wondering whether the examination of another of Radical Orthodoxy's ancestors is worth the effort. One might hope to bracket the question of whether Radical Orthodoxy stands on the shoulders of giants or figments of its own construction, and instead to focus on its fundamental concerns and suggestions, apart from its historical retrievals. Yet it is precisely because of the way that reading Hamann, and Milbank on Hamann, forces us to deal with the matters of historical retrieval and linguistic portrayal that Hamann's importance to Milbank comes to seem exceptional, and ultimately, revelatory of an internal incongruence within Radical Orthodoxy, which deepens the more determinedly the movement suppresses it. Hamann's thought and Milbank's appreciation of elements of it tell us that nothing matters as much as how we interpret and relate history, how we place ourselves within it, and how we may describe and therefore face up to our worldly commission.

Condescension and the Meta-Critical Standpoint

Milbank is sensitive to Hamann's contention that, insofar as God "speaks" in a manner human beings can understand, he speaks through history and the happenings of the natural world, which must be experienced with human sensibility and interpreted in human terms. As Milbank writes, for Hamann, "we can never have an abstract faith in God as author of nature, sustaining the reality of things, without *reading* these things in their specific, revealed and always *historical* contingency as the primary divine language."[3] History is not only a species of divine revelation for Hamann; he makes

---

and the radical pietists (Franz Heinrich Jacobi in particular) are responsible for the best ideas of modern philosophy. I leave it to the reader to judge whether Milbank's assurance that Kantianism was "quickly abandoned" is indicative of Milbank's level of competence in assessing the history of philosophy. Milbank relates the excesses of Kantianism and the "main lines of the German philosophical legacy" to Nazism, and implies that Hamann and the radical pietists present a track which could have opposed Nazism from within that same culture, in *Being Reconciled: Ontology and Pardon,* 24 (Hereafter, "BR"). The quote with which this paragraph ends, which attributes to Hamann (and Herder and Jacobi) the creation of an alternative to German romanticism and idealism, which fail insofar as they "isolate something 'given' apart from a faithful reception of the divine 'gift,'" is taken from John Milbank's *The Word Made Strange: Theology, Language, Culture,* 2. (Hereafter, "WMS").

3. *RO*, 27.

the stronger claim that only in the enactment and interpretation of history and nature can anything *like* a divine narrative be read.[4] I emphasize that Hamann describes something "like" a divine narrative because Hamann insists that insofar as anything is revealed, it is in a human language "to the creature through the creature"; we do not encounter, let alone master, the unmediated will or intention of God.[5] Rather, we contend with ourselves, exercising our freedom, and hoping our projections about divinity strike at a truth we cannot confirm. The crux of faith, for Hamann, is the hope that the relationship we posit between human-created and divine-creator exists in a meaningful way, as we continue to acknowledge, often through rational analysis, the character and conditions of our own hopeful positing.[6] Likewise, for Hamann, we understand our desire and our presumption in the analogical terms available to us. The dyad of "creator-created," so essential to Christian theology, is sustained by its analogical relation to our everyday experience of creations and their creators. Our experiential and intellectual strictures dictate our reliance on analogy, but whether this analogy successfully applies to the transcendent source it is meant to describe remains the stuff of hope or faith, not the confirmation of evidence. Hamann therefore depicts knowledge and language as a translation, "from a tongue of angels into a human tongue": insofar as the world appears to us, it is disposed to our expression, even more, it tends to appear *as* expression, to be grasped only insofar as it is expressed, as if the world and its history were a divine language, articulating itself over time, always in a human idiom.[7]

---

4. "Just as nature was given to us to open our eyes, so history was given to us to open our ears" in James C. O'Flaherty, *Hamann's Socratic Memorabilia: A Translation and Commentary*, 64.12–13.

5. Haynes, "Speak, that I may see you!—This wish was fulfilled by creation, which is a speech to creatures through creatures; for day unto day utters speech, and night unto night shows knowledge" from *Aesthetica in Nuce*, in *Hamann: Writings on Philosophy and Language*, 65. See also *Aesthetica in Nuce* (as well as a number of other of Hamann's writings, translator's notes, and exceptional interpretive essays) in Gwen Griffith Dickson, *Johann Georg Hamann's Relational Metacriticism*.

6. For characteristic statements of faith, see for example: "But perhaps all history is more mythology than this philosopher [Bolingbroke] thinks, and is, like nature, a book that is sealed, a hidden witness, a riddle which cannot be solved unless we plow with another heifer than our reason" *Socratic Memorabilia* 65.9–13, (O'Flaherty translation); and "Reason is given to you not that you may become wise, but that you may recognize your foolishness and ignorance" (Hamann to Kant July 27, 1759) in *Immanuel Kant: Philosophical Correspondence 1759–99* by Zweig.

7. See, for example, the letter Hamann writes Herder after reading a pre-press copy of Herder's *Treatise on the Origin of Language*: "God throws language *through* people—who

In Hamann, the idea that existence as we know it could only be the result of divine self-limitation entails the corollary that the existence we know is a limited phenomenon by its very nature; this shows up pointedly in our faculty of reason, which desires to know its own source and full scope, but which is able to grasp neither. As Hamann puts it in a personal letter, "since Adam's fall, all *gnosis* is suspicious to me, like a forbidden fruit."[8] Hamann connects divine condescension to human epistemic limitation without fail; though his descriptions tend to be accompanied by a poetic or mythic imagining of the scene of divine condescension, the bottom line is always the same: we may be known by God, but we do not know him.[9]

Milbank is attracted to Hamann's persistent defense of history as the site of divine revelation because he takes it to be the forerunner of his own position of "meta-narrative realism."[10] Where Hamann argues that the original condescension of God to the world and the fallenness of terrestrial life situate us permanently within an immanent field, Milbank's most vital proposal—that philosophy, social theory, and all of social and political life must return to their theological sources and submit to a renewed theology's judgments and ends—is "ensured" and "justified" by "a genuine metanarrative realism," which is authorized to interpret all of human history in light of the Christian mythos.[11] For Milbank, Hamann is such an important ally because his metacritique of transcendental philosophy both establishes the

---

doubts it? Who has? . . . That he does not throw mystically, but through nature, animals, a pantheon of speaking lutes; that he speaks through the urgency of human needs or wishes—who has taken this up more than I?" Hamann to Herder, August 1, 1772 in Arthur Henkel and Walter Ziesemer, *Briefwechsel*.

8. Hamann to Bucholz June 26, 1785, in *Briefwechsel* (*op. cit.*)

9. See for example Hamann's *Biblical Meditations*: "'Come,' says God, 'we will come down from heaven. Let us go down.' This is the means by which we have come closer to heaven: the condescension of God to earth"; see also the description of Apollo's condescension throughout Hamann's *Socratic Memorabilia* (e.g., at 68.32–35; 71.4–7; 71.15–18), and Hamann's connection of the ignorance which therefore characterizes the human mode of being with the wisdom of Socrates, who begins and ends by recognizing his lack of knowledge. See too Hamann's reference to Job 36:26: "Behold, God is great, and we know him not" in *Disrobing and Transfiguration: A Flying Letter to Nobody, the Well Known*, which is representative. In Haynes (*op. cit.*), 230.

10. Milbank uses the terms "metanarrative realism" to designate his own interpretative proposal in *Theology and Social Theory: Beyond Secular Reason*. (Hereafter, "*TST*.")

11. "The *logic* of Christianity involves the claim that the 'interruption' of history by Christ and his bride, the Church, is the most fundamental of events, interpreting all other events [. . . yet] a genuine metanarrative realism [. . .] ceases to be *only* a privileged set of events, but rather becomes the whole story of human history which is still being enacted and interpreted in light of those events" (*TST*, 388).

ubiquity of language in all functions of higher order cognition, and holds that the history of events and ideas constitutes a divine speaking to and through the world which must yet be engaged and interpreted. The human and divine logos are linked, in human forms of expression which project their divine accompaniments. Hamann upsets the "purification" of human reason from language, tradition, and experience; at the same time, he speaks of our most characteristically human possession —language—as a fount of divine being, or our truest access to it.[12] Thus, Milbank's own reliance on historical interpretation, and the essential dogma he lays down for Radical Orthodoxy, expects that the association with Hamann allows it a "metacritical," linguistic perspective on the failings of philosophy and theory, and by the same token, a "metanarrative about how God speaks in the world in order to redeem it."[13]

In order to draw out the difference between Hamann's suggestion that history be read as the site of divine discourse, carried out in human terms, and Milbank's assertion that the superiority of Radical Orthodoxy's theological position rests on a metanarrative realism authorized to judge all historical discourses through a set of Christian tropes, it is necessary to describe Hamann's enterprise in some more detail. As I have already suggested, the whole of that enterprise pivots on the notion of divine *Herunterlassung*, God's self-limitation or condescension in creation.[14] Taking up the idea as he first encounters it in Luther, Hamann returns persistently to the image of the fallen world as a godly self-negation we can neither account for nor overcome; God's inexplicable self-reduction "makes way" for the world and the finite beings who inhabit it. Divine condescension entails a vision of creation as the loss of undivided abundance; the world and its inhabitants are

12. *Metacritique of the Purism of Reason* in Dickson (*op. cit.*) and Haynes (*op. cit.*). See also Jere Paul Surber, *Metacritique: The Linguistic Assault on German Idealism*.

13. *TST*, 422.

14. I have analyzed Hamann's thinking about condescension, as well as his meta-critical position and his theory of language, in more detail elsewhere: Terezakis, "Language and Immanence in Hamann"; Terezakis, *The Immanent Word: The Turn to Language in German Philosophy 1759–1801*; Terezakis, "Is Theology Possible After Hamann?" My discussion of these notions here repeats the findings of those works. There is also considerable discussion of these themes in the literature on Hamann. I have cited already the interpretive essays of Dickson; for further discussion of the notion of condescension see also W. M. Alexander *Johann Georg Hamann: Philosophy and Faith*. For important secondary discussions of Hamann that relate closely to the notion of condescension see O'Flaherty (*op. cit.*); John R. Betz, *After Enlightenment: Hamann as Post-Secular Visionary*; Oswald Bayer "Gegen System und Struktur: Die Theologische Aktualität Johann Georg Hamanns"; and Josef Nadler, *Johann Georg Hamann. Der Zeuge des Corpus mysticum*.

effectively incomplete, and our lack of completion marks our understanding of the world. Unlike his theological precursors, however, Hamann is unwavering in his determination to take the epistemological consequence of divine condescension seriously. Since our creation, such as we can conceive of it, is initiated by a condition of constraint, our form of knowing cannot be comprehensive. The limitation that characterizes our intellectual activities tells us something about the confines of human discursive abilities, but nothing of the world or of God beyond this constraint. The real cause of our limitation cannot, therefore, be conclusively explained: condescension is itself a metaphorical image which makes sense of the inexplicable act of creation. Hamann's greatest invectives are issued against those who claim knowledge of what they cannot know—most especially of metaphysical first principles or the mind of God; his regard is granted foremost to those who maintain and question the limits of their knowledge—thus Socrates is the subject of Hamann's first work and is thereafter his lifelong ideal.[15]

Hamann develops upon the traditional notion of fallenness by arguing that while the cause and full scope of divine condescension in creation cannot be rationally mastered, the encounter with that which exceeds us may yet be detected where language attempts a description of divinity or its creative power, and succeeds only in describing its own attempt. Being, insofar as we can know it and speak of it, shows up as language; yet where traditional ontological argumentation inevitably fails, language necessarily entails and demonstrates its own existence. The epistemological limit that follows from recognition of the notion of divine condescension requires that ontology be supplanted with the study of discursive practices.[16]

Several ideas fundamental to Hamann's thinking extend from his argument in defense of divine condescension. The first, as we have seen, is the idea that *what is* shows up as language or expression.[17] Regarding

15. The entirety of the *Socratic Memorabilia* bears this out. For just a couple of examples: "Socrates lured his fellow citizens out of the labyrinths of their learned Sophists to a truth in the inward being, to a wisdom of the secret hearts," and "The ignorance of Socrates was a sensibility. But between sensibility and a theoretical proposition is a greater difference than between a living animal and its anatomical skeleton. The ancient and modern skeptics may wrap themselves ever so much in the lion skin of Socratic ignorance; nevertheless they betray themselves by their voices and ears. If they know nothing, why does the world need a learned demonstration of it? Their hypocrisy is ridiculous and insolent."

16. As Hamann writes in a 1787 letter to Jacobi: "What is called Being in your language, I would rather name the Word." Haman to Jacobi, in vol. 7 of *Briefwechsel*, 175.

17. Hamann does not fully endorse the position later called "expressivism," most

attempts to know the divine and to describe it, these expressive acts may tell us something important about the scope of language, but they do not burst through language into transcendence. As such, descriptions of God, his will, and his doings must have a metaphorical or a regulative function. To believe in God is not to assert that a set of properties belong to him, but to recognize one's own desire for connection with a force one can only imagine. Though our cognitive activities cannot be secured by a transcendent or objective foundation, and though we cannot know that *from which* the "original" translation occurs, we assert a continuity between humanity and divinity and thus establish a tradition of reading human logos as analogous to divine logos. It is this tradition upon which we rely, and which we hope points, in the excess of linguistic meaning, to the excess of human meaning. "Everything divine . . . is also human; because a human being can neither act nor suffer except by analogy to its nature. [. . .] This *communicatio* of divine and human *idiomatum*," Hamann writes, "is a fundamental law and principle key of all our knowledge."[18]

The second consequence of Hamann's conception of divine condescension is likewise one we have already touched upon: the nature of genuine faith. Hamann cites with relish (in a letter to Kant) Hume's ironic statement that one cannot "eat an egg and drink a glass of water without faith [*Glaube*]" because he agrees with the pronouncement, and takes it to be an appropriate corollary of Hume's skepticism and of his own.[19] In denying that the principle of causality or any metaphysical first principle can be

---

famously by Charles Taylor, in a set of essays which credit Hamann for being among the first to develop the position. That position, as has been often noted, is nicely summed in Wittgenstein's dictum "the limits of my language are the limits of my world." I discuss some of the ways that Hamann's linguistic theory blends elements of later "expressive" and "truth conditional" approaches to language in (2006) *op. cit.* For Taylor's discussion of expressivism: Taylor, *Human Agency and Language* and Taylor, "The Importance of Herder."

18. Dickson translation (*op. cit.*).

19. Hamann to Kant July 27, 1759: "The Attic philosopher, Hume, needs faith if he is to eat an egg and drink a glass of water. [. . .] Reason was not given to you to make you wise but to make you aware of your folly and ignorance . . . If he needs faith [*Glaube*] for food and drink, why does he deny faith when he judges of matters that are higher than sensuous eating and drinking? [. . .] If Hume were only sincere, consistent with himself—." in *Correspondence*, Zweig (*op. cit.*) 41–42. As Manfred Kuehn allows in notes to his description of Hamann's reading of Hume, the final paragraph of section 10 of Hume's first *Enquiry* "might indeed suggest" a reading of Hume consistent with fideism. Manfred Kuehn, *Kant: A Biography*. See too the *Socratic Memorabilia* 73.20: "Our own existence and the existence of all things outside us must be believed [*muB geglaubt . . . werden*] and cannot be determined in any other way."

The Poverty of Radical Orthodoxy

proven, Hume argues that we form ideas about the connections between events, beliefs which involve the desire for or anticipation of some set of apparent connections. Hamann is not merely being playful when he takes up this Humean notion of *Glaube* and insists on its significance. Indeed, according to Hamann, we get on in the world with faith, or a cognitive impulse which affirms what appears to be present and anticipates its conditions and possible products. If we look candidly for the ground of existence, like Hume, we will find nothing but human habits of inference. Hamann upholds Humean skepticism and denies the rational veracity of traditional metaphysics no less than theology—and he does so over two decades before the appearance of Kant's critical project. Yet, Hamann argues, it is with *Glaube* that we live in the world and make whatever everyday sense of it we do, and this same *Glaube* animates the "determination to believe" in God and the Christian religion. Again, Hamann tells Kant that Hume knew the truth in spite of his jest, for when Hume argues that no reasonable person could believe in miracles or the Christian creed, he is right; as Hume knows, such a person is "moved by faith . . . conscious of a continued miracle in his own person."[20] The faith or belief with which we make everyday assumptions about the world may be unreflective, but once it is examined, and the alternative systems meant to certify the resources of the real are questioned, then honesty demands that we admit the miraculous quality of everyday experience, and it allows us to choose to maintain the miraculous in our will to believe religiously. The choice to believe religiously necessarily entails, for Hamann, this preservation of the miraculous; the miraculous and our open, acknowledged inability to "subvert it to the principles of the understanding" must permanently belie truth claims about the being or intentions of God.

Hamann emphasizes the supreme human freedom which must follow from divine condescension; human beings are left to interpret a world without the possibility of complete or conclusive confirmation, yet only on this account are we free. Milbank rightly recognizes the proto-existentialism of Hamann's thinking on freedom, but refuses its consequence. For Hamann, "freedom is the maximum and minimum of all our natural powers, as well as both the fundamental drive and the final goal of their entire orientation, evolution, and return."[21] We are determined ultimately "neither by instinct

---

20. Hamann to Kant (*op. cit.*), 42.

21. *Philological Ideas and Doubts* in Haynes (*op. cit.*), 155. The rest of the quotes on freedom in this paragraph are taken from this essay and continue to use Haynes's translation.

nor sensus communis," Hamann writes, neither by natural law nor human custom, but "everyone is his own legislator." Moreover, without "the perfect law of freedom, man would not even be capable of imitation, the basis of all education and invention." Hamann's defense of the fundamental, existential fact of human freedom is unwavering; he goes on to argue that all cognitive abilities, including the moral conscience, stem from the primary actuality of freedom and are determined insofar as they are freely exercised. It is an act of our freedom when we gather the "determination to believe" which is faith, and only as an ongoing, freely undertaken positing that faith persists. As will be the case with each of these central positions, we must return to the Hamannian portrayal of freedom shortly in order to compare it with the substitute offered by Milbank, in the name of Hamann.

Before doing so, one further differentiation of a Hamannian concept is required. Hamann names his position "metacritical" in his *Metacritique of the Purism of Reason*, a brief review of Kant's *Critique of Pure Reason*. Hamann takes it that Kant's critical turn begins with the appropriate recognition that epistemic procedures require justification. But he charges that Kant is still shoring up a notion of reason unequipped to justify the epistemological principles he employs, for Kant has emptied reason of its actual dependencies: on tradition and custom; on experience and "everyday inductions"; and, most importantly, on language.[22] So while Kant rightly understands the continuation of philosophy (qua critical) requires the foundation for knowledge claims, or the criteria with which they will be judged, be made explicit, Kantian reason is disingenuously put forward as able to describe and adjudge the claims of "subjective universality" as if it were not itself bound by language and the contingencies to which it is otherwise subject. Kant aims to show reason to be independent of language, yet relies upon linguistic analogies to construct reason's ideal propositions. Moreover, Kant fails to allow that language, which belongs to both sensibility and intuition, is their "shared root."[23] Hamann's metacritical position is initially aimed at Kant, but is presented as a review of any metaphysical system unclear about its own conditions of possibility; these include its linguistic dependencies as well as the way in which experience and historically contingent tradition affect its presentation of human thinking. The metacritical position is also a skeptical standard in its own right, in that it holds

---

22. See the Dickson translation and well as the Haynes translation (*op. cit*).

23. Hamann's *Metacritique* appears in Dickson, Surber, and Hayes, (*op. cit.*, all). Kant allows that "our cognition springs from two fundamental sources of the mind" at A50/B74.

that nothing—beyond our own natural languages—ultimately undergirds epistemological categories and transcendental procedures. Following from the idea of divine condescension, human epistemic practices are necessarily limited by our inability to know the source or ground of Being; what we can know about are our discursive practices, and these tell us much about the ways in which human reason remains bound to linguistic acts, usage, tradition, and experience—but the history of language and reason is a human history, and if that history has a transcendent source which might authorize its claims, this cannot be rationally ascertained.[24]

Hamann's problem with Kant's first *Critique*, then, though he argues it as impishly as usual, revolves around one of the most consequential insights in eighteenth century thinking: the attempted project of dissociating thought and language, with its presentation of the laws of thought as if logic rendered them and the transcendental procedure followed from them, *itself* remains dependent upon the "ordinary" language of everyday experience, which it reproduces in an abstract form obligated by the same problems that led to the attempted dissociation in the first place. As Jere Paul Surber has detailed in his assessment of the metacritical position, Hamann argues that transcendental discourse cannot itself escape the fact it, too, is a linguistic construction mirroring the concrete judgments of experience.[25] After the metacritique issued at Kant, the key question remains "how are any judgments possible?" But instead of the promise of transcendental philosophy, it leads us to *Sprachkritik*, with its examination of the historically specific, contingently composed conditions of any given judgment. No judgment, in other words, can be assessed as purified from its circumstance, but each tends to reveal the creative resources of natural language. The metacritical position contends that the only legitimate way forward for thinking involves engaging language as philosophy first, even as the position undermines the possibility of traditional epistemology, along with the newly minted transcendental project. Hamann's metacriticism decisively upsets, by contextualizing, any attempt to derive logically the veritable ground of cognitive objectivity and normative authority.[26]

24. Hamann goes to lengths to argue the exclusively human derivation of language in his *Herderschriften* as well as his personal letters to Herder. See for example the quote from Hamann's August 1772 letter to Herder in footnote 7, above.

25. Surber (*op. cit.*), 14ff.

26. Hamman's metacritical position is succinctly described in James R. Walker's review of Daniel Dahlstrom's *Philosophical Legacies: Essays on the Thought of Kant, Hegel, and Their Contemporaries*.

Conservatism and the Mind of God

Milbank claims Hamann as the primogenitor of Radical Orthodoxy because, he says, Hamann is (along with Jacobi) the source of a "genuinely anti-liberal *radical* orthodoxy."[27] Hamann and Jacobi are "even greater conservative revolutionaries than Luther himself," though Milbank's intervention is required by the fact they have been only ignored or travestied by theologians in general and by Karl Barth in particular. Not only does Barth evade and misconstrue the character of radical pietism, he furthers a dominant trend in the history of ideas, which likewise evades and misconstrues the theological source of a great deal of modern thought. In his contribution to the *Radical Orthodoxy* manifesto, Milbank pinpoints in the thought of Duns Scotus the start of the trouble which pietism later addresses, for Scotus disconnects philosophy from theology when he suggests a consideration of Being "in abstraction from the question of whether one is considering created or creating being." Scotus's proposition engenders the possibility of an ontology and an epistemology independent of and transcendental to theology. During the Reformation, this separation deepens, with philosophy authorizing itself to study Being, and an acquiescent theology deteriorating into labored positivism. Unlike Luther (a point Milbank stresses), Hamann and Jacobi challenge this entire legacy at the root; such is the substance of their description as conservative revolutionaries.

Milbank published the Radical Orthodoxy manifesto in 1999; it was reprinted in 2001 without any amendment to the rhetoric of the "conservative revolutionary." This dating leaves the disposition of Milbank's notion of "conservatism" in question, for in *Theology and Social Theory*, first published in 1990 but also reprinted in 2001, Milbank identifies as conservative those approaches to theorizing he is against. Transcendental idealism is said to be just as conservative as Cartesian philosophy, in that it naively or disingenuously attempts to "conceal the abyss" exposed with the finding that language is a creative, expressive source of meaning, rather than a transparent representation of reality.[28] In this narrative then, it is conservatism which reacts against Milbank's heroes. Milbank identifies as distinctively conservative the position which, in the face of the "abyss," attempts to secure meaning and the stability of discourses with a perverse

---

27. *RO*, 23 (Milbank's emphasis). Subsequent quotes in this paragraph are taken from this same essay.

28. *TST*, 150ff.

adherence to human subjectivity, falsely making the human subject into the unsullied derivation of language and the particularities of practice.

Other of Milbank's declarations of value are more obviously those of religious and social conservatism: he maintains the Christian church is "indispensible for salvation" and other religions and social groups, however "virtuous seeming," are "on the path of damnation." While this sort of rhetoric may seem ill-suited to a serious work of scholarship, it is nevertheless how Milbank clarifies his role as a theologian, who must be able to judge, from the perspective of the church, "what is going on in other human societies."[29] Other schools of theology cannot be trusted to do the work of interpretation, for, as much of Milbank's work is devoted to showing, these positions sanction secularism and open the gates to nihilism, and have made of the church a "hellish anti-Church."[30] Radical Orthodoxy, or Milbank himself, is the one able to interpret all other events from the perspective of Christ and the church, and he proposes to submit social theory, political practice, and ontology, to a theology recrowned as "queen of the sciences." Milbank therefore argues for the articulation of a Christian "cultural code" through which all events and institutions can be read; he criticizes Aquinas, among others, for allowing the Christian church to be understood as separate from the political sphere, and as specializing merely in the inward life of its adherents. That sort of move inappropriately separates the "secular" from the "spiritual," and forces us to miss, in activities like "tending gardens, building bridges, sowing crops, caring for children," their true Christian character. And again, it is the supposed defenders of the church who are partially to blame for the loss, insofar as they have argued or allowed for a special "sphere of interest" that belongs to the church, when they ought to have known that since Being itself is permeated by the Christian logos, all extant institutions are extensions of the Christian word and should be read as such. "Better then," writes Milbank, "that the bounds between Church and state be extremely hazy, so that a 'social' existence of many complex and interlocking powers may emerge . . ."[31]

Milbank is especially adroit at calling out any theory which cannot justify its procedures, or which lacks (intentionally or in spite of itself) access to an objective or transcendent source of normative or epistemic authority. This is why, for example, he judges the "peaceful transmission of

---

29. This and the previous quotes are from *TST*, 387–88.
30. Ibid., 433.
31. Ibid., 408.

difference" in Gadamerian hermeneutics "would be splendid as theology," but remains "specious as philosophy": for nothing ultimately justifies the transmission for which Gadamer aims.[32] Yet the justification for Milbank's own positions—the authority of his metanarrative realism and the sanction whereby his interpretation of the Christian logos is known to be the intellectually and morally *right* interpretation of all discursive activity—is based directly and categorically on his appropriation of the meta-critical position he claims to take over from Hamann.

Milbank correctly identifies a consequence of Hamann's metacritical standpoint: since sensuous, historically determined language always already saturates our reasoning, we cannot analyze reasoning apart from its discursive acts, nor can we separate "categories" of cognition from the stuff of experience. As we saw in the previous section, this is how Hamann rejects the conceits of Kant's critical turn: in effect, he one-up's the level of "critique" in Kant to include the sensuous and contingent conditions of reason's possibility, thereby upsetting the separation of sensible and intelligible at the heart of Kant's project. Milbank correctly judges that "this metacritique enmeshes us more deeply in physical finitude than even Kant would allow"; immediately, however, he adds, "but on the other hand, it also makes it less easy to draw the Kantian boundary between 'legitimated' knowledge of finitude, and illegitimate pretensions of knowledge in the infinite."[33] Milbank is gearing up for an incredible assertion here, one which encapsulates his theological endeavor. Whereas, for Hamann, the metacritical standpoint leads to skepticism about all metaphysics and returns us to our dependencies on language and experience, Milbank claims that a metacritical application grants no less than divine insight. Milbank explains that inasmuch as Hamann proves the dependency of human reason on language and experience, we can no longer claim to know with certainty what the limitations of the understanding really are. Milbank continues, "and in that case, it becomes impossible to demonstrate that the 'understanding,' or human discursive thought, is clearly limited to judgment of the finite and must not trespass beyond these bounds." Presumably, Milbank means that if language and experience are the limiting factors for reasoning, and language and experience (qua unfolding history) are actually divine, then—contrary to being real limitations at all, our participation in language and history link us directly into the mind of God.

32. Ibid., 417.
33. Ibid., 151.

Milbank says as much in his *Radical Orthodoxy* contribution: "We correspond to the other only insofar as our expressions approximate the entire expression of the thing by *the mind of God*, which is the thing's actual existence over against nothing." Likewise, in contrast to the illegitimate legacy which separates philosophy and theology as well as reason and revelation, for "the Church Fathers . . . both faith and reason are included within the more generic framework of participation *in the mind of God*."[34] Yet it is precisely this sort of rational confidence about the Absolute that Hamann ridicules, in his *Metacritique*, when transcendental philosophy displays it: "Since, after two-thousand years, no knowledge has been gained in the search beyond experience, reason . . . promises its impatient contemporaries . . . that it will produce that universal and unerring stone of wisdom so necessary to Catholicism and despotism."[35]

Milbank devotes himself to "the relevance of language for theology," averring that the "foundations of theology are linguistically mediated," yet he justifies the notion of a human language which participates in divine language with the allegedly metacritical insight that our knowledge is not really regulated by language at all, but delivered, through language, into a form of knowledge which surpasses the human.[36] Although Hamann goes to lengths (for indeed, this is the sum and substance of his project) to show human thinking happens within human language, that anything we learn we learn in a language "to the creature through the creature." And though he routinely chides his contemporaries for making knowledge claims like those he associates with the false "stone of wisdom," Milbank claims not to transgress the limitations Hamann recognizes as linguistically mediated precisely by claiming access to a divine language which he is certain corresponds with our own. Milbank often toys with the rhetoric of faithful humility to the mysteriousness of divinity, but his claim of access into the divine mind is not a testimonial of personal faith, but a blatant assertion, made with the full weight of epistemic certitude.[37] Milbank tells us he

---

34. *RO*, 29, 24, my italics.

35. *Metacritique* (Surber translation).

36. These quotes are taken from *WMS*, 2, though Milbank references this same agenda throughout his works.

37. Janz argues Milbank sophistically plays down the idea of "transcendence" so as to avoid this sort of criticism. Instead, Janz maintains, Milbank prefers to speak of hidden and subterranean "depths," within the immanent, which nonetheless serve as bridges to the transcendent. Janz zeros in on Milbank's insinuation that, given the invisible and secreted nature of said depths, his own prophetic efforts are required (*op. cit.*, 399).

knows what the divine logos is about, as well as how to use it to interpret history *in toto* and in all of its manifesting particulars.

This speaks to the incongruence I have called characteristic of Milbank's thinking. Milbank seems to understand the emphasis on epistemic limitation and empirical embeddedness that are distinguishing features of Hamann's work. He seems also to be deeply attracted to these features, citing them frequently and adorning his texts with similar language. Yet these same ideas require of us a genuine praxis: if one agrees with them, one must abstain from certain kinds of metaphysical commitments, truth claims, and assertions of knowledge. Milbank cites the great "either/or" on which he, and Radical Orthodoxy, stake themselves.[38] Yet the real "either/or" of this narrative is not to be found in the opposition between philosophy and theology, but between an authenticity able to affirm the consequence of the forms of human limitedness it encounters, and bad faith, or a false consciousness which claims it alone transcends all evident limitations and remains justified by the source of its transcendence.

Milbank is a sensitive enough reader of Hamann to have encountered the reality that is "analogously continuous" in Hamann's work, but not a confident enough thinker to accept the context of the insight, which indicates that analogies are those fully human constructions which allow us to make use of our epistemic limitations.[39] One need not review the awesome resources—beginning with Plato and extending through Neoplatonism and the church fathers, though the German idealists and beyond, marshalled on behalf of the potential of analogical thought, and meant to either establish or question the true derivation of analogy—for Milbank plainly bases his "metanarrative" insights on the thought he knows to be harnessed by Hamann, and in this thought, nothing can guarantee the analogies, the regulative positing, and the faith upon which we nevertheless depend.

---

38. For example, in *RO*, 32, where Milbank writes: "Hence it is indeed for radical orthodoxy an either/or: philosophy (Western or Eastern) as a purely autonomous discipline, or theology: Herod or the magi, Pilate or the God-man."

39. Elsewhere, I have explained how Hamann advocates, on at least one occasion, the climb from analogy to anagogy, or from regulative orientation in thinking to spiritual interpretation and "performative" completion. However, Milbank does not take up the possibility of anagogy as Hamann imagines it, perhaps because, as I have argued, even this openly theological notion is inoculated against theological hubris in Hamann's description: the degree to which one must become an "unknower" on the ladder of anagogical ascent is severe, and the final miracle of revelation is, in addition to being a disclosure of infinite divine power, also a "miracle of such infinite silence, that makes God as nothing..." In *Sämtliche Werke*. (Hereafter "*N*") II 204.8–14. (See my 2006, 2007 *op. cit.*)

Following Hume, Hamann makes fun of the philosopher's inability to ground the categories of causality, necessity, and relation, for each of these are nonetheless structural features of the natural language upon which we rely. This is the rub for Hamann: when we inappropriately abstract from linguistic features like these, we generate a series of concepts confused about their own derivation.[40] Still, there is sense in speaking of the "linguistic a priori" or the "metaphysics of language," if what we are speaking about are the rules and the context within which a natural language is utilized. Milbank, as we have been following, goes in the opposite direction. He begins by claiming "we are free to make 'eminent' or 'analogical' use of these categories [causality, necessity, and relation] in imagining the infinite and the relation of the infinite to the finite," and ends by claiming there is, in fact, "no vantage point from which one can 'round upon' the bounds of finitude and determine what is confined to the finite alone"[41] In other words, Milbank shifts in the space of a few paragraphs from reminding us of our freedom to use analogy poetically, to claiming that because we have *only* analogical and speculative insight into certain categories, precisely these must be the mysterious route into infinity, into the very mind of God. Milbank skips the regulative step in Hamann's path, and thus abandons the modus operandi of the metacritical position. At bottom, Milbank's argument amounts to no more than that very traditional fallacy: the appeal to ignorance. Like the creationist who argues for a "God of the gaps," Milbank is telling us that because he does not know why (or the extent to which) our finitude and fallibility are bound by experience and language, these are ultimately unknowable things. Moreover, it is our ignorance which proves the hand of God is at work.[42] Milbank's is in fact that special case of the

---

40. Cf Hamann's letter to Jacobi of December 1784: "Metaphysics has its scholastic and courtly language; I am suspicious of both [. . .] I suspect that our entire philosophy consists more of language than reason, and of the misunderstandings of innumerable words, the prosopopoeia of the most arbitrary abstractions . . . indeed, even the most common figures of speech of the sensus communis have given rise to a world of questions, the posing and answering of which are equally unfounded" in *Briefwechsel* (*op. cit*).

41. TST, 151–52.

42. Milbank therefore takes a position no less daft than that recently put forward on one of the premier creationism websites (www.creationism.org), titled "Johann Georg Hamann (1730–1788), Preacher of Christ in the Wilderness of the Enlightenment." The article is written by Ellen Myers, who tells us that "Hamann realized from the very beginning of his walk with Christ that philosophers who do not take Christ as their starting point are not 'neutral' but rather dedicated to presuppositions of their own. This is why, for instance, they deny the creation account of the Bible, and seek to substitute for it a

argument from ignorance, the fallacy of personal incredulity: he means us to accept the idea that since he cannot imagine how the immanence of human knowledge is imposed by human language, then it is not imposed by human language. Instead, language must grant access to the same transcendent realm imagined by Milbank's own sect of Anglican Christendom. Likewise, Milbank says since he cannot imagine how we, being bounded, can ascertain the real bounds of human finitude, then finitude must not be bounded after all, but must run into infinity. Milbank's position can be summarized: "if I do not know the nature of the boundary marked by language, then it is not knowable, and therefore, the boundary is meaningless." It may be hard to believe a body of theorizing so complex rests upon such commonplace fallacious argumentation, but that does not mean it does not: the form of Milbank's approach, even without the details of his scholarly maltreatments, is self-refuting. Attentiveness to the entitlement of Hamann's metacritical position would have suggested a different track.

Once Milbank's basic move is identified, it becomes readily apparent throughout his work. Milbank refers us to Charles Taylor's notion of the "background dimension" necessary for making sense of experience and "getting right" our contentions, yet from this insight into human cognition that Taylor locates in the thought of Herder, Milbank veers hard to claim "from this background of the implicit . . . it is impossible to exclude the pressure upon us of a transcendent and infinite reality."[43] Once again then, the argument from personal incredulity: "because I cannot imagine that this allegedly immanent framework truly *excludes* a transcendent right of entry, then it does not; in fact, it necessarily *entails* a transcendent right of entry."

'story' of their own which would 'explain creation as a natural event.'" And: "While biblical creation is fundamental and crucial in Hamann's thought, he covers a wealth of other subjects pertinent and profitable from the Christian biblical perspective in the social sciences and humanities." Milbank might also agree with Myers about feeling "greatly blessed by [her] preliminary study of Hamann's valiant and profound contributions to Christian apologetics for his own time and even more strongly for our own. He anticipated [. . .] yes, the creationist movement since the 1960s." Milbank would certainly agree with Myers on the importance of "the unity between creation and redemption in the eternal Providence of God and the importance of allowing no autonomy whatever to man and man's reason [. . .] in our own neo-pagan age." Myers, "Johann Georg Hamann." Academics who would prefer not to deign to the inanity on display on the creationism website should note that compliance with Milbank's movement already implies their connivance with just that.

43. *TST*, 152. Taylor's argument may be found in 1985, 1991 (*op. cit.*).

Or once more, Milbank argues (fairly, I find) that, insofar as Hamann and Herder deny the possibility of rationally ascertaining the cognitive or normative ground of judgment, they identify *metaphor* as the origin, genesis, or ultimate resource of discursive activity (in other words, as I have argued, our epistemic limitation entails the fact that, like Socrates, we can say what things are *like* but not what things are). But from this assessment, Milbank concludes that "if metaphor is fundamental, then religion ceases to be a mystery *in addition to* the mystery of humanity itself."[44] Of course, *that* the ground of our alleged objectivity shows up as a metaphorical construction means nothing of the kind about religion, devotion, or ritual; indeed, if it implies anything about these, it is their basic irrelevance vis-à-vis the cognitive need for metaphor, and their subsumption under the more primary force of metaphoricity.

By creating a body of work that hinges upon just these assertions, Milbank relinquishes the Hamannian metacritical standpoint he claims to follow.[45] Hence, he continues to play two, irreconcilable tunes throughout his oeuvre, with no means of linking them together. On the one hand, Milbank admits the uncertainty with which human intellectual endeavors are fraught, and he seems to object to attempts to make God or his properties the subject of epistemic claims. God is, rather, "unclassifiable," while good religion invokes an "openness to the strange." On the other hand, Milbank claims that because God is "not an object of our knowledge," no human discourse has "any secular or scientific autonomy in relation to theology," and Christian theology must get on with its true mission of subjugating all other discourses to its ends.[46] Christian theology is authorized on this front by Christian theology itself, which nevertheless refers to its "transcendent source" for sanction. Should the new theology fail in its mission, and at every moment that it has not yet accomplished it, nihilism prevails, and all that is meaningful in human life ebbs away. So Milbank tells us Radical Orthodoxy is aligned with that (Hamannian, but also Platonic, empiricist, and pragmatist) tradition which is open to the "strange and unclassifiable," but his arguments begin and end with the guarantee that we are, after all, a

---

44. WMS, 106.

45. When I make the case that Milbank skids inappropriately from the Hamannian retrieval of faith in everyday experience to arguments from personal incredulity about Being, I have not implied that theological modes clearer about their metaphysical commitments cannot claim to be reason-based, but only that Milbank's alleged metacritical methodology should commit him to a different form of skepticism, and ultimately, of faith.

46. WMS, 2–3.

mise en abyme in the mind of God, a narrative contained within and justified by the greater narrative of our creator. This guarantee flies in the face of the Hamannian construal of knowledge, faith, and freedom.

Hamann's Leap and Milbank's Guarantee

As Milbank tells it, Hamann radically challenges the Scotist legacy in two essential ways: first, Hamann argues that no finite thing can be known, "*not even to any degree,*" apart from its ratio to the infinite. Second, Milbank explains, Hamann argues that the truth or value of nature rests exclusively upon its supernatural ordination.[47] I have argued the very notion of "the infinite" is a regulative projection in Hamann; it is something we think about insofar as it can be compared to our experience and insofar as our language limits what can be said about it. When we nonetheless leap with faith into the hope for the existence of the infinite, our metacritical standpoint obliges us to remain clear about the finite, immanent conditions of our assertion of faith. Likewise, Hamann's discussion of nature consistently focuses upon its sensuousness, which Hamann speaks of most when he discusses the tangible pleasure of human sexuality.[48] To encounter nature is to meet a physically demanding, corporeal reality, which may be read as the very body-being of God, but which Hamann never describes as a mere quotient to be measured out and reckoned in relation to an available "infinity." When we encounter nature (as we continuously do), we engage with bodies and changing phenomena that are often compelling, as in the case of our own bodily needs. But if we are assured, as Milbank would assure us, that bodies are not really bodies and nature not really nature, nor the limitations of our experience as they appear to be, then that which Hamann considers the site of our embrace of divinity would be emptied of the features which, for Hamann, characterize it.

Milbank seems to consider the possibility that Hamann would oppose the attribution of these arguments to himself, and he even quotes Hamann, in a letter to Jacobi, refusing to allow the idea Spinozism (or everything contained in the formulation *Deus sive Natura*) leads to nihilism, and calling Jacobi "too otherworldly."[49] Yet here Milbank only notes Hamann's

---

47. RO, 24 (Milbank's emphasis).

48. For example, in the *Essay of a Sibyl on Marriage*, in Dickson (*op. cit.*).

49. RO, 26. The letters quoted are those of January 23, 1785 and April 27, 1787 in *Johann Georg Hamann: Briefwechsel* (*op. cit.*).

"strange peevishness" is refusing to go along with Jacobi and therefore with Milbank's own reading. Likewise, Milbank admits if Hamann has a fault, it is in his tendency "to *replace* altogether a sense of an analogical ascent to God, or of a continuously deepened participation in divine eternity, with the notion of God's kenotic adaptation to us [. . .] This . . . does not allow for the New Testament notion that God became man in order to incorporate us into the Trinity—to make us indeed more heavenly and spiritual . . ."[50] Having understood as much, however, Milbank straight away adds that here, at least, Jacobi should be read as "balancing out" Hamann, and the two of them thus taken as a pair, even though "Hamann's attitude to Jacobi is strange and problematical."

There is another possibility however; for Hamann cannot be faulted, accused of peevishness, or of being a strange friend if his own, avowed position is that the contingency of history and the sensuousness of nature *are* the sites of divine being, *insofar as* we can conceive of such things; and further, that we can continue to think about and respond to this conception of divinity in an acknowledged analogy to our own nature, language, and experience.

Milbank's theological program requires the pre-emption of what he takes to be the modern philosophical conceptions of finitude, contingency, subjectivity, and material nature, by the properly Christian narrative which places them within a framework that confirms in advance infinitude, certainty, and divine omnipotence, the supernatural character of embodied life, and the containment of all individual beings within divine Being. This confirmation makes the world reliable and guarantees the consequence of one's individual, immortal life. Nonetheless, it is just this sort of guarantee and reliability that bankrupt authentic religious experience, Hamann tells us. What is necessary and reliable is not thereby ennobled, unless, Hamann teases, we would want to say the "infallible and unerring instinct of insects" trumps human reasoning at every turn.[51] As we saw, Hamann is adamant in claiming, with Job, "God is great and we know him not." Hamann also aligns himself with Socrates in this regard: one is wise who knows how little he knows. For Hamann, our ignorance is the condition of possibility for our freedom, not our guarantee of divine intervention. Freedom is, again, the seat of our consciousness, attentiveness, our ability to think abstractly, and our moral conscience; freedom is the human being's most

50. *RO*, 31.
51. *Philological Ideas and Doubts*, Dickson translation (*op. cit.*).

"perfect law," making each into his own legislator. For Hamann, the God who condescends to earth is the God who leaves us free. The "gift" of free will is the corollary of divine agency, but its actual recognition and exercise requires the God who has given the gift become a human ideal; for if God's existence is known to be more than *our* ideal, then everything, after all, is guaranteed, and free will becomes a barren concept.

Hamann's thinking about individual free will and the onus to cultivate the self locate him closer to the "liberal-humanist" model of self-creation than Milbank can allow. But Hamann is resolute: we know individuals qua agents, as free, unique expressions of personality, and our agency is not equipped with hidden parachutes, for one either leaps into the unknown, or one never really leaps at all. Hamann does privilege the universality of narrative, and he certainly adores the narratives available in Scripture, but he is sensitive to a point that Milbank, in his role as an adjudicator of the church, must overlook. Hamann understands we choose to perform a reading (paradigmatically, of Scripture) that characterizes our freedom within a certain narrative, and he recognizes to narrate freedom is to give it a kind of determination. To articulate the *mythos* of human free will in a particular way is to express the individuality of one's reading in tandem with the individuality of the theological object.[52] In other words, the interpretation of texts is both an act and an expression of free individuality, and the God about whom one speaks, in such a case, is known as an individual. Each of us therefore creates our own profession of faith, and to attempt to universalize that articulation as doctrine or to enforce it as rule is to make a shift from individual event to authoritarian imposition.

No careful reader of Kierkegaard could be surprised to uncover this Hamannian position, for what Kierkegaard famously lauds in Hamann is hardly the "Christendom" for which Milbank has appointed himself speaker. And like Kierkegaard, Hamann deserves the term "radical"—not

---

52. I am indebted to the writings of Edward P. Butler for this insight. Butler analyzes neither Hamann nor Milbank; rather, much of his work is devoted to the theological exploration of the agency of divine individuals insofar as it manifests in narrative and iconic representation. See for example "Polytheism and Individuality in the Henadic Manifold"; "The Theological Interpretation of Myth"; "Offering to the Gods: A Neoplatonic Perspective"; and "The Gods and Being in Proclus." In "God's Care for Human Individuals: What Neoplatonism Gives to a Christian Doctrine of Providence," his keynote address to *Neoplatonism and Its Legacy: The 2009 Annual Conference on Christian Philosophy*, Wayne J. Hankey utilizes Butler's work to show how engagement with the divine can be understood as an encounter between individuals, in which divine individuality is mirrored in human individuality.

because he is an "anti-liberal," "anti-Enlightenment," "conservative revolutionary," but, on the contrary, because his venture weeds out, from the mystery of existence and the unadulterated responsibility we must take for our own, all promises of transcendence, no matter if they are amplified by the church, the academy, or the state.

Milbank's greatest fear—or at least the justification for his martial agenda—is, again, the impending threat of nihilism. The reason philosophy must be usurped, other theologies undercut, and secularism in all its manifestations rejected, is that each of these is geared to end in the great Nihil. Yet reading Hamann should tell us there is an absolute difference between the nihilism of exhaustion and the recognition of individual, existential freedom. Though both the "nihilistic" and the "existential" positions hold that a transcendent guarantee means nothing, only the latter allows us to continue to narrate a life of meaning, and refuses any panacea, which eases its difficulties at the cost of denying the mystery of human freedom. Milbank's conflation of what I've called the existential possibility with what he calls the nihilistic threat leads him to issue an ultimatum, which he credits Hamann with originating. Milbank relates that sense in which, for Hamann, "to be human means . . . that we must reckon with an immense depth behind things." Milbank continues: "There are only two possible attitudes to this depth: for the first, like Kant, we distinguish what is clear from what is hidden: but then the depth is an abyss, and what appears, as only apparent, will equally induce vertigo. This is why critical philosophy, the attitude of pure reason itself, is also the stance of nihilism. [. . .] The second possibility is that we trust the depth, and appearance as the gift of depth, and history as the restoration of the loss of this depth in Christ."[53]

By now it should be clear the Hamann I read, and, I believe, the Hamann who Kierkegaard read, would say this "depth" is the necessary context of the leap of faith, the only guarantor of human freedom, and as such, the condition of our rational and moral maturity—but only if it remains a gulf, and is not exchanged for the promise of everlasting surety. Hamann's *Socratic Memorabilia* tells us the maieutic art was developed precisely because we do not know what lurks in the depths until it is articulated and analyzed; oftentimes, what has been hiding behind appearances is naïve or politically dangerous. Moreover, the figure of Socrates reminds us the beautiful-bodied are not always the good-souled, as disappointing as that may be. Rather, our task is to risk vertigo (a fine description of the philosopher's sense upon

53. *RO*, 32.

leaving and returning to the cave), and to provoke and engage the logos which, once born from each psyche, becomes amenable to judgment. Of course, Milbank would remind us that he's already refused philosophy on Radical Orthodoxy's behalf—but then he has also refused Hamann, and with him, the means of connecting this language of appearances and contingency with the hope for a language of presence, staked on infinity.

Milbank would like Radical Orthodoxy to be that theology which transcends the opposition between finitude and infinity, the demands of materiality and the promise of spirituality, in order to recover the primal, persistent generativity of the Christian God. In order to develop his position, Milbank returns to the iterative embeddedness of human reason probed by Hamann, and uses the insight as an anchor for his chronicle of the misbegotten creation of the secular realm. At the same time, however, this very insight, and the perspective on human thought and history it affords, disallows Milbank's advancement of the church dogmas upon which he insists, and undermines his own claims of expertise. Because Milbank's theology cannot suffer critique, contextualization, or even comparison with bodies of thinking that make different use of its favored images, it loses its standing as a study of discourses about divinity. Likewise, having made his central doctrine about the divine presence in human epistemic and linguistic practices dependent upon an argument from personal incredulity, Milbank's theology has left no further resource but the appeal to authority to sustain its claim of access to the mind of God, a claim it uses to insist upon its own mandate to arbitrate social theories and practices. In effect, then, though Milbank seems to see himself as a prophet, his theology ceases to be a genuine theology at all, and must be understood as intricate apologetics for an authoritarian, predictably conservative socio-political agenda.

Bibliography

Alexander, W. M. *Johann Georg Hamann: Philosophy and Faith*. The Hague: Martinus Nijhoff, 1966.

Bayer, Oswald. "Gegen System und Struktur: Die Theologische Aktualität Johann Georg Hamanns." In *Johann Georg Hamann: Acta des internationalen Hamann-Colloquiums*, edited by Bernhard Gajek. Frankfurt am Main: Vittorio Klostermann, 1979.

Betz, John R. *After Enlightenment: Hamann as Post-Secular Visionary*. West Sussex: Wiley-Blackwell, 2009.

Butler, Edward P. "Offering to the Gods: A Neoplatonic Perspective." *Magic, Ritual, and Witchcraft* 2:1 (2007) 1–20.

———. "Polytheism and Individuality in the Henadic Manifold." *Dionysius* 23 (2005) 83–104.

———. "The Gods and Being in Proclus." *Dionysius* 26 (2008).

———. "God's Care for Human Individuals: What Neoplatonism Gives to a Christian Doctrine of Providence." Keynote address, Neoplatonism and Its Legacy: The 2009 Annual Conference on Christian Philosophy, Conference at Fransican University of Steubenville.

———. "The Theological Interpretation of Myth." *The Pomegranate: The International Journal of Pagan Studies* 7:1 (2005) 27–41.

Dickson, Gwen Griffith. *Johann Georg Hamann's Relational Metacriticism*. New York: Walter de Gruyter, 1995.

Hankey, Wayne J. "Radical Orthodoxy's *Poiesis*: Ideological Historiography and Anti-Modern Polemic." *American Catholic Philosophical Quarterly* 80:1 (2006) 1–21.

Hankey, Wayne J. and Douglas Hedley. *Deconstructing Radical Orthodoxy: Postmodern Theology, Rhetoric and Truth*. Aldershot: Ashgate, 2005.

Haynes, Kenneth. "Aesthetica in Nuce." In *Hamann: Writings on Philosophy and Language*, translated and edited by Kenneth Haynes, 60–95. New York: Cambridge University Press, 2007.

Hedley, Douglas. "Should Divinity Overcome Metaphysics? Reflections on John Milbank's Theology beyond Secular Reason and Confessions of a Cambridge Platonist." *The Journal of Religion* 80:2 (April 2000) 271–98.

Henkel, Arthur, and Walter Ziesemer. *Briefwechsel*. Frankfurt am Main: Insel, 1955–79.

Janz, Paul D. "Radical Orthodoxy and the New Culture of Obscurantism." *Modern Theology* 20 (2004) 362–405.

Kuehn, Manfred. *Kant: A Biography*. Cambridge University Press, 2001.

Lovin, Robin. Review of *Theology and Social Theory: Beyond Secular Reason* by John Milbank. *The Journal of Religion* 74:1 (January 1994) 113–14.

Milbank, John et al. *Radical Orthodoxy*. New York: Routledge, 1999.

Milbank, John. *Being Reconciled: Ontology and Pardon*. New York: Routledge, 2003.

———. *Theology and Social Theory: Beyond Secular Reason*. Cambridge: Blackwell Publishers, 1990.

———. *The Word Made Strange: Theology, Language, Culture*. Cambridge: Blackwell Publishers, 1997.

Myers, Ellen. "Johann Georg Hamann (1730–1788), Preacher of Christ in the Wilderness of the Enlightenment." No pages. Online: http://www.creationism.org/csshs/v07n3p19.htm.

Nadler, Josef. *Sämtliche Werke*. Historische-Kritische Ausgabe. Vienna: Herder, 1949–1957.

———. *Johann Georg Hamann. Der Zeuge des Corpus mysticum*. Salzburg: Otto Müller, 1949.

O'Flaherty, James C. *Hamann's Socratic Memorabilia: A Translation and Commentary*. Baltimore: Johns Hopkins, 1967.

Smith, Anthony Paul, and Daniel Whistler. Introduction for *After the Postsecular and the Postmodern: New Essays in Continental Philosophy of Religion*. Newcastle upon Tyne: Cambridge Scholars Publishing, 2010.

Stackhouse, Max. Review of *The Word Made Strange: Theology, Language, Culture* by John Milbank. *The Journal of Religion* 78:4 (October 1998) 640–41.

Surber, Jere Paul. *Metacritique: The Linguistic Assault on German Idealism*. Translated by Jere Paul Surber. Amherst: Humanity Books, 2001.

Taylor, Charles. *Human Agency and Language*. Philosophical Papers I. Cambridge, New York: Cambridge University Press, 1985.

———. "The Importance of Herder." In *Isaiah Berlin: A Celebration*, edited by Edna and Avishai Margalit. Chicago: University of Chicago Press, 1991.

Terezakis, Katie. "Language and Immanence in Hamann." *Graduate Faculty Philosophy Journal* 27:2 (November 2006) 25–50.

———. *The Immanent Word: The Turn to Language in German Philosophy 1759-1801*. New York: Routledge, 2007.

———. "Is Theology Possible After Hamann?" In *Hamann and the Tradition*, edited by Lisa Marie Anderson. Evanston, IL: Northwestern University Press, 2011.

Walker, James R. Review of *Philosophical Legacies: Essays on the Thought of Kant, Hegel, and Their Contemporaries* by Daniel Dahlstrom. *Notre Dame Philosophical Reviews* (January 2009). No pages. Online: http://ndpr.nd.edu/review.cfm?id=15006.

Wisse, Maarten. Review of *Deconstructing Radical Orthodoxy* by Wayne J. Hankey and Douglas Hedley. *Ars Disputandi* 8 (2008) 10–17.

Zweig, Arnulf. *Immanuel Kant: Philosophical Correspondence 1759-99*. Translated by Arnulf Zweig. University of Chicago Press, 1967.

4

The Less Sublime Allure of the Paradox

Some Kierkegaardian Provocations to John Milbank[1]

Leo Stan

In his compelling introduction to the creationistic gist, Trinitarian theology, liturgical materiality, and anti-secularist ecclesiology of the Anglo-Saxon school of Radical Orthodoxy, James K. A. Smith[2] assigns the Danish philosopher and religious writer, Søren Kierkegaard (1813–1855), a marginal, although not necessarily negligible, place in the historical palimpsest of his topic. More exactly, Kierkegaard comes across as a precursor to Radical Orthodoxy on the basis of his adhesion to an anti-rational "counter-modernity,"[3] by virtue of which he raised fundamental objections to the Enlightenment agenda.[4] Smith also observes—rightly so, in my view—that Kierkegaard's creationism accords with the basic creed of Radical Orthodoxy.[5] Moreover, within a genealogical perspective, he remarks that Kierkegaard's rebuttal of the autonomy of philosophy has been fruitfully appropriated by

---

1. This article has been made possible through a generous postdoctoral grant offered by the Social Sciences and Humanities Research Council of Canada, to which I extend my full gratitude.
2. Smith, *Introducing Radical Orthodoxy*.
3. Ibid., 54.
4. Ibid., 32–33 and 76 note 7.
5. Ibid., 88.

the most prominent member of the movement, John Milbank.[6] However, regarding the trope of desire, Smith's tone becomes critical. He points out that in contrast to Radical Orthodoxy—which thinks desire along the lines of a Trinitarian soteriology favorable to *eros*[7]—Kierkegaard advocates a kind of "private . . . love affair with the absolute."[8]

Eight years prior to Smith's informed propaedeutic, Kierkegaard had already entered the inclusive purview of Radical Orthodoxy via a substantial essay, authored by John Milbank and entitled "The Sublime in Kierkegaard."[9] Probably due to its reduced relevance within the overall economy of the volume, this article appears only once in Smith's *Introducing Radical Orthodoxy*, namely in the bibliography. The present study is, therefore, meant to fill a particular gap in James Smith's approach. That is, going beyond Smith's laconic observations about the Danish thinker, I aim to critically explore the distinctive way in which John Milbank interprets a few Christian tropes in Kierkegaard's thought. In a sense, my goal is infinitely more modest than Smith's since I deal with a narrow issue concerning a single member of Radical Orthodoxy. Yet, not unlike Smith, while concerning myself with some theoretical particularities of Radical Orthodoxy, I will bring to surface certain limitations of Milbank's encounter with Kierkegaard. In addition, on a constructive note, I briefly indicate a few unexplored areas opened by Milbank's exegesis, which the vast field of Kierkegaard studies cannot afford to ignore.

1. Ontology, Universality, Subjectivity

John Milbank commences the above-mentioned article by noting that some of Kierkegaard's categories transpire as "quasi-ontological,"[10] i.e., as coevally ontological and existential.[11] Milbank specifically envisions the notion of the

---

6. Ibid., 151.

7. Smith references here Ward's *Cities of God*, 172, 174.

8. Smith, *Introducing Radical Orthodoxy*, 246. Hereby, Smith uncritically appropriates a mere shibboleth—now long outdated—regarding Kierkegaard's alleged spiritual solipsism. In point of fact, Kierkegaard makes the opposite case in WL. For authoritative and comprehensive commentaries in this regard see Jamie Ferreira, *Love's Grateful Striving*.

9. Milbank, "The Sublime in Kierkegaard." The article was reprinted two years later in Philip Blond, *Post-Secular Philosophy*. Throughout this essay, references will be to the second edition; henceforth SIK.

10. SIK, 68.

11. Ibid., 71.

moment, repetition, anxiety, and *inter-esse*. Even if Kierkegaard's dialectic of being and becoming interests Milbank only marginally, the latter's argument could be reinforced by the fact that Kierkegaard conceives of these two concepts in antagonistic, although interconnected, terms.[12] Thus, Kierkegaard's partial ontology may have also been conjectured from the principle that "the medium of being [*Væren*]"—which "implies growth and composure"—must be distinguished from "the medium of becoming [*Vorden*]"—which is the natural environment of the single individual's free, *angst*-ridden resolutions and acts.[13] More importantly, Kierkegaard senses the portentous quality of this distinction when he combats Spinoza and Schleiermacher for having "esthetically-metaphysically"[14] ascribed religiousness a purely ontological meaning; whereas, for him, the true religion "is essentially to be conceived ethically,"[15] that is to say, as inextricable from personal inward striving.[16] Put differently, Kierkegaard's almost exclusive concern has been with the person's Christian self-becoming, more precisely, with the relational structure of a finite subjectivity that is ceaselessly called to become an unrepeatable self before God and the God-man. Therefore, in conjunction with Milbank we can conceivably argue that Kierkegaard was a mild "saboteur" of classical religious ontology or that his "apparently 'existential' categories . . . are also 'anti-ontological.'"[17]

12. See, for ex., *Pap. X2 A 324/JP* 263.

13. *Pap.* IX A 450/ *JP* 2011.

14. *Pap.* X2 417/ *JP* 3853. The word "aesthetically" encompasses ethical irresponsibility or personal disengagement.

15. *Pap.* X2 417/*JP* 3853.

16. Schleiermacher, Kierkegaard elaborates, "represents everything in the sphere of being (*Væren*). How it becomes (*vorder*) in the sense of coming to exist (*blive til*) and in the sense of being maintained does not really concern him. [However,] Every Christian qualification is characterized by the ethical oriented to striving. From this comes fear and trembling, and the you shall; from this [comes] also the possibility of offense etc. This is of minor concern to Schleiermacher. He treats religiousness in the sphere of being." *Pap.* X2 A 416/*JP* 3852. See also *Pap.* X2 417/*JP* 3853. For Kierkegaard's critiques of Spinoza see *PF* esp. 40–2 and *Pap.* VII1 C 1–4/*JP* 4319–4322.

17. SIK, 71. Here it must be added that Kierkegaard's opposition to ontology should not be overstated. There are instances when Kierkegaard deems being secondary in relation to the category of quality, whereas the latter is pivotal in his understanding of human existence. See *Pap.* IV C 66, 67/*JP* 1598, 1599. At the same time, Kierkegaard continues to consider being commensurable with intensiveness or interiority. That, I claim, may be an indirect reference to being's inescapable interrelatedness with becoming. See *Pap.* XI1 A 500/*JP* 2103. *Pap.* XI2 A 64 / *JP* 2104. This aspect is in full accord with Anti-Climacus's processual view of selfhood: "Insofar as [the self] is itself, it is the necessary, and insofar

At this juncture, Milbank takes a significant step. He states that Kierkegaard's subjectivity is intrinsically tied to "an alternately and indeterminately creative and destructive process."[18] Of these two processes, however, Milbank tends to favor the negative one. Thus, to him the Kierkegaardian self appears "endlessly liable to fracture and postponement," or "simultaneously preconstituted and deconstituted by a repetitious dynamic which permits only an illusory self-mastery."[19] Consequently, while going back to Kierkegaard's categories, Milbank's preliminary conclusion is that they "prevent us affirming any universal identities or even sites of identity."[20]

Particularly striking here is not so much the viable attempt at deconstructing Kierkegaard's anthropology.[21] What surprises us is the secular setting, wherein Milbank chooses to couch these observations; although, as we will see below, he is not unaware of theological roots of Kierkegaard's psychology. The most puzzling, however, remains the fact that Milbank turns a blind eye to Kierkegaard's open affirmation of a universal site of personal identity.[22] It is to this issue that I turn now.

---

as it has the task of becoming itself, it is a possibility." SD 35. Kierkegaard's category of "being-in-and-for-itself" might be of additional relevance here. See *Pap.* X4 A 581/*JP* 536. *Pap.* XI2 A 133/*JP* 1449. *Pap.* X4 A 636/*JP* 4902. *Pap.* X4 A 474/*JP* 6793.

18. SIK, 69.

19. Ibid. Hence, the suspicion that Kierkegaard's anthropology may not be incompatible with poststructuralism, a possibility which Milbank quickly dismisses. See SIK, 69, 72, 76. I fully subscribe to Milbank's argument. The classical appropriation of Kierkegaard in the poststructuralist environment is offered by Gilles Deleuze in *Difference and Repetition*. For the broad contours of poststructuralism see Johannes Willem Bertens, *The Idea of the Postmodern. A History*.

20. SIK, 71.

21. However, this interpretive trend is not completely without problems. Some of the difficulties related to deconstructing Kierkegaard, in general, have been shortly, yet trenchantly, outlined by Sylvia Walsh in "Kierkegaard and Postmodernism." Walsh's caveat is worth quoting here: "Far from embracing deconstruction or irony except as a strategy for dismounting untruth in whatever form it may appear, Kierkegaard's thought constitutes an implied critique of postmodernism just as much as it was explicitly as well as implicitly critical of Hegelian idealism and German romanticism. From his standpoint— which is not the standpoint of irony, but of striving in humility, love, faith, and hope—to realize that which is existentially true and upbuilding in life, postmodernism would appear, I suspect, as another form or perhaps the culmination of romanticism, neither postmodern nor truly modem in its Nietzschean aestheticism." Ibid., 121.

22. This is true only of SIK. Somewhere else, Milbank advocates an entirely different view. With Kierkegaard, he will come to realize, "the finite has taken on the weight of an infinitely disclosive significance, such that the personhood or 'personality' of the human being breaks entirely, as Jacques Maritain and Emmanuel Mounier taught, the bounds of

To begin with, contrary to Milbank, Kierkegaard does admit that inwardness—probably the central category of his thought—represents the "universally human."[23] Second, he recognizes that nothing is more indispensable to the proper encounter with human alterity than the all-encompassing notions of humankind, fellow citizen, and especially the neighbor.[24] Next, in *Either/Or* II, Kierkegaard has the paragon of ethics, Judge William, define the self's constitution as a unitary compound of universality and particularity.[25] Which is why William warns that "[not] until the individual himself is the universal, not until then can the ethical be actualized."[26] His explanation is also worth heeding: "The universal human being is not a phantom, but every human being is the universal human being—that is, every human being is shown the way by which he becomes the universal human being. The person who lives esthetically is an accidental human being; he believes he is the perfect human being by being the one and only human being. The person who lives ethically works toward becoming the universal human being."[27]

Further, in *Concluding Unscientific Postscript*—on which Milbank relies considerably—the pseudonym Johannes Climacus declares that since "[every] human being must be assumed to possess essentially what belongs *essentially* to being a human being," a consistent "subjective thinker" must become "an instrument that clearly and definitely expresses in existence the

---

her 'individuality'—she becomes distinct precisely at that point where her action cannot be seen as a mere example of a general principle and, rather, becomes 'equal' in significance to humanity taken as a whole." Slavoj Žižek and John Milbank, *The Monstrosity of Christ*, 168. Milbank never illumines this possible self-contradiction.

23. *PV*, 25–26.

24. *EO* II, 328–32. *WL* 72–73, 147. *Pap.* II A 462/JP 2384. Additional comments can be found in Paul R. Sponheim, *Kierkegaard on Christ and Christian Coherence*, 145ff.

25. *EO* II, 263–4; see also 259. On this occasion, I should remind that of all Kierkegaardian pseudonyms, Milbank considers Anti-Climacus "Kierkegaard's spokesman for ethical immediacy." SIK 76. Yet, this title ought to be assigned to judge William, given Kierkegaard's intention to project Anti-Climacus as the pseudonym with the highest Christian (i.e., primarily salvific) consciousness. I have dealt with the irreconcilable differences between judge William's ethics and Anti-Climacus's soteriology in Leo Stan, *Either Nothingness or Love*, 20–43, 59–73, 101–11, 119–21.

26. *EO* II, 255.

27. Ibid., 256. See also *CUP*, 356: "To will to be an individual being . . . with the help of and by virtue of one's difference is flabbiness. But to will to be an individual existing human being . . . in the same sense as *everyone else* is capable of being—that is the ethical victory over life and over every mirage, the victory that is perhaps the most difficult of all in the theocentric nineteenth century." Italics mine.

essentially human."[28] This essentialism proves instrumental to ethics inasmuch as the individual acquires a paradigmatic status by merely assuming an ethical mode of existence; hence, Climacus will argue, the universalist trait of ethics.

When questioning above the secular undertones of Milbank's approach, I had in mind the prominence of Kierkegaard's universalism within the confines of religion. To detail, Kierkegaard's scorn for the equation of individuality with a set of psychological or socio-political differences issues from the belief in a religiously sanctioned universality.[29] On this very basis, Kierkegaard deplores the existence of individuals "who have inhumanly forgotten that everyone should fortify himself by means of the universal divine likeness of all people, have forgotten that therefore, whether a person is man or woman, poorly or richly endowed, master or slave, beggar or plutocrat, the relationships among human beings ought and may never be such that the one worships and the other is the one worshiped."[30] It is no wonder, then, that universality figures amongst the defining attributes of Kierkegaard's fideism. Thus, as if counteracting all future indictments of solipsism or callous indifference towards the spiritual condition of others, Kierkegaard remarks that "the person who wishes [faith] for himself wishes it for every human being, because that by which another person has faith is not that by which he is different from him but is that by which he is like him; that by which he possesses it is not that by which he is different from others but that by which he is *altogether like all.*"[31]

But the controversy of Milbank's thesis is much ampler. In Kierkegaard's thought the universal subject gains even more salience once it enters the terrain of Christianity, the epicenter of which lies in spiritual equality.[32] The Danish thinker warns that the Christian religion has "deeply and forever memorably [imprinted] the kinship of all human beings—because the kinship is secured by each individual's equal kinship with and relationship to God in Christ; because the Christian doctrine addressed itself equally to each individual, teaches him that God has created him and Christ has redeemed him; . . ."[33] Neighbor love is no exception, either. Kierkegaard

28. *CUP*, 356; italics mine.
29. See Howard and Edna Hong's Historical Introduction to *EUD*, xix and note 26.
30. *WL*, 125.
31. *EUD*, 10; italics added.
32. Kierkegaard calls it "the blessed equality of the essentially Christian." *WL*, 70.
33. *WL*, 69. See also *M* 180 where Kierkegaard remarks that "God wants Christianity to be proclaimed unconditionally to all, therefore the apostles are very simple, ordinary

rests assured that the very notion of neighbor is broad enough to allow every Christian to love humanity *per se* in every single individual.[34] It is for no other reason, he further clarifies, that neighbor love is to obstruct any concern with "removing this or that dissimilarity, or with eliminating all of them in a worldly way;" rather, upon practicing agape the believer should "devoutly [concern] himself with permeating his dissimilarity with the sanctifying thought of Christian equality . . ."[35]

2. Reason vs. Paradox: An Epic Battle

As a theologian with extensive knowledge of Western philosophy, John Milbank boldly reopens the long-standing debate on faith's relation to reason in Kierkegaard.[36] First, he observes that in *Philosophical Fragments*, "Kierkegaard proceeds to reinvent, or to repeat, a different logos, associated not with the 'identity' of Socrates (attained through recollection), but with the 'identity' of Christ."[37] At the same time, probably with an eye to the fruitful encounter between Greek philosophy and early Christian theology, Milbank puts forward the original thesis that "absurdity and paradox are not, in the first place, attributes of faith as opposed to reason, but on the contrary, the inner suppressed reality of (Greek) reason itself."[38] Conceivably relying on his indebtedness to Radical Orthodoxy, Milbank goes even further and contends that with Kierkegaard "'absurdity' and 'paradox' now become names *for* (a higher) reason, and what appeared acutely

---

people, therefore the prototype [i.e., Jesus] is in the lowly form of a servant, all this in order to indicate that this extraordinary is the ordinary, is open to all . . ." Kierkegaard thus evaluates as unchristian to "independently [want] to deny kinship with all people, with unconditionally every person." *WL*, 74. On the "essential humanity" attained via religion, see *TA* 88–89, 93. Sponheim, *op. cit.*, 149 note 85.

34. Even if "no one has ever seen *humanity*," Kierkegaard holds, when practicing neighbor-love "'humanity' is the essential specification." *WL*, 147. See also Pia Søltoft, "The Presence of the Absent Neighbor in *Works of Love*." See also Amy Laura Hall, *Kierkegaard and the Treachery of Love*, 175–76.

35. *WL*, 73.

36. For the larger background of this discussion see Smith, *Introducing Radical Orthodoxy*, 143–84.

37. *SIK*, 72.

38. Ibid., 71. Milbank specifically targets *PF*, 54–67. For a slightly different formulation of the same argument see Žižek and Milbank, *The Monstrosity of Christ*, 169–70.

embarrassing for reason turns out, on the contrary, to disclose the true order and possibility of human thought."[39]

For Milbank, all of this indicates that in elaborating Christianity's contrastive rapports with the Greek logos, *Philosophical Fragments* is driven by a proto-deconstructive teleology.[40] The originality of this hypothesis should be immediately remarked. However, given my present aims (and scholarly expertise), I will set this particular issue aside in the hope that future research will elucidate its exegetical promise. What I wish to dissect instead is the conjecture that Kierkegaard makes use of a discretely hierarchical notion of rationality.[41] *Pace* Milbank, I will claim that a) in *Philosophical Frag-*

---

39. SIK, 71. In *The Monstrosity of Christ*, 177, Milbank states that, in fact, Kierkegaard's "attempt to find a common logic throughout Christian belief ensures that doctrine is not reduced to a random series of revealed declarations, and that a Christian understanding of reason can be presented in continuity with a rational comprehension of the role of revelation." As intriguing as it may sound, for Milbank, Kierkegaard incarnates "the most hyperrational of all Western philosophers." Ibid., 217.

40. SIK, 72.

41. This thesis may accord with Milbank's surmise that Kierkegaard's "linking of faith with reason (and vice versa) restores a basically Catholic perspective . . . " See also *The Monstrosity of Christ*, 112 and 117, where Milbank holds that Kierkegaard can be seen as "a radically Catholic humanist alternative to" the "dialectical (Lutheran, Behmenist, Kantian, Hegelian) version of Christian doctrine." (Puzzlingly enough, Milbank also speaks of a Hegelian dimension of Kierkegaard's subjectivity; idem, 180–81.) Regarding Catholic humanism, Milbank relies on the fact that Kierkegaard, *pace* Luther, underscored the inseparability between faith and works. Idem, 219 note 5. The theme of Kierkegaard's Catholic leanings is too vast to be treated in a footnote. However, on this particular trope Milbank has against him Kierkegaard's insistence on the infinite need for grace as a result of humankind's infinite culpa (*EO* II, 339–54) and corruption (*SD*, 75ff). Also, the traces Kant and Hegel did leave on Kierkegaard's thought are deeper than Milbank acknowledges. See also notes 103 and 118 below. As to Kierkegaard's attachment to works, it should be taken *cum grano salis*. Although The Epistle of James has a special place in his heart, Kierkegaard admits the true believer is to resist the temptation to build one's salvation on any work whatsoever; instead she must ascribe every soteriological power to God only. *EUD*, 272. (Note also the Lutheran echoes of this theological stance.) The intimate link between faith and incertitude—given that throughout this life the awareness of salvation never takes away the possibility of perdition—can be interpreted to the same effect. See *EUD*, 270. *CUP*, 203–5, 209–10, 446. What Milbank forgets, I hypothesize, is Kierkegaard may appropriate the importance of works—after all, he was a stark defender of human freedom and of the individual's incumbent responsibility before the divine—but coevally resist viewing them as justificatory. In other words, the self remains ultimately impotent concerning salvation as *fait accompli*. At the same time, the individual must *freely* suffer for the Truth and for the accomplishment of all other religious tasks while believing in the *possibility* of redemption. In the last resort, both genuine faith and salvation are attributable to divine grace only. I defended this point on the basis of

ments, the failure of the Greek *logos* occurs due to the relational structure and "heroic"—i.e., self-sacrificial—potential of reason; and b) considering Kierkegaard's *soteriological* framework—that is to say, his insistence on the exceptionally *non-Greek* character of sin,[42] divine incarnation, and Christian historicity—reason may prove reprehensibly hubristic, which is an epiphenomenon of its sinful nature. In other words, as I read him, Kierkegaard draws on the *heteronomous* assumptions of Christian theology when thematizing the *inevitable* fallibility of human understanding, in general, and of the Greek logos, in particular, vis-à-vis faith.

Apart from his better-known rebuttal of some attempts at rationally demonstrating the existence of God,[43] Kierkegaard often brings to light the ceaseless tension, if not mere incompatibility, between the workings of reason and the divine truth. Thus, in the journals he admits that no exclusively intellectual investigation can render God's existence obvious.[44] In *The Book on Adler* we are told that religion is the realm of individuality, inwardness, contradiction, and existential decision in lieu of intellectual concepts.[45] Somewhere else, Christianity's primordial concern—which is the existence of singular persons—is contrasted with the vacuous notional apparatus of pure philosophy.[46] To explain himself Kierkegaard holds that, as God is "absolutely different,"[47] the way he reveals himself to us will be either plainly absurd or shrouded in numinous mystery. Consequently, only faith is entitled to strive for seeing through the paradoxical veils of the absolute, and that while battling the uncertainty, anxiety, and despair within.

---

numerous references to primary texts in *Either Nothingness or Love*, 158–61. Finally, with Milbank's thesis in mind, it would be interesting to compare and contrast the Catholic doctrine of social ethics with Kierkegaard's meditation on the ethical repercussions of neighbor love. See note 8 above.

42. See, for instance, *SD*, 82.

43. *PF*, 37–48. *EUD*, 242 and *Pap.* V A 7/*JP* 1334.

44. *Pap.* VIII1 A 327/ *JP* 1358.

45. *BA* 164. Since "thinking draws its breath in immanence," "all thought ceases . . . in the sphere of the paradoxical-religious and faith." *BA*, 175, 180. Consequently, "[even] if thought considered itself capable of assimilating the doctrine, it cannot assimilate the way in which the doctrine came into the world, because the essential paradox is specifically the protest against immanence." *BA*, 176.

46. *Pap.* X3 359/*JP* 1409.

47. *Pap.* V B 5/*JP* 3081. *Pap.* VI A 123 / *JP* 4430. For God as "the wholly Other," see also *CUP*, 217. Steven Shakespeare, *Kierkegaard, Language, and the Reality of God*, 198–210, 227–39. Stan, *Either Nothingness or Love*, 122–71.

From such statements, critics inferred the existence of an irreconcilable divorce between *fides* and *ratio*. As a result, they promptly purported that Kierkegaard is in essence an irrational fideist.[48] Nevertheless, genuine as the opposition between divine acts and human comprehension (*Forstanden*) may be, Kierkegaard's faultfinders did not pay enough attention to the unexpected role Kierkegaard assigns to the latter in both *Philosophical Fragments* and the *Postscript*. Below I will show how in matters of faith Climacus finds the highest and *indispensible* function of logos to be that of self-denial.[49] My additional suggestion will be that whether reason's deliberate auto-da-fé is part and parcel of a "higher" rationality in Milbank's sense remains highly debatable.

In the third chapter of *Philosophical Fragments*,[50] Climacus sets out to delineate the contradiction brought about by the idea of an absolute deity, who is fully embodied in a single individual and has as much historical-existential actuality as anyone of us. Upon trying to come to grips with this enigma, Climacus develops the following argument. If "the paradox is the passion of thought;" and if "the ultimate potentiation (*høieste Potens*) of every passion is always to will its own downfall," then the apex of a passionate kind of thinking is reached when understanding—which I take as inseparable from logos—*wills* to collide with something "unknown" (*det Ubekjendte*)[51] and be vanquished thereby. For Climacus, the most salient feature of *Forstanden* is that it "cannot stop reaching [the unknown] and being engaged with it."[52] Further, if *Forstanden*'s willed struggle with

---

48. This charge has a substantial history behind it. See, for ex., William Barrett, *Irrational Man*. Brand Blanshard, "Kierkegaard on Faith," 5–23; Murphy, A. E. "On Kierkegaard's Claim that 'Truth is Subjectivity'"; Herbert M. Garelick, *The Anti-Christianity of Kierkegaard*; Louis P. Pojman, *The Logic of Subjectivity: Kierkegaard's Philosophy of Religion*. However, much more reliable treatments of Kierkegaard's fideism can be found in Jeremy Walker, "The Paradox in *Fear and Trembling*"; Robert Herbert, "Two of Kierkegaard's Uses of Paradox,"; Karen L. Carr and Philip J. Ivanhoe, *The Sense of Antirationalism. The Religious Thought of Zhuangzi and Kierkegaard*, esp. 42–57; Steven M. Emmanuel, "Kierkegaard's Pragmatist Faith,"; C. Stephen Evans, "Faith as the Telos of Morality: A Reading of *Fear and Trembling*," 9–27; Oliva Blanchette, "The Silencing of Philosophy," 29–65; Marilyn Gaye Piety, "Kierkegaard on Rationality."

49. One might wonder if that cannot be said of *Fear and Trembling*, as well.

50. *PF*, 37–48.

51. Ibid., 37, 39.

52. Ibid., 44. This openness is also reciprocated by the divine. Climacus states that the paradox (that is, the God incarnate) "wills this downfall of the understanding, and thus the two have a mutual understanding." *PF*, 47. Arguably, the "mutual understanding" here could be an instantiation of a higher logos Milbank found at work in Kierkegaard's

the inconceivable is not only ceaseless but also bound to fail,[53] then the unknown it collides against must be *radically different*. Consequently, *det Ubekjendte* must needs be "something that thought itself cannot [ever] think,"[54] i.e., a god or something utterly divine.

In brief, human understanding is structurally marked by the inchoate incapacity to cognize the absolutely different, although it is endlessly and passionately drawn to the impenetrability of this otherness. Moreover, insofar as *Forstanden* is able to aspire to know the unknown, albeit ensuring its own downfall in the process; that is to say, insofar as *det Ubekjendte* is transcendent, absolutely unknowable and therefore divine—rather than the byproduct of the human mind—then *Forstanden* is able to encounter the Other only because the Other has decided to *reveal* himself.[55] Hence, the utter impotence of logos without the prior manifestation of "the god."

My core thesis is that within the limits of *Philosophical Fragments*, logos, albeit powerless with regard to grasping the divine other's radical difference, plays a vital role in the struggle for faith by means of a *willed self-failure*. Subsequent to the collision with and inevitable fiasco before *det Ubekjendte*, reason has to let go, as it were, so that the truth may dwell in inwardness through faith. By an unforeseeable twist Climacus thus implies that the fideistic relation to the Other is improbable to a logos that does not imitate Christ, so to speak, that is to say, to an intellect that resists self-offering. I do not hereby argue that Kierkegaard surreptitiously defends a

---

theology. Pace Milbank, my view is that significant problems arise once we enter the terrain of soteriology, and that because reason is perfectly susceptible to the corrupting impact of sin. When analyzing the crippling effects of the latter, Alastair Hannay detects two ways in which Kierkegaard saw reason as potentially sinful: through its imperialistic penchants, that is to say, when reason strives to appropriate and explain everything in its path; and through its prideful self-sufficiency. For Hannay, the fact that faith ceaselessly appears to reason as absurd or offensive constitutes a supplementary sign of rationality's maculate roots. Alastair Hannay, *Kierkegaard*, 96–106. See also *SD*, 119 where it is stated that thinking as such is impermeable to the reality of sin.

53. Hence its paradoxicality. Salvation is no less paradoxical because it is contingent upon a deity, which must reveal to human understanding both its absolute difference from humankind (which issues from sin) and its kinship with all humans by virtue of divine love. See *PF*, 46–47. Evidently, no *Forstand* will ever be capable of overcoming such contradiction. Noteworthy here is also the heterogeneity between human comprehension and a type of otherness that can reach us only through revelation, see *Pap*. V B 5:8/*JP* 1340. On the same issue see Steven M. Emmanuel, *Kierkegaard and the Concept of Revelation*, 37, 72.

54. *PF*, 37.

55. Ibid., 46.

"suicidal" type of reason. In my reading, he analogically links a combative (or pathos-laden) rationality[56] with the broader task of kenotically allowing the divine to perform its salvific function in one's interiority.

So far, we established that faith on the Climacan account should be preceded by a willed self-sacrifice of logos. We should add that reason's kenosis is also endless as the understanding remains in constant clash with all the paradoxes of Christianity. Moreover, only this collision is able to mediate the individual's passionate decision for faith against offense, while the continuance of faith is contingent upon the incessant awareness of the perplexing core of one's belief. In Kierkegaard's thought, therefore, *ratio* is to keep the fire of contradiction burning, to fuel consciousness with the vexing facet of the exigencies of salvation, whereas *fide* is expected to assume the unadulterated contradictions of Christianity and resist against their offensiveness.[57]

As I understand it, Climacus's argument is the God-relationship would lack something crucial if *Forstanden* did not relentlessly strive to reach a qualitatively different unknown in full awareness of its breakdown. In this precise sense, then, faith ca*nn*ot do without reason. Otherwise stated, the deliberate collapse or self-emptying of logos is integral to the very possibility of faith.[58] Further, the decision to believe must be renewed time and again against the paradoxical backdrop of a logos which willfully stalls before the numinous transcendence. It is crucial to remember that the individual is not hereby invited to cultivate a stoic resignation apropos of *Forstanden*'s impotence. Rather, one is encouraged to openly assume the breakdown of logos in order to pursue the God-relationship in a kenotic form: more exactly, to become receptive to the Other's love and ultimately to triumph.

Equally worthy of mentioning is Climacus's distinction between what I would call the relational paradox and the ontological paradox. The first type of paradoxicality indicates that "the eternal . . . is a paradox by being related to an existing person."[59] As to the ontological paradox,[60] it refers to the act of

---

56. The combative dimension of *Forstanden* consists, more exactly, in passionately *willing* against its own nature to *lose* the battle with the unknown or god. This view pivots on a *relational* structure of human faculties.

57. *CUP*, 224–25, footnote.

58. To which we should immediately add the indispensability of divine grace. See note 41 above and notes 89 and 114 below.

59. *CUP*, 205. See also ibid., 218.

60. Or, the paradox of identity, by virtue of which eternity is thought to be one with or concealed within historicity, albeit qualitatively and eternally different. *CUP*, 209:

divine incarnation, conceived by Kierkegaard in opposition to—or at least outside the ambiance of—the Hellenic logos.[61] Going back to John Milbank, I surmise "a deconstructed Greek logos"[62] may be applicable solely to the relational paradox. In contrast, Climacus (and probably Kierkegaard himself) qualifies the ontological paradox as incommensurable to the Greek rationality as such. It is on no other ground that the same pseudonym defines the absurd as "the contradiction that something that can become historical *only in direct opposition to all human understanding* has [actually] become historical."[63] Similarly, Johannes de Silentio, the pseudonymous author of *Fear and Trembling*, while in the grip of a candid effusion, acknowledges "the prodigious paradox that is the content of Abraham's life." He immediately confesses his thought is "constantly repelled" by it, that he "cannot penetrate it" even "by a hairsbreadth."[64] Moreover, every time he tries to probe into the unyielding mystery of faith, de Silentio's mind becomes "paralyzed."[65] In his turn, Climacus rests assured that in Christianity "the maximum of any eventual understanding is to understand that [the paradox of incarnation]

"The paradox came into existence through the relating of the eternal, essential truth to the existing person. Let us now *go further*; let us assume the eternal, essential truth *is itself* the paradox. How does [this latter] paradox emerge? By placing the eternal, essential truth together with existing. Consequently, if we place it together *in the truth itself*, the truth becomes a paradox . . ." Italics mine.

61. SD, 100, 116, 127–8. This idea goes back to Paul who calls the incarnate God "an offence to Jews and folly to Gentiles." 1 Cor. 1:23. Climacus is in full agreement with Paul on this issue; see CUP, 213. Contrast this point with Milbank's hypothesis that "Kierkegaard makes a significant return to Plato . . . and thinks again of truth as something at issue between temporal flux and the non-representable, eternal 'other' of time." SIK, 71. See also *The Monstrosity of Christ*, 169–70, 217. Milbank additionally ignores Anti-Climacus's tenet that sinfulness—a purely Christian category—is exceptionally non-Socratic. SD, 80–2, 87–96. Here it might also be useful to remember that Climacus holds Plato responsible for the emergence of Hegelian speculative dialectics (CUP, 206 footnote), to which the Kierkegaardian pseudonym opposes the religion of paradox and transcendence, i.e., religiousness B.

62. SIK, 72.

63. CUP, 211; italics added. See also CUP, 210f where we read that "[it] is by way of objective repulsion that the absurd is the dynamometer of faith in inwardness."

64. FT, 33. While struggling with "the prodigious paradox of faith, a paradox that makes a murder into a holy and God-pleasing act, a paradox that gives Isaac back to Abraham again," Johannes de Silentio insists that "no thought can grasp" such contradictions, since "faith begins precisely where thought stops (*hører op*)." FT, 53. Consequently, the declared *telos* of *Fear and Trembling* "is to have . . . the paradox appear in [its] *absolute* dissimilarity." FT, 85; italics added.

65. FT, 33.

cannot be understood."⁶⁶ On this issue he is in full agreement with his putative twin, Anti-Climacus, who concurs that "to believe is indeed to lose the understanding in order to gain God."⁶⁷

3. Subjectivity Redux

Previously, I expressed serious doubts about Milbank's view that the Kierkegaardian selfhood is non-universalizable. However, when tackling the same theme from the vantage of repetition, the novelty of Milbank's hermeneutical enterprise is undeniable.⁶⁸ The argument starts with the realization that, as conceived by Kierkegaard, repetition (*Gjentagelse*) harbors the possibility of an infinite dissolution, while being, on the other hand, of a "chronically aporetic"⁶⁹ nature. Next, Milbank connects the structural self-destructive deadlock of repetition with subjectivity itself. "Where every identity," he writes, "is a repetition, and every repetition traverses a difference, then the identity can also be undone through the very movement which constitutes it. And the isolated moments which remain as the fragments of this deconstruction are not, of course, inviolable atoms, but themselves repeated identities which can in turn be undone, and so on ad infinitum."⁷⁰

Needless to note that, thus understood, *Gjentagelsen* becomes a negatively charged category. For Milbank, that is also why Kierkegaard affirmed the subject's identity only "precariously"⁷¹ and why the self "must remain endlessly in question."⁷² Moreover, Milbank observes that unlike Descartes and Kant, Kierkegaard preserves the rift between subject and object, insisting that "it must always remain in place, that there can never be any perfect correspondence between the two, precisely because their relationship is not one of mirroring . . . "⁷³ Which implies that far from being "the

---

66. *CUP*, 214.

67. *SD*, 38. For the same idea, this time related to the unconditional imperatives of the New Testament, see *Pap*. X4 A 581/*JP* 536. *Pap*. XI2 A 133/*JP* 1449.

68. Milbank takes Kierkegaard's repetition as a "subversive" or "suspended ontological category" which is intrinsically linked with *anxiety* and indispensable to understanding human identity. SIK 68, 71. Even if Kierkegaard does not explicitly make the former connection, Milbank's approach to this issue remains compelling.

69. SIK, 68.

70. Ibid.

71. Ibid., 69.

72. Ibid.

73. Ibid., 70. Concerning Kierkegaard's reception of Descartes, it is much more ambivalent than Milbank implies. Anders Moe Rasmussen has recently shown that

locus of interiority" or the domain of private self-consciousness, Kierkegaard's subject finds itself "'within' a perpetual transition that it can never survey in a theoretical manner from without."[74] More specifically, selfhood is "necessarily suspended between material motion on the one hand, and symbolic, linguistic operations on the other."[75] In this sense, Milbank suggests that the aporetic kernel of repetition—i.e., the paradoxical and constitutive inscription of difference within identity—can be extended to human nature as such. Kierkegaard's human is, therefore, "the difference between nature and humanity, yet is both."[76]

By means of a multilayered argumentation that cannot be faithfully summarized here, Milbank concludes that by interweaving the subject's indeterminacy—which, we said, stems from a self-undermining repeatability—with a new conception of God and human resolution, Kierkegaard propounds a type of inwardness that "conforms to no universal norms."[77] Additionally, Kierkegaard lays the ground for "a subjective 'decision' for atheism and anti-humanism,"[78] wherein Milbank detects a dangerously nihilistic tendency.

Here Milbank's interpretation is much less substantiated than the one discussed in the opening section of this essay. Before showing why that is so, I should remark first that Milbank draws an incomplete picture of Kierkegaard's category of spirit (*Aand*). He sees Kierkegaard's *Aand* as "that which binds soul (thinking possibility) and body (living actuality) together."[79] Even though he does not give specific bibliographical references,

---

Kierkegaard filtered Cartesian thought through the Hegelian lens of Hans L. Martensen, the "arch-opponent" of the Danish philosopher. A. M. Rasmussen, "René Descartes: Kierkegaard's Understanding of Doubt and Certainty," 11–22; see esp. 15–7. However, what complicates things is that Kierkegaard projected Descartes into an existentialist mind frame. With that in mind, in *FT* he praises Descartes for having honestly acknowledged that the verities revealed by God are always far superior to the truth of reason, especially when the former may go against the dictates of the latter. *FT*, 5–6. Besides Descartes, we should not forget G. E. Lessing's possible influence on Kierkegaard's take on subjectivity. See in this sense, Curtis L. Thompson, "Gotthold Ephraim Lessing: Appropriating the Testimony of a Theological Naturalist," 77–112; esp. 88, 101. See also Alastair Hannay, *Kierkegaard: A Biography*, 287.

74. SIK, 70.

75. Ibid. For a possible Kierkegaardian critique of this point see *TA*, 66–8.

76. SIK, 70.

77. Ibid., 72.

78. Ibid., 69. The same idea is expressed in Žižek and Milbank, *The Monstrosity of Christ*, 199.

79. Ibid., 70.

the commentator could have reached this conclusion via the soteriological anthropology of *The Concept of Anxiety* and *The Sickness Unto Death*. *The Concept of Anxiety* does, indeed, conceive of human nature as a synthesis of opposites (the physical/the psychical, temporality/eternity, finitude/infinity). And since this "synthesis is unthinkable if the two [components] are not united in a third,"[80] the third entity is precisely the spirit. On the other side, although not entirely different, the perspective unfolded in *The Sickness Unto Death* is much more inclusive. In this book, Anti-Climacus appropriates the definition of selfhood from *The Concept of Anxiety* but adds an essential proviso. The spiritual self, he says, cannot be reduced to a synthetic relation. The spirit is rather "the relation's relating itself to itself."[81] Moreover, *Aanden* is instituted, rooted in, and supported by divine transcendence, and cannot exist otherwise. Consequently, whenever it takes a stance toward itself or its surrounding environs, the spirit implicitly relates itself to its holy origins and ground.

My suspicion is that Milbank passes too quickly over the insurmountably derived status of subjectivity in Kierkegaard.[82] This negligence lies at the origin of an oversimplification. Namely, Milbank never explains how we could reconcile Kierkegaard's "willed, contingent subjectivity"[83] with the creationist, Providence-centered psychology that underpins *The Sickness Unto Death* and Kierkegaard's edifying corpus as a whole. Indeed, human identity may be divisible into heteronomous identities which are in their turn subjected to further fragmentation. The problem is that Kierkegaard's anthropology is coevally predicated upon a foundational moment, which Milbank apparently integrates within the purview of the subject in lieu of God. By contrast, Kierkegaard would say that the possibility of "a subjective 'decision' for atheism and anti-humanism"[84] is and can be granted solely by a divine creator who lovingly places freedom before any other attribute of human nature.[85]

Still, there does exist a topical vista in Kierkegaard's thought, which could be more conducive to Milbank's thesis. I refer to Kierkegaard's appropriation of sin and its continuance. Although it surfaces now and then in

---

80. *CA*, 43.
81. *SD*, 13.
82. See also Žižek and Milbank, *The Monstrosity of Christ*, 170.
83. SIK, 71.
84. Ibid., 69.
85. See *Pap.* VII1 A 181/*JP* II 1251. Reprinted in *M* 390–2.

The Concept of Anxiety, this theme is carefully detailed in *The Sickness Unto Death*.[86] However, my view is that even in this case Milbank cannot avoid all difficulty. For, although he accepts the perpetuity of sin, Kierkegaard also advises his readers to *endlessly* and boldly struggle against evil and sin with a view to an authentic self-becoming.[87] As to the infinity of spiritual efforts, it suffices to remind that, notwithstanding the antagonistic relation between God and the sinful individual, believers, according to Kierkegaard, must *continually* endeavor to realize the onerous tasks set by the absolute for the sake of religious individuation.[88] In other words, one's persistent sinfulness must needs be counteracted through an equally endless *agon*, the success of which is guaranteed solely by grace.[89] At the same time, if one does not deliberately struggle for the attainment and preservation of faith, then the continuity belongs to sin/despair, and discontinuous are only the latter's epiphenomena.[90]

In short, *contra* Milbank, Kierkegaard implies that repetition's disintegrating capacity and subjectivity's indeterminacy are perpetually challenged, when not plainly neutralized, by the *normative* continuity of the inner striving to live as a singular person before the absolute. Perhaps, Milbank's discussion of subjectivity and repetition is apposite only so far as

---

86. *CA*, 32–5, 37, 47, 52. *SD*, 105–31.

87. See *EUD*, 7–29, 79–101. David J. Kangas, "J. G. Fichte: From Transcendental Ego to Existence," 67–95; 79.

88. Milbank is not completely oblivious to the ideal of ethico-religious continuity in Kierkegaard. See his statement that Kierkegaard's "repetition is affirmed in order to uphold ethical 'continuity,' consistent identity, divine transcendence and atonement..." *SIK*, 72. However, Milbank does not pursue this line of thought in any detail.

89. Milbank resists this Lutheran logic, although it clearly underpins the overall teleology of *Philosophical Fragments*. (An excessive affirmation of grace could downplay Kierkegaard's importance for Catholic theology, which Milbank struggles to defend.) Moreover, when he refers to "the transition from a ruinous to a positive paradox," that is, from the failure of the Socratic to the acceptability of Christ-centered absurdity, Milbank argues that "the new bridge thrown across the abyss is not the work of the abyss, but of willed, contingent subjectivity." *SIK*, 71. (Later on, Milbank seems hesitant about this point; see *SIK*, 79–80, note 44.) In contrast, Climacus ascribes the power of reopening the channel between the sinful immanence and the loving transcendence solely to God. *PF*, 14–21. As I understand it, that is exactly the inexorable and unconditional necessity of grace in the salvific process of self-becoming. See, for ex., *Pap*. X3 A 470/*JP* 4933.

90. Compare in this sense Milbank's overall depiction of the Kierkegaardian selfhood to Anti-Climacus's definition of despair as the possibility which lacks all contact with necessity. See *SD*, 35–7.

Kierkegaard's polymorphic description of the aesthetic self[91] is concerned. Further, the "willed, contingent subjectivity" prioritized by Milbank may be more reminiscent of Judge William's ethical model[92] rather than Kierkegaard's full-fledged Christian anthropology.[93]

4. Ideality and Metaphysics

Besides its aporetic nature and proclivity toward inward dissolution, John Milbank takes note of the "anti-metaphysical"[94] weight of Kierkegaardian repetition. When he expands on this specific point, Milbank relies on the Climacan diptych, *Philosophical Fragments* and the *Postscript*.[95] However, the problem is that these two works speak only obliquely to Kierkegaard's "New Testament Christianity," whose creationistic-salvific kernel is frontally addressed in *The Sickness Unto Death* and *Practice in Christianity* (to refer to the pseudonymous literature), and in *Upbuilding Discourses in Various Spirits* or *Christian Discourses* (as regards the upbuilding corpus).

The second impediment Milbank runs into concerns the extent to which Kierkegaard opposed metaphysics. To be sure, considering Kierkegaard's adamant affirmation of the self's anxious finitude and risk-laden resolutions; or of God's inscrutable incognito and "pure subjectivity"[96]—to whom one opens oneself only through an ever renewable faith haunted by uncertainty—we could concede Milbank's overall judgment. Still, should Milbank's metaphysical share any affinity with "onto-theology" in Heidegger's sense—and I do not see why not[97]—then his conjecture must be set against the much more intricate backdrop of Kierkegaard's cosmology. Due

---

91. See *EO* I, 17–43, 217–30, 281–300. For a concise formulation of the same idea see *EO* II, 255–56.

92. See *EO* II, 215, 223, 249, 262–63.

93. I understand Kierkegaard's anthropology as a fruitful encounter between monotheistic creationism, a dynamic (or processual) view of subjectivity, and Christian soteriology (with a particular emphasis on sin and salvation). Milbank completely ignores the first, explicitly appropriates the second, and only marginally touches upon the third. See SIK, 73.

94. SIK, 68.

95. *PF*, 23–36. *CUP*, 189–251.

96. *Pap.* XI2 A 133/*JP* 1449.

97. When expanding on Kierkegaard's anti-idealism, Milbank equates the "theoretical metaphysics" that Kierkegaard "decisively abandoned" with the Cartesian and Kantian-German traditions of idealism. SIK, 69. Consequently, given Heidegger's repeated attacks against Cartesian metaphysics, my assumption concerning onto-theology is plausible.

to space constraints and the fact I explored this theme somewhere else,[98] I limit myself to reminding that a large part of Kierkegaard's religious oeuvre coheres with the traditional worldview of monotheistic creationism, and thus with the onto-theological presuppositions of Western metaphysics.[99]

The issue that I wish to develop in this section regards Kierkegaard's non-idealistic side, which Milbank links with the anti-metaphysical attitude mentioned above. Milbank's argument is, shortly put, that Kierkegaard bypassed traditional metaphysics because he "consistently" infused faith with skepticism,[100] while challenging the idealist paradigm of subjectivity.[101] I find the latter contention contestable from a genealogical, as well as systemic perspective. Concerning the genealogical aspect, the interested reader might want to consult the recent research which suggests that historically, Kierkegaard did *not* make such a clear-cut break with German idealism.[102]

---

98. Leo Stan, "The Lily in the Field and the Bird in the Air: An Endless Liturgy in Kierkegaard's Authorship." Id., *Either Nothingness or Love*, 122–225.

99. Therefore, we can say that to a definite degree, Kierkegaard thinks like a classical Judeo-Christian metaphysician. For instance, he does not hesitate to declare that God represents the other-worldly, infinitely heterogeneous, and unchangeable maker, ground, and sustainer of everything that is and becomes, the human self included. In this restricted sense, Kierkegaard's theological assumptions do not contradict the guiding postulates of onto-theology.

100. SIK, 69. On this occasion Milbank alleges that Kierkegaard entertained a particular enthusiasm for the Greek skeptics. SIK, 71. This tenet, however, needs much more textual confirmations than Milbank offers. The commentator rests his case on *Johannes Climacus or De omnibus dubitandum est* (a very early text never published in Kierkegaard's lifetime), *The Concept of Irony* (an academic work later repudiated by Kierkegaard due to its clear Hegelian overtones and assumptions), and the *Postscript* (a book signed with a pseudonym that occupies a middle ground in Kierkegaard's authorial pantheon). SIK, 78, note 19. For the relative importance of Climacus see note 138 below. In response to Milbank my thesis—which I cannot develop here—is that Kierkegaard may not be more than an agnostic in ethico-religious matters. For details see Stan, *Either Nothingness or Love*, esp. 226–85.

101. As a side note, Milbank claims that Kierkegaard considered modern idealism "a variant (though an especially degenerate one) of the ancient Socratic knowing and self-knowing self." SIK, 70. Hereby Milbank passes too quickly over the fundamental role played by self-knowledge and consciousness in becoming ethical; see *EO* II, 258–60, 265. The same can be stated of Kierkegaard's frank and quite passionate admiration for Socrates, who represents the peerless embodiment of "the subjective thinker." See *CUP*, 204–10, 247–49.

102. Milbank contemplates this possibility in *The Monstrosity of Christ*, 180–81. For Kierkegaard's relation to the idealist tradition see *Kierkegaard and His German Contemporaries*, Tome I, *op. cit.*, particularly the articles on Kierkegaard's interaction with the philosophy of J. G. Fichte, Hegel, Kant, and Schelling. See also next note and note 118 below.

(To give just one example, as Jon Stewart has meticulously documented, a significant portion of Kierkegaard's philosophical authorship is simply unintelligible outside Hegel's thought and terminology.[103]) But perhaps, the historical approach is insufficient when attempting to settle the problem of Kierkegaard's relation to idealism. That is why under the heading of systemic perspective I will briefly indicate the polymorphous sense in which Kierkegaard remains an idealist notwithstanding his disagreements with speculative philosophy.

Ideality occupies the center stage from the very beginning of Kierkegaard's activity. Even before the publication of *Repetition*, more exactly in the second tome of *Either/Or* (February 1843), Kierkegaard has the ethicist William develop a very elaborate and quite original understanding of self-becoming along the lines of immediacy, self-choice, temporality, intersubjectivity, and repentance. For my purposes here, it should suffice to recall that for Judge William, ethical individualization requires the free choice of an "ideal self" which is integral to one's identity, and yet "absolutely different"[104] from one's immediate determinations. Judge William explains: "The self the individual knows is simultaneously the actual self and the ideal self, which the individual has outside himself, as the image in whose likeness he is to form himself, and which on the other hand he has within himself, since it is he himself. Only within himself does the individual have the objective toward which he is to strive, and yet he has this objective outside himself as he strives toward it."[105]

Sure enough, this sense of ideality may seem too ego-oriented, almost bordering on solipsism.[106] We should then turn our attention to the other

---

103. Jon Stewart, *Kierkegaard's Relations to Hegel Reconsidered*. Id., "Kierkegaard's Phenomenology of Despair in *The Sickness unto Death*." As to Kierkegaard's relation to Hegel the reader might want to compare and contrast SIK, 72 with *Pap.* V C 1/*JP* 2345.

104. *EO* II, 215.

105. *EO* II, 259. Also idem, 215: "This self that [one] chooses in this way [i.e., ethically] is infinitely concrete, for it is he himself, and yet it is absolutely different from his former [aesthetic] self, for he has chosen it absolutely. This self has not existed before, because it came into existence through the choice, and yet it has existed, for it was indeed 'himself.' The choice here makes two dialectical movements simultaneously—that which is chosen does not exist and comes into existence through the choice—and that which is chosen exists; otherwise it was not a choice." I tried to explore the labyrinthine path of this ethical theory in *Either Nothingness or Love*, 20–43. For the specific meaning of ethical "concretion" or immediacy see *EO* II, 255–56, 262–63.

106. This would be the prototypical Levinasian criticism of Kierkegaard. Emmanuel Levinas, "Existence and Ethics." However, Levinas never cites *Either/Or* in his unsparing criticisms of Kierkegaard.

two important senses of ideality in Kierkegaard's corpus. We have first the ground-breaking passage from *Two Ages*, where Kierkegaard conveys his version of truly being-with-one-another:

> If the essential passion is taken away [from individuals], . . . and everything becomes meaningless externality, devoid of character, then the spring of ideality stops flowing and life together becomes stagnant water—this is crudeness . . . When individuals (each one individually) are essentially and passionately related to an *idea* and together are essentially related to the same idea, the relation is *optimal* and normative. Individually the relation separates them (each one has himself for himself), and ideally it unites them. Where there is essential inwardness, there is a decent modesty between man and man that prevents crude aggressiveness; . . . Thus the individuals never come too close to each other in the herd sense, simply because they are united on the basis of an *ideal* distance. The unanimity of separation is indeed fully orchestrated music.[107]

Given Kierkegaard's spirit-oriented anthropology, nothing should deter us from equating the "idea" or ideality referred to here with the ethico-religious selfhood, for which the individual, we said, is to strive continually. This possibility is confirmed by a late diary entry (dated 1854), in which Kierkegaard meditates on the interrelatedness between the qualitative—a notion which is quintessential to his understanding of the singular subject—and (the Christian) ideality which is subsequently equated with the "purity of spirit." To quote Kierkegaard again:

> An orientation toward quality, always an eye to quality, is required for the honesty of ideality (which is purity of spirit or is spirit) . . . [However, with] the aid of mediocrity's cheap dishonesty, Christendom has managed to lose the prototypes completely. We need to reintroduce the prototypes, make them recognizable. . . . But with respect to what is a qualitative level different from oneself, even though one is, if you please, the closest approximation, the essential thing is that one has the honesty of ideality not to accept approximations but to uphold only qualities, so one finds one's sole joy in pointing out what is a quality higher.[108]

A related sense of exemplarity compels Kierkegaard to warn against the interference of collectivities in one's personal God-relation, as the sole

---

107. *TA*, 62–63; italics mine.
108. *Pap.* XI1 A 476/*JP* 1812; reprinted in *EO* II, 455–57.

purpose of crowds is to keep one away from the ideality of religion.[109] Moreover, he insists the ideals delineated in the New Testament are so high because they are a trustworthy witness to God's "infinite majesty."[110] That said, when the individual comes "face to face with the [Christian] ideal" he is just "a poor wretch,"[111] for whom the need for grace becomes more stringent than ever.

The salient affirmation of this ideal distance surfaces when Kierkegaard takes cognizance of the infinite abyss between the sinful self and God.[112] An equally potent sense of ideality is also retained when Kierkegaard reflects on the imperative imitation of Christ. In this regard, he does not shy away from underlining the decisive and unattainable ideality comprised even in the God-man's earthly existence. Thus, Jesus Christ—who is God's most faithful, "suffering servant"—appears to Kierkegaard as the sole "prototype of the essential human perfection."[113] In contrast, probably by virtue of his anti-Pelagian propensities, Kierkegaard takes humans' religious imperfection to be unsurpassable in this life; hence, again, the perennial necessity of God's assistance in the struggle for salvation.[114] Highly relevant here is also the concept of "sacred history" (*den hellige Historie*), premised as it is on Christ's ideality.[115]

Sure enough, John Milbank is aware of Christ's paradigmatic stature when observing that for Kierkegaard, the God-man's atonement "can only

---

109. WA, 229. BA 318. M 460.

110. *Pap.* XI2 A 133/JP 1449. Kierkegaard decided to publish *The Sickness Unto Death* pseudonymously in order to disclose the radical ideality of the Christian religion. *Pap.* X1 A 548/JP 6446: "It is absolutely right—a pseudonym had to be used [for *The Sickness Unto Death*]. When the demands of ideality are to be presented at their maximum, then one must take extreme care not to be confused with them himself, as if he himself were the ideal." Quoted in Howard and Edna Hong, Historical Introduction to *The Sickness Unto Death*, xx. See also PC 90 where Kierkegaard opposes "the enormous criterion of [religious or Christian] ideality" to any self-deifying and therefore, spiritually threatening establishment.

111. *Pap.* X3 A 470/JP 4933.

112. SD, 122.

113. UDVS, 197.

114. M, 423: "To the degree that a person becomes more and more aware of how infinitely ideal the prototype is, yes, that he is heterogeneous by a full quality, to the same degree grace must be more and more affirmed." See also *Pap.* X5 A 88/JP 1922.

115. PC, 64: "Christ's life upon earth, the sacred history, stands alone by itself, outside history." For a more detailed discussion of this issue side by side with Kierkegaard's three-staged theory of existence, see my essay "Kierkegaard on Temporality and God Incarnate."

be appropriated if it is 'repeated' in every redeemed individual: its 'once and for allness' is not a substantive 'something' which each individual can 'possess' through mere affirmation; though it is once and for all because it 'has happened,' this is also a *transcendental* moment which *keeps on happening*, and continues to be 'over' before one is aware of its presence."[116]

But even if he specifies that the advent of Christ represents an "intrusion" which makes possible "a historical and intersubjective project of imitation,"[117] Milbank still does not sufficiently explicate what lies behind this "intrusion."[118] As I understand it, the latter bespeaks the infinite qualitative difference between God (or the God-man) and humankind, a difference which is reinforced by the equally endless gap between *any* of Jesus's disciples and "the exemplar" himself as a *human* being.

5. Ontological Rupture and Sin

In his dealings with Kierkegaard's subversion of idealism, John Milbank concludes "[no] abyss sunders us, the knowing subjects, from reality, but rather reality is itself incessantly fractured between the actual and the possible, and within this rift 'subjectivity' comes to be/becomes possible."[119] Whereas that may be true within the boundaries of *Repetition* and *The*

---

116. SIK, 81 note 52; italics added.

117. SIK, 72.

118. Milbank notes only that Kierkegaard's Christ stands for "that universal identity which arises through its happening again, differently." Hence, the existence of an unprecedented Christological identity which "[exhibits] 'consistency,' and yet [remains] indeterminately open to the future;" or which resembles "a repetition that discovers inexhaustible variety in 'the same'" and wherein "desire is ceaselessly renewed." SIK, 72. I debate Milbank's contention because first it neglects the endless qualitative difference between God/Christ and the rest of us. Second, it argues that, once conscious of this difference, we must postulate a religious ideality that does not immediately square with the anti-idealism Milbank detects in Kierkegaard. If tempted to sharply dissociate between the idealism envisioned by Milbank and Kierkegaard's Christian-soteriological ideality, the reader can consult Ronald M. Green's discussion of the affinities between Kierkegaard and Kant apropos of radical evil, the consequent need for grace, and Christian ideality. Green, "Kant: A Debt both Obscure and Enormous." See also id., *Kierkegaard and Kant: The Hidden Debt*; Id., "Kierkegaard's *Philosophical Fragments*: A Kantian Commentary." Another exploration of Kierkegaard's metaphysics in the proximity of Kantian religion can be found in J. Heywood Thomas, "Revelation, Knowledge, and Proof."

119. SIK, 70. Arguably, echoes of Slavoj Žižek's (Lacanian) ontology could be heard in this statement. Žižek, *The Parallax View*, esp. 61–63, 167, 242, 281; id., *How to Read Lacan*, esp. ch. 2, 22–39. Let us not forget, however, that Žižek and Milbank are separated by insuperable differences. See *The Monstrosity of Christ*, op. cit.

Concept of Anxiety, the question is whether the same judgment can be applied to the religious epistemology put forward in Kierkegaard's larger corpus. I am inclined to answer in the negative and here is why.

In his pedantic reflections on the dialectic of despair, Anti-Climacus explicitly acknowledges the possibility that subjectivity be split against itself.[120] As I already alluded to the highest ontological hiatus, according to Kierkegaard, namely, that between the immanent and the transcendent, I regard the inner uncertainty pertaining to faith and salvation, as well as the anxious core of the subject's freedom (both of which lay at the center of Milbank's reading), as mere echoes of the "infinite qualitative difference." The principal and most passionate exponent of this rift between us and the real—i.e., the divine—is again Anti-Climacus, who unwaveringly recognizes that "[as] sinner, man is separated from God by the most engulfing qualitative abyss (*Qvalitetens meest svælgende Dyb*)."[121] Moreover, in the case of forgiveness this difference appears to him as *eternal* and *irrevocable*,[122] a creedal statement that goes against the very core of Radical Orthodoxy.

When discussing the topic of sin, Milbank engages in a genealogical exercise. He surmises that Kierkegaard has reintroduced transcendence into the philosophical discourse by "rewriting the Augustinian account of human fallenness."[123] Unfortunately, Milbank's approach to fallenness is complicated by frequent detours through Kant—and his category of the sublime—and poststructuralism. To be sure, my intention is not to engage Milbank on the terrain of Kantianism or postmodern philosophy. My only goal below is to gesture towards Kierkegaard's multifaceted appropriation of sin in order to question some of Milbank's assumptions and interpretive strategy.

When he explains Kierkegaard's reinsertion of transcendence within the boundaries of philosophy, Milbank remarks that in the eyes of the Danish thinker "the 'original,' innocent relationship to God . . . included that

---

120. His insightful analysis of demonism should be emphasized here. See *SD*, 67–74, 108–10 and *CA* 118–36. For illustrations of the despaired self's conflictual volition, see *SD*, 49–67 and note 155 below.

121. *SD*, 122; translation slightly modified. God is also the most real because omnipresent. *CD*, 180. *WL*, 140, 268, 383, 414–15, 465.

122. Anti-Climacus writes that since "God is separated from man by the same engulfing qualitative abyss when he forgives sins," then "there is one way in which man could *never in all eternity* come to be like God: in forgiving sins." *SD*, 122; translation slightly modified and italics added.

123. SIK, 73.

uncertainty pertaining to relationship with the unknown/unknowable, though this then took the form of a 'pleasing anxiety' entirely devoid of terror . . ."[124] If attempting to unpack this succinct and dense quote, one could—adequately, I think—suppose that Milbank amalgamates the different accounts of sin delineated by Johannes Climacus and Vigilius Haufniensis.[125] To be absolutely fair, the treatment of sinfulness from *Philosophical Fragments*, *The Concept of Anxiety*, and *The Sickness Unto Death* is ambiguous enough to lend itself to misconceptions or give rise to controversies. Nevertheless, it is generally accepted that *The Concept of Anxiety* presents a quasi-transcendental approach—which is the end result of the improbable encounter between "scientific" psychology and Christian dogmatics[126]— through its interest in the general *possibility* of sin and the way sinfulness disseminates throughout human history. Contrastively enough, *The Sickness Unto Death* tends to turn a blind eye to the advent of original sin and its transcendental-dogmatic dimension; instead, it scrutinizes the dialectic of personal despair, an existential phenomenon which it deems universal and eventually equates with sin.[127]

This perspectival nuance aside, Milbank fails to notice the dangers involved in combining several soteriological views from Kierkegaard's *pseudonymous* corpus. Here, I have in mind the peculiar profile of each pseudonym, which Kierkegaard treated with extreme care. Thus, we should remember that the personalities of Kierkegaard's pseudonyms vary to a significant degree, ranging from an ironic jocosity to the most upbuilding (and even prophetic) solemnity. That is also why we cannot afford to dismiss too quickly their theoretical specificity, whereupon the differences between their *religious* views become all the more crucial.

---

124. Ibid.

125. To whom one could safely add Anti-Climacus.

126. See the subtitle of *CA*: "A Simple Psychologically Orienting Deliberation on the Dogmatic Issue of Hereditary Sin."

127. For instance, questions about the contribution of the human race to the perpetuation of sin are hardly raised in *SD*. The stress falls rather on the singular individual's relation to sin and its cure, faith. Indispensable here is Lee C. Barrett's "Kierkegaard's 'Anxiety' and the Augustinian Doctrine of Original Sin," 35–61; esp. 47. Note also that the creationist dimension of the Christian religion is much more momentous in *SD* than *PF* and *CA*.

To exemplify, Kierkegaard sketches Johannes Climacus as an "ironic dialectician"[128] who knows everything about humor.[129] Climacus is also portrayed as a "loafer"[130] who is "able to dance lightly in the service of thought;"[131] or as a potentially frivolous pamphleteer.[132] From this characterization we can easily deduce the hypothetical nature of *Philosophical Fragments*.[133] The same can be stated about the *Postscript*, given its Climacan imprimatur and its self-designation as an "imaginatively constructing" pamphlet.[134] Moving to Vigilius Haufniensis (the pseudonymous author of *The Concept of Anxiety*), Kierkegaard envisions him as "a psychological observer," who, without lacking in "poetic originality," makes prodigious use of "*Experimenter*" (i.e., thought-experiments or imaginary constructions).[135] It is not without surprise to discover that, in spite of his proverbial vigilance, Haufniensis is oftentimes capable of deceiving his fellow humans for the sake of trenchant and impeccable psychological observations.[136] When we get to Anti-Climacus, things are less ambivalent and more earnest. His intended sobriety can be guessed first from the subtitle of *The Sickness Unto Death*: "A Christian Psychological Exposition for Upbuilding and Awakening." Second, Kierkegaard himself confesses that in comparison to Anti-Climacus, both Climacus and Haufniensis appear as "lower pseudonimities."[137] Therefore, as if drawing a boundary between himself and his pseudonyms, Kierkegaard feels he is entitled to occupy the median position between Climacus and the latter's far superior counterpart, Anti-Climacus.[138]

128. See Howard and Edna Hong, Historical Introduction to *PF*, xvii.

129. Worthy of further inquiry is the way in which Climacus's theory on spirit-oriented humor relates to Milbank's reading of the role and status of textual sublimity in Kierkegaard. *CUP*, 431–524, 505, 550–55. See also Hugh S. Pyper, "Beyond a Joke: Kierkegaard's *Concluding Unscientific Postscript* as a Comic Book."

130. *PF*, 5.

131. Ibid., 7.

132. Ibid., 5, 109.

133. See also the title of *PF*'s opening chapter: "Thought-Project."

134. *CUP*, 361.

135. Witness Haufniensis's poetical self-portrait from *CA*, 54–6 and *Pap*. V A 34/*JP* 5732.

136. One could even go as far as saying that Haufniensis's behavior is not incongruous with the inquisitive, yet essentially impassioned, attitude of the secular psychiatrist in his or her dealings with the patient.

137. See Howard and Edna Hong, Historical Introduction to *SD*, xxi and notes 58, 59.

138. *Pap*. X1 A 517/*JP* 6433: ". . . whereas Johannes Climacus places himself so low

What this indicates is that by indiscriminately bringing together (as Milbank inadvertently does) the dissimilar accounts of sin voiced by various pseudonyms, we forcibly disregard the complex teleology and existentially formative *Bildung* of Kierkegaard's authorship. Furthermore, the theological paternity and particularity of each pseudonymous account would not be less affected, were we to treat the pseudonyms as holistically and harmoniously complementing one another.

John Milbank's next thesis on the Fall states that "Where Augustine located the transcendental sin as 'pride.' . . . Kierkegaard substitutes fear, which swims in the medium of acknowledged uncertainty. The only way out of this condition is to travel to the end of despair, to discover that despair does indeed lurk beneath the indeterminate series of finite project—and then paradoxically to invest our hope and love in infinite indeterminacy itself. A leap into the void by which faith heals anxiety."[139]

Leaving aside the forced juxtaposition between fear and anxiety,[140] the controversial points expressed in this quote go in several directions. First, for Kierkegaard, faith could never irrevocably heal anxiety due to the everlastingness of the sin-generating anxiety and the dutiful continuity of repentance.[141] On the other side, counter to the centrality of the "infinite qualitative difference," to which I briefly alluded above, Milbank turns Kierkegaard into a crypto-Pelagian when implying that the tribulations of anxiety and despair could be (definitively?) overcome by experiencing them "to the end." True enough, Anti-Climacus assures us that even in the grips of the darkest despair the self is still given the possibility of redemption.[142] At the same time, Anti-Climacus nowhere conditions faith or the cure for despair on experiencing the latter's apex. In this manner, he

---

that he even says that he himself is not a Christian, one seems to be able to detect in Anti-Climacus that he considers himself to be a Christian on an extraordinarily high level . . . I [Kierkegaard] would place myself higher than Johannes Climacus, lower than Anti-Climacus."

139. SIK, 73.

140. For the sharp difference between the two see Martin Heidegger's cogent elaboration of anxiety, which is directly inspired by Kierkegaard. Martin Heidegger, *Being and Time*, ¶40, 228–35. Furthermore, the collation between anxiety and despair poses tremendous problems within the limits of Kierkegaard's corpus.

141. Vigilius's defense of the requisite continuity of repentance is completely omitted by Milbank.

142. And that because for God everything is possible, including the deliverance of the most evil. SD, 38–41, 70–71.

implies that there exist despairing selves who genuinely strive for salvation without *ever* reaching the level of the demonic (which is the most intense expression of despair).

Thirdly, one can find in Kierkegaard's oeuvre at least two instances when religious hope and love do not necessarily target an "infinite indeterminacy." Quite the opposite. Take the (paradoxical) centrality of earthliness in *Fear and Trembling*, in view of which Johannes de Silentio rejoicingly declares that "[temporality], finitude . . . is what everything revolves on."[143] It is for no other reason that on Silentio's account, Abraham's undeterred faith primarily envisions *this life*, more exactly, the *historically* determined promise that God's chosen people will spring from Isaac's seed. The second instance has to do with the fact that, when exploring the tropes of sin, salvation, and hope, Kierkegaard consistently projects them against the background of *Christology* in lieu of an indeterminate religiousness. In the same vein, spiritual love or *agape* has a definite target: the actual neighbor one sees and in whom one is to love humanity *in toto* through the mediation of divine love.[144]

Fourthly, regardless of their obvious affinities, the Kierkegaardian category of sin cannot be reduced to the mere substitution of an objectless fear for the Augustinian *vanitas*;[145] or to "a perverse repetition that undoes

---

143. *FT*, 49; translation amended. This omission is quite puzzling since in his polemic against Slavoj Žižek, Milbank fruitfully deploys Kierkegaard's idea from *FT* that finitude can be thought as divine gift to the faithful. See *The Monstrosity of Christ*, 199. Moreover, Milbank appreciates that the religious "suspension of the ethical" as depicted in the same book "appears somehow to recapitulate and redeem 'the aesthetic'" SIK, 76. However, I hold that the aesthetic—taken as *determinate* immediacy—problematizes Milbank's emphasis on an all-pervasive indeterminacy.

144. *WL*, 154–74.

145. *Contra* Augustine, Kierkegaard shies away from addressing the bodily determinations of sinfulness. On this issue I rely on Elaine Pagels's *Adam, Eve, and the Serpent*, which describes how for Augustine, original sin is sexually transmissible. Contrast this point with the relation between sexuality and sinfulness from *CA* 48, 53, 67, 79, 190–95. Moreover, besides Augustine, Kierkegaard's soteriology remains unthinkable without the Lutheran-Pietistic tradition of Christianity. See Bruce Kirmmse, *Kierkegaard in Golden Age Denmark*; Lee C. Barrett, "Kierkegaard's 'Anxiety' and the Augustinian Doctrine of Original Sin." With that in mind, Milbank's suggestion that Kierkegaard's ethico-religious may be paralleled with Nietzsche's "Dionysiac" (SIK, 71 and 78 note 25) is no more than a formal association. The Pietistic influence on Kierkegaard's biography (particularly, his early encounter with the worldview of the Moravian Brothers) should be enough in evincing the incompatibility between Nietzsche's "Dionysiac" and Christian soteriology. See also note 148 below.

repetition and induces self-enclosed anxiety."[146] Undeniably, Kierkegaard understands sin in this sense, too, but he additionally examines numerous other manifestations of spiritual corruption within the confines of will, consciousness, memory, and, as we saw earlier, logos itself. Besides, in contrast to Augustine's ecclesiology, he views any collectivist interference in religious matters as utterly heretical, deserving nothing else than scorn and fervent rebuttal.[147] Taken together, all of these aspects additionally prove that Kierkegaard is much more antagonistic towards Pelagianism than Milbank allows.[148]

Kierkegaard's counter-Pelagianism can be seen at work even in the books recurrently cited by Milbank. For instance, despite his insistence on the initial guiltlessness of every individual, Haufniensis brings to light a historical-communal determination of anxiety, which leads to an incremental

[146]. SIK, 75. I delineate the complexity of this issue in *Either Nothingness or Love*, 74–121.

[147]. I sketched this line of thought in Stan, "The Hidden Ethics of Soteriology: A Reconsideration of Kierkegaard's Understanding of the Human Other." For a fuller development see Stan, *Either Nothingness or Love*, 226–85. Equally relevant here is the—sometimes frustrating—scarcity of Kierkegaard's mediations on the possibility and nature of a truly religious community in contradistinction to the centrality of *ecclesia* in Augustine. As relevant is the doctrinal eminence of the church, which has lain at the center of Martensen's polemic against Kierkegaard. See *M*, 360–65. This is yet another difference from the ecclesiology of Radical Orthodoxy as discussed in James K. A. Smith, *Introducing Radical Orthodoxy*, chps. 4, 6, and 7. See also Milbank's attempt to unearth a hidden "linguistic" ecclesiology in Kierkegaard without, however, sufficiently developing it. *The Monstrosity of Christ*, 211.

[148]. To be precise, Milbank holds that Kierkegaard occupies the middle ground "between Pelagianism and essentialization of 'the sin of the race.'" SIK, 81 note 52. My position stresses to a larger extent the latter possibility. A confirmation in this sense lies in the relative substantiality sinfulness acquires especially in its higher forms; see *SD*, 106–7. See also *WA*, 30 where Kierkegaard realizes that fallenness and evil reached such amplitude that only an infinitely patient and loving deity could counteract them. Lee Barrett convincingly showed how Kierkegaard displays "clear affinities with the confessional Lutheran tradition in its *opposition* to semi-Pelagianism, [namely by] insisting that original sin involves a *corruption of all capacities* (not just the lower appetites), that it does entail guilt (and not just a nonculpable debility), and that it is universal." Barrett, "Kierkegaard's 'Anxiety' and the Augustinian Doctrine of Original Sin," 51; italics mine. With *PF* in mind, Lee Barrett argues that, even if he "is neither a doctrinaire Augustinian nor a pure Pelagian," "Climacus undercuts the basic foundations upon which all these doctrinal options were based." Barrett, "The Paradox of Faith in *Philosophical Fragments*: Gift or Task?," 261. On Kierkegaard's explicit opposition to Pelagianism see *SD*, 81. *CA*, 34–35, 37. Another important question related to this issue is how compatible is Kierkegaard's version of sin with Milbank's preference for the theological articulation of evil and original sin as privation. See John Milbank, "Darkness and Silence. Evil and the Western Legacy."

accumulation of *Angest*. The climax of this process is reached when anxiety about sin starts producing sin.[149] Moving to Climacus, his expertise on humor and witty pamphleteering notwithstanding, he is not at all unfamiliar with the perpetuity of sin.[150] In his turn, Anti-Climacus warns against the degradation of spirit because of its sheer ubiquity,[151] while his notorious gravity makes him realize that "sin is a position that on its own develops an increasingly established continuity."[152]

One final point is in order here regarding John Milbank's tenet that Kierkegaard's anthropology harbors nihilistic undertones.[153] From a theological point of view, nihilism overlaps in significant ways with Kierkegaard's depiction of existential demonism. Accordingly, on Kierkegaard's evaluation, only a demonic self is capable of circumventing all universal determination. Thus, demonism prides itself upon an illusive self-mastery, predicated on the arrogant ability to (re)create itself. In point of fact, argues Anti-Climacus, the kind of identity cultivated by the demonic—that is to say, an identity self-invented *ex nihilo*—remains forever arbitrary, fictitious, temporary, and therefore existentially vacuous.[154] By implication, when Milbank discerns a proto-nihilistic sense of self-realization in Kierkegaard, that may be indicative of the self-immured, alterity-loathing, and spiritually defiant selfhood[155] which does not have very much in common with the follower of Christ, the practitioner of neighbor love, or the (sublime) knight of faith.

---

149. *CA*, 73. For the vicious self-replication of sin see *CA*, 53; *SD*, 105ff. Lee Barrett, "Kierkegaard's 'Anxiety' and the Augustinian Doctrine of Original Sin," 46.

150. "The untruth," he writes, "is not merely outside the truth but is polemical against the truth, which is expressed by saying that [the disciple] himself *has forfeited* and *is forfeiting* the condition [of truth] . . . he uses the power of freedom in the service of unfreedom . . . and in this way the combined power of unfreedom grows and makes him the slave of sin." *PF*, 15, 17; italics added.

151. According to Anti-Climacus, humans are "so much in the power of sin that [they have] no idea of its *wholly encompassing nature*." *SD*, 105; italics mine. See also idem, 22–28, 113.

152. *SD*, 106.

153. SIK, 72.

154. *SD*, 68–69.

155. Ibid., 71, 80, 106, 113. Milbank's interpretation is far more appropriate to Kierkegaard's depiction of double-mindedness and despair in terms of a self-conflicted volition; see *UDVS*, 24–35.

6. Relative Voluntarism?

Milbank's elaboration of Kierkegaardian subjectivity draws to a large extent on a particular understanding of volition. What the British theologian brings into focus is Kierkegaard's realization of the ingrained undecidability that undermines each and every project. For Milbank, this goes hand in hand with Kierkegaard's subversion of "the self-percipient Cartesian/idealist subject."[156] Moreover, Milbank observes that on the problem of decision, Kierkegaard's approach is highly ambiguous, if not aporetic. More explicitly, Kierkegaard's subject is required to decide—that is to say, to overcome or reach over the "inevitably engulfing abyss"[157] of repetition—but without ever being sure of "having decided what one appears to have decided."[158] Milbank goes on to say that Kierkegaard's resoluteness is thus meant "to affirm absurdly and without grounds such-and-such a repeated continuity,"[159] while at bottom, the "'deciding' subject" is nothing more than "a 'textual' subject."[160]

In speaking of decision against the backdrop of absurdity and groundlessness,[161] Milbank unintentionally pledges allegiance to the hermeneutic trend initiated by the political thinker and historian of ethics, Alasdair MacIntyre, who has taken Kierkegaard to task for the postulation of an allegedly irrational transition from aesthetic hedonism to ethical responsibility, and even to religious fideism.[162] MacIntyre's interpretation has attracted severe criticisms from a broad cadre of Kierkegaard scholars.[163]

---

156. SIK, 69.

157. Ibid.

158. Ibid. Put otherwise, the *aporia* lies in the fact that "Our decisions are preinscribed in conditions of innocence, sin and redemption, which no single person invents. And yet, what is preinscribed here is the constant necessity for the event of decision." SIK, 76.

159. SIK, 69.

160. Ibid.

161. See SIK, 70 where Milbank affirms that "the question of truth is only resolvable by an *unfounded* decision concerning our own self-development;" italics added.

162. Alasdair MacIntyre, *After Virtue: A Study in Moral Theory*. See also MacIntyre's remarks in John J. Davenport and Anthony Rudd, *Kierkegaard after MacIntyre: Essays on Freedom, Narrative, and Virtue*, 339ff. Revelatory in this sense may be John Milbank's ample and critical dialog with MacIntyre from Milbank, *Theology and Social Theory. Beyond Secular Reason*.

163. *Kierkegaard after MacIntyre*, op. cit. See also Matthew D. Mendham, "*Eudaimonia* and *Agape* in MacIntyre and Kierkegaard's *Works of Love*."

If one discerns substantial intellectual affinities between MacIntyre and Milbank, such criticisms might be extensible to the latter.

Be that as it may, what concerns me here is the scepticism or agnosticism that Milbank deems momentous in Kierkegaard's theory on decision—the immediate consequence being that the subject's inner continuity is utterly unfathomable. Of equal interest is Milbank's consequent remark that Kierkegaard does not go further than a mere textual (that is, abstract or vacuous) form of subjectivity. I fully agree with Milbank as regards the first point. Johannes Climacus reveals and elaborates the link between risk, the ethico-religious decision, and the qualitative leap, based on the inevitable limitations of the individual's knowledge of all the consequences of his or her free acts. Climacus remarkably reveals the gap between one's existential knowledge and every momentous decision. Such gap becomes even more evident when Climacus conceives the subjective truth as contingent on an "objective uncertainty."[164]

The danger, though, is to overemphasize the "void," against which repetition must be willed, and thus to completely lose sight of the object or content of one's decision.[165] Also, Milbank's insistence on the centrality of the text in the genesis of subjectivity might gratuitously marginalize the pivotal role of passion in Climacus's psychology. It is well-known that in his existential heuristics, Climacus defends the necessity of appropriating the

---

164. *CUP*, 203.

165. Paramount in this sense is Judge William's dialectic of ethical self-choice. William writes: "The person who has ethically chosen and found himself possesses himself defined in his entire concretion. He then possesses himself as an individual who has these capacities, these passions, these inclinations, these habits, who is subject to these external influences, who is influenced in one direction thus and in another thus . . . the self that is the objective [of choosing oneself] is not an abstract self that fits everywhere and therefore nowhere but is a concrete self in living interaction with these specific surroundings, these life conditions, this order of things. The self that is the objective is not only a personal self but a social, a civic self . . . [The ethical person] transfers himself from personal life to civic life, from this to personal life. Personal life as such was an isolation and therefore imperfect, but when he turns back into his personality through the civic life, the personal life appears in a higher form." *EO*, II 262–63. See also Sylvia Walsh, "Kierkegaard and Postmodernism," 121, where we read: ". . . in the flux of life we must choose a face, a name, a character, a lifeview, an ethic by which to identify ourselves and be identified by others. If we do not attempt to integrate ourselves in such a manner our very indecision will itself decide the matter and constitute a choice of the aesthetic." See also Kierkegaard's insistence (via Climacus and Anti-Climacus) that faith envisions primarily the *historicity* of Christ.

truth "with the most passionate inwardness."[166] Therefore, pathos is constitutive of every genuine decision,[167] which in tandem with the historical determinations of one's ethical-religious decisions, becomes a noteworthy *counterweight* to the subject's indecision. To overemphasize the undecidable is to ignore both the dense concreteness of one's choices and the centrality of volition in Kierkegaard's religious self-becoming.

Speaking of volition, we should not forget either that Anti-Climacus considers it the only faculty capable of unifying the given and the possible, or the abstract and the palpable.[168] Faith, too, is for him unthinkable without a strong sense of will.[169] Volition is as necessary in coping with the adversity of the world when the disciple follows in Christ's earthly steps.[170] That being so, the inner endurance of the religious endeavor is contingent on a renewable decision which is *never* unsure as to "what one appears to have decided."[171] In short, my argument is that the undecidability of one's salvation is underscored by Kierkegaard as much as the self's pathos-laden, concrete, equally dramatic and joyful,[172] exertions for the sake of redemption.

7. The Dialog Has just Begun

No matter how critical, no future assessment of Radical Orthodoxy's rapports with Kierkegaard can (nor should) ignore Milbank's merit in opening a few brand new vistas in a field which otherwise may seem exhausted and even on the wane. The first issue I want to pinpoint in this sense regards Milbank's thought-provoking interpretation of existential aesthetics, in particular his parallel between seduction (or aesthetic repetition) and marriage (that is, ethical repetition).[173] Interesting biographical observations are

166. *CUP*, 203. For more on the centrality of passion see ibid., 197, 230, 354, 509.

167. Lee Barrett, "The Paradox of Faith in *Philosophical Fragments*," 267–68, 271, 274–77, 279.

168. *SD*, 32, 37. *Pap.* VIII2 B 150:6/*SD*, 149.

169. *SD*, 26, 29, 78, 80. Volition is also of great consequence to faith, granted its central place in the dialectic of despair. *SD*, 43, 81, 99–100, 106.

170. *Practice in Christianity*—where Anti-Climacus offers his inimitable version of *imitatio Christi*—is dominated through and through by the volitional tenor of Kierkegaard's existential Christology. See also *Pap.* X3 A 470/*JP* 4933. *Pap.* X3 A 471/*JP* 4934.

171. *SIK*, 69. Moreover, were Milbank's emphasis on undecidability fully tenable, then Kierkegaard's attack against equivocation—as a perfect excuse *not* to decide and act—would not make too much sense. See *TA*, 77ff.

172. *CD*, 93–159. *UDVS*, 155–212.

173. *SIK*, 71, 78–79 note 28.

made when Milbank places Kierkegaard's personal faith side-by-side with the engagement episode.[174] No less praiseworthy is that, unlike a legion of Kierkegaard scholars, Milbank perceptively realizes that Kierkegaard "'saves' philosophy by transforming it, without remainder, into theology."[175] But most promising by far is Milbank's engagement with the fascinating and controversial work, *Fear and Trembling*. Milbank suggests that, insofar as "Abraham's sacrifice of Isaac is an anti-sacrifice" or "a completely pointless sacrifice," then "there is, after all, nothing really 'beyond' the ethical."[176] That is to say, because it turns out to be a "ban on murder" or "a faithful refusal of death," the teleological suspension of the ethical comes to ground an ethics that excludes both murder and sacrifice.[177] Not to be missed either is Milbank's high regard for the religious "transvaluation" of the aesthetic in *Fear and Trembling*,[178] an aspect insufficiently researched in the enormous extant literature on this particular book.

Overall, John Milbank succeeds in initiating an animated discussion of Radical Orthodoxy's theo-philosophical position vis-à-vis Kierkegaard. But the conversation should not end here. I hope the present chapter is a mere preamble to a multidirectional and necessary dialog.

ABBREVIATIONS OF KIERKEGAARD'S WRITINGS

BA   *The Book on Adler*. Translated by Howard V. Hong and Edna H. Hong. Princeton, NJ: Princeton University Press, 1998.
A   *The Concept of Anxiety*. Translated by Reidar Thomte and Albert B. Anderson. Princeton, NJ: Princeton University Press, 1980.
CD   *Christian Discourses*. Translated by Howard V. Hong and Edna H. Hong. Princeton, NJ: Princeton University Press, 1997.
CUP   *Concluding Unscientific Postscript to Philosophical Fragments*. Translated by Howard V. Hong and Edna H. Hong. Princeton, NJ: Princeton University Press, 1992.

174. Ibid., 80 note 50.
175. Ibid., 72.
176. Ibid., 74.
177. Ibid., 75. Or, as Milbank wonderfully puts it, "In the Abraham story one sees how the ultimate vertical rupture of faith is supposed transcendentally to found and guarantee the continuity of ethical life, which is the life of the city. Only when we persist in continuity is salvation realized, but sustaining this achievement requires a constant reckoning with the unknown, a faith in the continued possibility of this continuity, despite all disasters." SIK, 75.
178. SIK, 76.

EO   *Either/Or*. 2 vols. Translated by Howard V. Hong and Edna H. Hong. Princeton, NJ: Princeton University Press, 1987. Cited by volume number and page number.

EUD   *Eighteen Upbuilding Discourses*. Translated by Howard V. Hong and Edna H. Hong, Princeton, NJ: Princeton University Press, 1990.

FT   *Fear and Trembling*. Translated by Howard V. Hong and Edna H. Hong. Princeton, NJ: Princeton University Press, 1983.

JP[179] *Søren Kierkegaard's Journals and Papers*. Edited and translated by Howard and Edna Hong. vols. 1–6. Bloomington: Indiana University Press, 1967–1978. Cited by volume number and entry number.

M   *The Moment and Late Writings*. Translated by Howard V. Hong and Edna H. Hong. Princeton, NJ: Princeton University Press, 1998.

Pap.[180] *Papirer*. Edited by P. A. Heiberg, V. Kuhr, and E. Torsting. Vols. 1–16. Copenhagen: Gyldendal, 1909–1948. Supplemented by Niels Thulstrup. Copenhagen: Gyldendal, 1968–1978.

PC   *Practice in Christianity*. Translated by Howard V. Hong and Edna H. Hong, Princeton. NJ: Princeton University Press, 1991.

PV   *The Point of View of My Work as an Author*. Translated by Howard V. Hong and Edna H. Hong. Princeton, NJ: Princeton University Press, 1998.

SD   *The Sickness Unto Death*. Translated by Howard V. Hong and Edna H. Hong. Princeton, NJ: Princeton University Press, 1980.

TA   *Two Ages*. Translated by Howard V. Hong and Edna H. Hong, Princeton, NJ: Princeton University Press, 1978.

UDVS *Upbuilding Discourses in Various Spirits*. Translated by Howard V. Hong and Edna H. Hong, Princeton, NJ: Princeton University Press, 1993.

WA   *Without Authority*. Translated by Howard V. Hong and Edna H. Hong. Princeton, NJ: Princeton University Press, 1997.

WL   *Works of Love*. Translated by Howard V. Hong and Edna H. Hong. Princeton, NJ: Princeton University Press, 1995.

---

179. For Kierkegaard's journals, reference will be made to the Danish edition of *Papirer* (see below), followed by the English translation from *Søren Kierkegaard's Journals and Papers* (see below). Thus, Pap. V B 55:4 indicates *Papirer*, vol. V, entry B 55:4. As to the English translation, I preserved the editors' original numbering of Kierkegaard's diary entries: for example, JP 52 refers to entry 52 from *Kierkegaard's Journals and Papers*.

180. See previous note.

Bibliography

Barrett, Lee C. "The Paradox of Faith in *Philosophical Fragments*: Gift or Task?" In *International Kierkegaard Commentary: Philosophical Fragments and Johannes Climacus*, edited by Robert Perkins, 261–84. Macon, GA: Mercer University Press, 1985.

———. "Kierkegaard's 'Anxiety' and the Augustinian Doctrine of Original Sin." In *International Kierkegaard Commentary: The Concept of Anxiety*, edited by Robert Perkins, 35–61. Macon, GA: Mercer University Press, 1985.

Barrett, William. *Irrational Man*. Garden City, NY: Doubleday, 1962.

Bertens, Johannes Willem. *The Idea of the Postmodern. A History*. New York: Routledge, 1995.

Blanchette, Oliva. "The Silencing of Philosophy." In *International Kierkegaard Commentary: Fear and Trembling and Repetition*, edited by Robert Perkins, 29–65. Macon, GA: Mercer University Press, 1993.

Blanshard, Brand. "Kierkegaard on Faith." *Personalist* 49 (1968) 5–23.

Carr, Karen L., and Philip J. Ivanhoe. *The Sense of Antirationalism. The Religious Thought of Zhuangzi and Kierkegaard*. New York: Seven Bridges, 2000.

Davenport, John J., and Anthony Rudd. *Kierkegaard after MacIntyre: Essays on Freedom, Narrative, and Virtue*. Chicago: Open Court, 2001.

Deleuze, Gilles. *Difference and Repetition*, translated by Paul Patton. New York: Columbia University Press, 1994.

Emmanuel, Steven M. "Kierkegaard's Pragmatist Faith." *Philosophy and Phenomenological Research* 51:2 (June 1991) 279–302.

———. *Kierkegaard and the Concept of Revelation*. Albany: State University of New York Press, 1996.

Evans, C. Stephen. "Faith as the Telos of Morality: A Reading of *Fear and Trembling*." In *International Kierkegaard Commentary*: *Fear and Trembling and Repetition*, edited by Robert Perkins, 9–27. Macon, GA: Mercer University Press, 1993.

Ferreira, Jamie. *Love's Grateful Striving: A Commentary on Kierkegaard's Works of Love*. Oxford: Oxford University Press, 2001.

Garelick, Herbert M. *The Anti-Christianity of Kierkegaard*. The Hague: Martinus Nijhoff, 1965.

Green, Ronald Michael. "Kant: A Debt both Obscure and Enormous." In *Kierkegaard and His German Contemporaries*, edited by Jon Stewart, 179–210. Tome I: Philosophy. Aldershot: Ashgate, 2007.

———. *Kierkegaard and Kant: The Hidden Debt*. Albany: State University of New York Press, 1992.

Hall, Amy Laura. *Kierkegaard and the Treachery of Love*. New York: Cambridge University Press, 2002.

Hannay, Alastair. *Kierkegaard: A Biography*. Cambridge: Cambridge University Press, 2001.

———. *Kierkegaard*. New York: Routledge, 1991.

Heidegger, Martin. *Being and Time*. Translated by John Macquarrie and Edward Robinson. Oxford: Basil Blackwell, 1962.

Hong, Howard, and Edna Hong. "Historical Introduction." In *Eighteen Upbuilding Discourses*, by Søren Kierkegaard. Princeton, NJ: Princeton University Press, 1990.

———. "Historical Introduction." In *Practice in Christianity*, by Søren Kierkegaard. Princeton, NJ: Princeton University Press, 1991.

The Poverty of Radical Orthodoxy

———. "Historical Introduction." In *The Sickness Unto Death*, by Søren Kierkegaard. Princeton, NJ: Princeton University Press, 1980.
Herbert, Robert. "Two of Kierkegaard's Uses of Paradox." *The Philosophical Review* 70:1 (1961) 41–55.
Kangas, David J. "J. G. Fichte: From Transcendental Ego to Existence." In *Kierkegaard and His German Contemporaries*, edited by Jon Stewart, 67–95. Tome I: Philosophy. Aldershot: Ashgate, 2007.
Kierkegaard, Søren. *The Book on Adler*. Translated by Howard V. Hong and Edna H. Hong. Princeton, NJ: Princeton University Press, 1998.
———. *The Concept of Anxiety*. Translated by Reidar Thomte and Albert B. Anderson. Princeton, NJ: Princeton University Press, 1980.
———. *Christian Discourses*. Translated by Howard V. Hong and Edna H. Hong. Princeton, NJ: Princeton University Press, 1997.
———. *Concluding Unscientific Postscript to Philosophical Fragments*. Translated by Howard V. Hong and Edna H. Hong. Princeton, NJ: Princeton University Press, 1992.
———. *Either/Or*. 2 vols. Translated by Howard V. Hong and Edna H. Hong. Princeton, NJ: Princeton University Press, 1987.
———. *Eighteen Upbuilding Discourses*. Translated by Howard V. Hong and Edna H. Hong. Princeton, NJ: Princeton University Press, 1990.
———. *Fear and Trembling*. Translated by Howard V. Hong and Edna H. Hong. Princeton, NJ: Princeton University Press, 1983.
———. *Søren Kierkegaard's Journals and Papers*. Edited and translated by Howard and Edna Hong. Vols. 1–6. Bloomington: Indiana University Press, 1967–1978.
———. *The Moment and Late Writings*. Translated by Howard V. Hong and Edna H. Hong. Princeton, NJ: Princeton University Press, 1998.
———. *Papirer*. Edited by P. A. Heiberg, V. Kuhr, and E. Torsting. Vols. 1–16. Copenhagen: Gyldendal, 1909–1948. Supplemented by Niels Thulstrup. Copenhagen: Gyldendal, 1968–1978.
———. *Practice in Christianity*. Translated by Howard V. Hong and Edna H. Hong. Princeton, NJ: Princeton University Press, 1991.
———. *The Point of View of My Work as an Author*. Translated by Howard V. Hong and Edna H. Hong. Princeton, NJ: Princeton University Press, 1998.
———. *The Sickness Unto Death*. Translated by Howard V. Hong and Edna H. Hong. Princeton, NJ: Princeton University Press, 1980.
———. *Two Ages*. Translated by Howard V. Hong and Edna H. Hong. Princeton, NJ: Princeton University Press, 1978.
———. *Upbuilding Discourses in Various Spirits*. Translated by Howard V. Hong and Edna H. Hong. Princeton, NJ: Princeton University Press, 1993.
———. *Without Authority*. Translated by Howard V. Hong and Edna H. Hong. Princeton, NJ: Princeton University Press, 1997.
———. *Works of Love*. Translated by Howard V. Hong and Edna H. Hong. Princeton, NJ: Princeton University Press, 1995.
Kirmmse, Bruce. *Kierkegaard in Golden Age Denmark*. Bloomington: Indiana University Press, 1990.
Levinas, Emmanuel. "Existence and Ethics." In *Kierkegaard: A Critical Reader*, edited by J. Rée and Jane Chamberlain, 26–36. Malden, MA: Blackwell, 2001.

MacIntyre, Alasdair. *After Virtue: A Study in Moral Theory*. Notre Dame: University of Notre Dame Press, 1981.

Mendham, Matthew D. "*Eudaimonia* and *Agape* in MacIntyre and Kierkegaard's *Works of Love*." *Journal of Religious Ethics* 35:4 (2007) 591–625.

Milbank, John. "Darkness and Silence. Evil and the Western Legacy." In The Religious, edited by John D. Caputo, 277–300. Oxford: Blackwell, 2002.

———. *Theology and Social Theory. Beyond Secular Reason*. 2nd ed. Malden, MA: Blackwell Publishing, 2006.

———. "The Sublime in Kierkegaard." *Heythrop Journal* 37 (1996) 298–321.

———. "The Sublime in Kierkegaard." In *Post-Secular Philosophy: Between Philosophy and Theology*, edited by Philip Blond, 68–81. New York: Routledge, 1998.

Murphy, Arthur E. "On Kierkegaard's Claim that 'Truth is Subjectivity.'" In *Reason and the Common Good*, edited by William H. Hay, Marcus G. Singer, and Arthur E. Murphy. Englewood Cliffs, NJ: Prentice Hall, 1963.

Pagels, Elaine. *Adam, Eve, and the Serpent*. New York: Vintage, 1989.

Piety, Marilyn Gaye. "Kierkegaard on Rationality." *Faith and Philosophy* 10 (1993) 365–79.

Pojman, Louis P. *The Logic of Subjectivity: Kierkegaard's Philosophy of Religion*. University, AL: The University of Alabama Press, 1984.

Pyper, Hugh S. "Beyond a Joke: Kierkegaard's *Concluding Unscientific Postscript* as a Comic Book." In *International Kierkegaard Commentary: Concluding Unscientific Postscript*, edited by Robert Perkins, 149–68. Macon, GA: Mercer University Press, 1997.

Rasmussen, A. M. "René Descartes: Kierkegaard's Understanding of Doubt and Certainty." In *Kierkegaard and the Renaissance and Modern Traditions*, edited by Jon Stewart, 11–22. Tome I: Philosophy. Burlington: Ashgate, 2009.

Shakespeare, Steven. *Kierkegaard, Language, and the Reality of God*. Aldershot: Ashgate, 2001.

Smith, James K. A. *Introducing Radical Orthodoxy. Mapping a Post-Secular Theology*. Grand Rapids: Baker Academic, 2004.

Søltoft, Pia. "The Presence of the Absent Neighbor in *Works of Love*." In *Kierkegaard Studies*, edited by Niels J. Cappelørn and Hermann Deuser. New York: Walter de Gruyter, 1998.

Sponheim, Paul R. *Kierkegaard on Christ and Christian Coherence*. London: SCM, 1968.

Stan, Leo. *Either Nothingness or Love. On Alterity in Søren Kierkegaard's Writings*. Saarbrucken: Verlag, 2009.

———. "The Hidden Ethics of Soteriology: A Reconsideration of Kierkegaard's Understanding of the Human Other." *Journal of Religious Ethics* 38:2 (June 2010) 349–70.

———. "Kierkegaard on Temporality and God Incarnate." In *Philosophical Concepts and Religious Metaphors: New Perspectives on Phenomenology and Theology*, edited by Cristian Ciocan, 237–54. Bucharest: Zeta, 2009.

———. "Kierkegaard's *Philosophical Fragments*: A Kantian Commentary." In *International Kierkegaard Commentary*: Philosophical Fragments *and* Johannes Climacus, edited by Robert L. Perkins, 169–202. Macon, GA: Mercer University Press, 1994.

———. "The Lily in the Field and the Bird in the Air: An Endless Liturgy in Kierkegaard's Authorship." In *Kierkegaard and the Bible*, edited by Lee C. Barrett. Tome II: The New Testament. Aldershot: Ashgate, 2010.

Stewart, Jon. *Kierkegaard's Relations to Hegel Reconsidered*. New York: Cambridge University Press, 2003.

———. "Kierkegaard's Phenomenology of Despair in *The Sickness unto Death.*" In *Kierkegaard Studies Yearbook,* edited by N. J. Cappelørn and H. Deuser, 117–43. New York: Walter de Gruyter, 1997.

Thompson, Curtis L. "Gotthold Ephraim Lessing: Appropriating the Testimony of a Theological Naturalist." In *Kierkegaard and the Renaissance and Modern Traditions,* edited by Jon Stewart, 77–112. Tome I: Philosophy. Burlington: Ashgate, 2009.

Thomas, J. Heywood. "Revelation, Knowledge, and Proof." In *International Kierkegaard Commentary:* Philosophical Fragments *and* Johannes Climacus, edited by Robert L. Perkins, 147–68. Macon, GA: Mercer University Press, 1994.

Walker, Jeremy. "The Paradox in *Fear and Trembling.*" *Kierkegaardiana* 10 (1977) 133–51.

Walsh, Sylvia. "Kierkegaard and Postmodernism." *International Journal for Philosophy of Religion* 29:2 (1991) 113–22.

Ward, Graham. *Cities of God.* Radical Orthodoxy Series. London: Routledge, 2001.

Žižek, Slavoj, and John Milbank. *The Monstrosity of Christ. Paradox or Dialectic?* Edited by Creston Davis. Cambridge, MA: MIT, 2009.

Žižek, Slavoj. *How to Read Lacan.* London: Granta Books, 2006.

———. *The Parallax View.* Cambridge, MA: MIT, 2006.

5

Girls and Boys Come Out to Play

*Feminist Theology and Radical Orthodoxy
in Ludic Encounter*

Jenny Daggers

> Girls and boys come out to play
> The moon does shine as bright as day
> Come with a hoop and come with a call
> Come with a good will or not at all
> Leave your supper and leave your sleep
> Join with your playfellows on the street
>
> English Nursery Rhyme

It was bound to happen. When, in Radical Orthodoxy's inaugural text, John Milbank's *Theology and Social Theory*,[1] Milbank sounded a critical blast against Liberation Theology, the scene was set for a showdown

---

1. John Milbank, *Theology and Social Theory: Beyond Secular Reason*. Milbank's critique of liberation theology is set out in his essay in this volume, 'Founding the Supernatural: Political and Liberation Theology in the Context of Modern Catholic Thought.'

between Radical Orthodoxy and feminist Liberation Theology. Twenty years later, the dust has settled: for many theologians and their broader constituencies, a clear demarcation between two kinds of theology has been reinforced in this noisy confrontation. On the one hand, conservative theologies reassert Christian doctrinal orthodoxy over against a secularized and multifaith world[2]; they claim the Christian Church as vehicle of salvation, while ignoring the havoc wrought in the exercise of ecclesial power throughout the long history of western Christianity. On the other hand, feminist and other liberation theologies make incisive critique of the exercise of power in the name of Christianity, and its consequences in the suffering of the poor and oppressed; further, they claim salvation as liberation to lie at the heart of Christianity.[3]

Radical Orthodoxy has certainly succeeded in stirring up theological debate, and bringing the contours of these two theological shapes into sharp focus. Contributors to the volume, *Radical Orthodoxy: A New Theology*, brought into view a British movement, which was subsequently extended by North American writings; critics came from many quarters.[4] The title of this current volume of essays, *The Poverty of Radical Orthodoxy*, invites further critique of the movement from liberationist perspectives. However, this contribution takes a different approach. In the somewhat surreal spirit

---

2. James Harvey SJ locates Radical Orthodoxy as "a creative protest against the 'Sea of Faith' . . . and fervent evangelical fundamentalism" in "Conclusion: Continuing the Conversation," 150; his first reference is to the movement based on Don Cupitt's book, *The Sea of Faith*. Thus Harvey locates Radical Orthodoxy as the most recent chapter in the long engagement of European Christian theology with (post)modern thought. While Harvey's critical reading takes issue with radical orthodox readings of Barth and "Catholic Transcendentalism" of *nouvelle théologie*, his discussion does not stray beyond the terrain of the Christian-secular reason debate: he is silent about the implications for radical orthodoxy of the expansion beyond the Eurocentric represented in liberation theology.

3. Some liberation theologians emphasise the thorough orthodoxy of this theological understanding and praxis: Jon Sobrino and Ignacio Ellacuría (eds) *Systematic Theology: Perspectives from Liberation Theology* is one example. Others, notably the editor of this volume, Lisa Isherwood, view orthodoxy as antithetical to the struggle for justice.

4. See John Milbank, Catherine Pickstock and Graham Ward (eds) *Radical Orthodoxy: A New Theology*. Editors and contributors, notably Gerard Loughlin and Philip Blond, also published subsequent monographs; Daniel Bell, *Liberation Theology after the End of History: The Refusal to Cease Suffering*; Stephen Long, *Divine Economy: Theology and the Market*. Some significant critical engagements are: Steven Shakespeare *Radical Orthodoxy: A Critical Introduction;* Rosemary Radford Ruether & Marion Grau (eds) *Interpreting the Postmodern: Responses to "Radical Orthodoxy"*; Gavin Hyman *The Predicament of Postmodern Theology: Radical Orthodoxy or Nihilist Textualism*.

of the nursery rhyme at its head,[5] I attempt to bring radical orthodox and feminist theological writings into playful encounter, akin to girls and boys playing on the moonlit street.[6] In so doing, feminist theology ameliorates the "poverty" of Radical Orthodoxy, and, for those who might welcome this move, a way is reopened for feminist theology to recover something of the riches of orthodoxy from their debasement during the long exercise of oppressive power within the Church.

I put feminist theology into play with Radical Orthodoxy through two specific encounters; the first—between Catherine Keller and John Milbank—I engineer myself, while the second—between Mayra Rivera and Catherine Pickstock—takes the form of my further reflection on Rivera's reading of Pickstock. I use the first encounter to throw up questions about the relation between feminist theology and Radical Orthodoxy, which I then pursue through the second.

Keller's Theopoetics Meets Milbank's Christological Poetics

In this first part of the essay, I have chosen to put Keller and Milbank into play together on the ground of aesthetic *poetics*, as this is a common theme in their respective work: John Milbank's "Christological poetics," articulated in *The Word Made Strange*, meets Catherine Keller's "theopoetics" in her *God and Power: Counter-Apocalyptic Journeys*. This first encounter takes place under four headings: first, the term *poetics* is located in each author's work; Milbank's Christological poetics and Keller's theopoetics are then examined in turn; finally, the political outworking of these two forms of theological poetics is clarified.

POETICS

Milbank clarifies that he writes in a "kindred ambience" to von Balthasar's insistence that revelation be understood as aesthetic, not merely as logical

---

5. The rhyme has a material basis that resonates with liberation theological concerns: children who were expected to work during the day could only play in the evening, by forsaking their supper and their sleep. http://www.rhymes.org.uk/a114-boys-and-girls.htm. (accessed June 16, 2010).

6. My project is thus akin to the "Charitable Interpretation" offered by John F. Hoffmeyer, though this desire to blur the boundaries between the two theologies is rather more queer in a feminist theologian.

and ethical. "Poetic" thus refers to "the realization or manifestation of the Beautiful."[7] Milbank further clarifies the derivation of his term *poetics* from Aristotle's *Nicomachean Ethics* and his (Milbank's) deployment of it. Aristotle resists the reduction of poesis to mere technique, by, as Malcolm Heath points out, valorizing metaphor as the most important feature of poetic language, and insisting the ability to perceive similarities is a natural gift, which cannot be taught as mere technique.[8] Milbank too insists on the priority of metaphor, arguing that humanity be understood as "fundamentally poetic being."[9]

It will be helpful to say more at this point on the poetic way of understanding, according to Milbank. Relying on Ricouer and Vico, Milbank reads Aristotle as combining *mimesis* and *mythos* in poesis: *mimesis* inaugurates a world, so setting up an *ethos* through employing a *mythos*.[10] The metaphoric act of poetry (Ricoeur) leads to the creation of "poetic or concrete universals" (Vico), providing a measure and a *telos* for human activity. These first poetic "reasons," in Milbank's view "[allow] more scope [than abstract reasons] for creative re-application to practical living."[11]

A final preliminary point for understanding Milbank's turn to poetics is to emphasise that "Christological poetics" must be read within the context of the surrounding essays in *The Word Made Strange*, where Milbank makes his case for the primacy of linguistic mediation, which, he maintains, theology must construe in a distinctive way, alert to the cultural mediation of poetically conveyed events.[12] Identifying an alternative modern tradition through Lowth, Hamann, Herder, and Vico, he traces "a seemingly surprising movement, whereby Christian thought moves away from a 'rationalist' to a more 'mystical' conception of language."[13] It is here that Milbank situates his poetics.

---

7. John Milbank, "A Christological Poetics," 123. He goes on qualify ". . . Beautiful, in contrast to the being of the beautiful object or the perception of beauty, which is the subject of aesthetics in the Kantian sense . . . [although] an ontology of the aesthetic object and a phenomenology of aesthetic experience are implicitly involved" in his following argument.

8. Heath, "Introduction," *Poetics* by Aristotle, x–xi.

9. Milbank, *The Word Made Strange*, 124.

10. Ibid., 127.

11. Ibid., 128–29.

12. Ibid., 2–3.

13. Ibid., 110.

Turning to Keller, "theopoetics" is the first word in her book, *God and Power*, appearing in the title of her Preface, though not sighted again before her final chapter. But, before "theopoetics" reappears to do its work, Keller speaks of the Spirit of creation which seems "to be revealing itself, but not making itself known—we only *know*," she says, "our own metaphors" which need to be "poetically alive" and "scripturally resonant."[14] Her poetic license mimics the "artful imagery of scripture," as when Keller borrows descriptions of the four mythical creatures who drove Ezekiel's chariot, who reappear in the Book of Revelation,[15] for her constructive re-vision of the Book of Revelation.

But it is in her turn from Omega to Alpha, from Revelation to Genesis, that Keller's theopoetics reappear. To the biblical poetics of Genesis, Keller brings hermeneutical insight informed by her readings of Derrida, Kristeva, and Irigaray, and postcolonial perspectives of Spivak and Bhabha. There is no explicit attempt to place her "poetics" within an intellectual genealogy, as with Milbank's claim upon Aristotle. But Keller does refer to the *khora* in Plato's *Timaeus* as "being creatively reread by theorists such as Julia Kristeva as a rhythmic embodiment of relation to the mother, by Derrida as the place of difference itself, and by postcolonial theory as the 'third space' or boundary zone."[16] Keller's poetics are more reminiscent of Kristeva's semiotic babblings, in Keller's resistance to closure in interpretation of the biblical text.

To summarize, I have sketched the Aristotelian derivation of Milbank's poetics, and its location within a wider theological argument for the primacy of linguistic mediation. Such mediation exceeds reductive rationalism, in the expression of alternative poetic "reasons," capable of creating poetic universals in which are inscribed both a measure and *telos* for human activity. As we will see, Keller's theopoetics allow a strategic re-reading of the text of Genesis, to resource her counter-apocalyptic journey, as she reads Revelation in the context of American empire. I have sketched here Keller's turn to metaphor, as a poetic license borrowed from biblical writers. These sketches are filled out below. I begin with Milbank's Christological poetics.

---

14. Keller, *God and Power*, 30–31.
15. Ibid., 69.
16. Ibid., 146.

Milbank's Christological Poetics

It will be helpful to clarify Milbank's preliminary discussion of poetic existence as specific activity and in relation to ethics before turning to his Christological poetics.

POETIC EXISTENCE AS FUNDAMENTAL ACTIVITY

Turning first to activity, the act and capacity to act are valorized by Aristotle, who turns from *poesis* to *praxis* to ensure the act remains "entirely outside the manipulative aspirations of technique,"[17] as Milbank puts it. In opting for *poesis*, Milbank is interested in the possibility of "a positive gain in being for the subject,"[18] which the turn to praxis obscures. He returns to the Jewish, Christian, and Islamic integration of the Neoplatonic notion of emanation with this Aristotelian focus upon act and potency; in so doing he makes with particular reference to Aquinas's notion of *virtus* or active potency.[19] What Milbank is interested in here is the double movement in which, on the one hand we are related to the products of *virtus*—we both identify with them as realizing our selfhood in relation to a *telos*—and, on the other hand, we are distinct from these products, as *virtus* is a property of the self who exceeds its products.

Milbank then takes the step—beyond Aquinas—of portraying humanity as a fundamentally poetic being, but a being in which this tension over relation between persons and human products persists. To speak in terms of *poesis*, rather than *praxis*, is to recognize that "*to act at all* is always to be dispossessed";[20] he does not set out to dispossess us of the capacity for an intentional act which is under our control, and thus properly our own (i.e. to dispossess us of a capacity for *praxis*). "To maintain, nonetheless, in the face of this circumstance, a doctrine of full moral responsibility, requires precisely *faith* that if we attend to God, he will graciously provide us, out of ourselves, with appropriate good performances."[21]

This situation is further complicated by the question of human intersubjectivity, given that grace is always humanly, culturally, mediated before and "after" its occurrence. This poetic view of action highlights

---

17. Milbank, *The Word Made Strange*, 124.
18. Ibid.
19. Ibid.
20. Ibid., 126.
21. Ibid.

a "simultaneous and risky openness both to grace and the possibility of sinful distortion" for which human persons are both responsible and not responsible. Every action is part of a series at both individual and cultural levels, and conversely the series constitutes but a single action, the work of humanity, co-partner in responsibility to God.[22]

Poetic Existence in Relation to Praxis or Ethics

Moving on now to Milbank's preliminary comments on poetic existence and praxis, Milbank begins with the statement, "ethical activity always occurs within the bounds afforded by our poetic representations," where these are committed to establishing the human *telos*. He is therefore speaking of "a single practical-poetic movement," opening a deeper potential in human behavior.[23] Contra Hegel, good intentions are not good enough to ensure a good act. Rather, "At most, we have to be *collectively* open to the receiving of better performed representations which can only 'occur' to us as the arrival of performed 'events.'"[24] Praxis has been absorbed within poetics.

CHRISTOLOGICAL POETICS

For Milbank, *poesis* "is an integral aspect of Christian practice and redemption."[25] The poetic being, humankind, in its *mimesis*, which both reflects and inaugurates the Christian *mythos* wherein *mythos* is always *mimesis*,[26] is necessary for the transcendental possibility of revelation, which, Milbank says, "may be defined as the intersection between the divine and human creations."[27] Issues of divine overtaking of human purpose arise,[28] and Milbank discusses the Old Testament record of the Hebraic poetic encounter with God in these terms, arguing that this problematic "points to the coincidence of divine purpose with human *telos*."[29] The "strongly poetic" words of Jesus and his works, "the work of the Father who

---

22. Ibid., 127.
23. Ibid., 129.
24. Ibid., 129–30.
25. Ibid., 32.
26. Ibid., 131.
27. Ibid., 130.
28. Ibid., 135.
29. Ibid.

sent me,"[30] interpellate poetic humanity into its *telos*, that is, into the repeated mimetic inauguration of the Christian *mythos*. The incarnate *Logos* is a full manifestation of the divine presence, as God's activity is at one with his being; this divine manifestation "automatically brings with it the realization, and so representation, of the true human *telos* within human history."[31] In this "poetic synthesis"[32] in the divine-human person of Christ, the divine both overtakes and fulfills human purposes.

Further, "Christian texts allow a rebirth of the human imagination by remembering that the *mythos* is something that opens up reality."[33] Imagination is directed in the very core of *poesis* "to the vision of Christ himself in the mysterious depths of his progression from the Father. Here our 'total hermeneutic situation' with regard to Christ *both* regards him aesthetically as he is given (Balthasar) *and* regards him *poetically* as he is still being given, reborn through our own spirit-inspired constructions."[34]

Keller's Theopoetics

"Spirit-inspired constructions" might be an apt way of characterizing Keller's theological genre, as our attention turns to her theopoetics. It will be helpful to clarify the overall nature of Keller's project in *God and Power*: as her title suggests, theopolitics provides the context in which she shapes her theopoetics. I will return to this point below. Keller takes the Book of Revelation "as master text and historicized context of all western theopolitics."[35] Her work is a theological response to post-9/11 American politics of empire.

God and Power seeks to make "culturally recognizable" an *apocalyptic unconsciousness* manifest in this contemporary American imperial messianism.[36] Theopoetics is deployed by Keller in her advocacy of a counter-apocalypse (itself a form of apocalypse),[37] allowing her to read the Book of Revelation differently: she disrupts the linear trajectory from Alpha to Omega, through a return to the beginning, to Genesis in order to articulate

30. Ibid.
31. Ibid., 135–36.
32. Ibid., 136.
33. Ibid., 141.
34. Ibid., 142.
35. Keller, *God and Power*, 55.
36. Ibid., viii.
37. Ibid., 88.

the possibility of "a nonlinear creativity from chaos."[38] This complementary biblical reading opens a way beyond theopolitics in the image of an omnipotent God, towards an ecologically sustainable vision of human co-creativity with the God whose spirit breathes on the waters.

Keller turns to verse 2 of Genesis: "And the earth was *tohuvabohu* (without form and wild) and darkness was on the face of *tehom* (deep, ocean, chaos) and *ruach elohim* was vibrating over the surface of the waters."[39] Her strategy is to uncover a tehomophilic biblical tradition, from which she suggests a theological interpretation, *creatio ex profundis*, as complement to the *creatio ex nihilo* tradition, which Keller claims is based on a longstanding and dominant tehomophobic reading of the biblical text.

Keller's theopoetics is a theopoetics of becoming, recognizing that the biblical genesis means becoming, and claiming that resurrecting *tehom*[40] is a symbolic strategy also for the becoming of women, resonant with a biblical trace in Genesis of an unfulfilled gynesis. Drawing on the eleventh century Jewish interpreter, Rashi, Keller argues for a tehomophilic interpretation which reads the creation account as one of co-creation, rather than as *creatio ex nihilo*.[41] And this is a *creatio continuo*, a continuum of all relations from which order and cosmos continually emerge.[42]

For Keller, theopoetics flows beneath and beyond our theopolitics.[43] Poetic language, which both reveals and hides, is capable of healing the wounds inflicted by theopolitical violence: its discourse of uncertainty is more effective than "just another sure truth."[44] "When God ceases to be a poetic invocation . . . and begins to control the political context, we no longer have to do with the God of Love, but with the idol of omnipotence."[45] So it becomes manifest that Keller, in her turn to metaphor, favours "poetically alive" and "scripturally resonant" metaphor-making which is "rich in justice."[46]

---

38. Ibid., xii.

39. Ibid., 137.

40. And with *tehom*, resurrection of Tiamat, whose link with *tehom* in the biblical creation story was clarified by late nineteenth century research, noting mythological parallels between the Babylonian creation story, *Enumu Elish*, and the biblical creation story.

41. Keller, *God and Power*, 145.

42. Ibid., 147.

43. Ibid., 149.

44. Ibid., 150.

45. Ibid., 151.

46. Ibid., 30–31.

The Poverty of Radical Orthodoxy

Poetics and Politics

Moving now to the encounter between Milbank and Keller, my discussion aims to bring out the political significance of these two theologies of poetics. I begin by noting similarities. First, they are both wary of modernist forms of liberatory praxis. The effect of Milbank's development of Aristotle's poesis, so that he (contra Aristotle) opts for poesis over praxis, is to refuse the possibility of praxis as act capable of achieving its end. This undermines the possibility of a committed liberatory praxis, capable of acting in order to achieve the end of liberation.[47]

Similarly, Keller is critical of unacknowledged liberation and feminist binary strategies,[48] which repeatedly set up liberatory and oppressive forces in opposition. Her postcolonial theology reads the apocalyptic biblical tradition so that it "may help us outgrow the pious prevarications of progressive theopolitics."[49] Keller resists a "theopolitics" that "however presumably progressive" encourages "chronic moral indignation"; she resists any reductive flattening of the world to ethics or politics alone.[50] In her view, both revolutionary and imperial messianic forms are equally "galvanizing, reductive and absolute" in their claims.[51]

Second, their respective turn to poetics elicits striking similarities in their articulation of their respective projects. So when Milbank says that "Christian texts allow a rebirth of the human imagination by remembering that the *mythos* is something that opens up reality," or when he urges us to regard Christ "*poetically* as he is still being given, reborn through our own spirit-inspired constructions," he speaks in a similar vein to Keller's spirit-inspired prose. When Keller speaks of theology—unlike religious studies or

---

47. Milbank, *The Word Made Strange*, 129 makes the opposite decision to Aristotle in valorizing poetics over praxis. Yet Milbank argues that, because poetic representation establishes *telos*, there is a single practical-poetic movement, so *praxis* and *poetics* cannot be separated. But Milbank says of Aristotle that "In *praxis* act and end are identical, in *poesis*, act and end are distinguished" (124), explaining that Aristotle opts for praxis to avoid the slide towards mere *techne* (with its Platonic tendencies), which may occur with poesis. Milbank shares Aristotle's concern, but develops poesis so as to emphasise its creativity and its function in revealing human *telos*. It is the distinction between act and end which effectively valorizes poetics over praxis, by refusing the possibility of praxis as act capable of achieving its end.

48. Keller, *God and Power*, 87.

49. Ibid., 104.

50. Ibid., 136.

51. Ibid.

Daggers | *Girls and Boys Come Out to Play*

even biblical studies—as cultivating an interiority, always within the biblical text, operating "within a tradition and community derived from the interpretation of a text,"[52] she articulates a perspective on theology which is close to that of Milbank.

A third point of similarity—related to the first—is that the turn to poetics for both represents a theological postmodernism. However, this is a similarity which is also a difference, given that Keller, as we have seen, embraces schools of postmodern and postcolonial thought, while Milbank resolutely rejects these as secularist in character; also that Keller values the modernist tradition of feminist process theology, which she now critiques, while Milbank is resolutely antimodernist.

But when we turn, finally, to their politics, differences between Milbank and Keller emerge in stark contrast, and it becomes clear that these thinkers do not meet but talk past one another. For Keller, it is impossible to speak of theology without speaking also of politics, hence her term theopolitics. "Theopoetics" arrives on the scene with an avowedly political purpose: to foster theopoetic justice, while resisting any urge towards a revolutionary messianism in response to post-9/11 American imperial messianism.[53]

For Keller, "the hope for a just and sustainable peace arises within a theological *post*modernism, predicated on a steadfast excavation of the systematic violence of the modern project of the last five hundred years."[54] Power needs recoding away from the theopolitics of power, which assumes "*a manic will to power called omnipotence*,"[55] towards a theopolitics of becoming. This desirous move draws upon the enriched matrix of spiritual codes represented in process, liberation, feminist, and ecological theologies, and their involvements in movements of globalization from below.[56]

In contrast, for Milbank, post-9/11 American militarism is an expression of "secularized absolute sovereignty and its empty pursuit of power,"[57] rather than of biblically-inspired theopolitics. Contextual theologies too are misguided in confusing secular politics with theology in their critique of empire, ancient and modern. Rather, for Milbank, representation of the

---

52. Ibid., 72.
53. Ibid., 136.
54. Ibid., 11.
55. Ibid., 30.
56. Ibid.
57. Milbank, "Sovereignty, Empire, Capital and Terror," 74; cited in Keller, *God and Power*, 124.

Christian *mythos* in existing development of doctrine is already complete and adequate, albeit obscured in recent capitulation to modern rationalism and therefore in need of rearticulated, poetic mimesis. There is no sense, in Milbank, of any problem in what Virginia Burrus calls "the heresiological habit" which accompanied the historical delineation of the orthodox and singular true faith,[58] nor is there any shadow of doubt in his certainty that theology plays no part in the contemporary machinations of "secularized sovereignty."

Where Milbank argues that the errors of secularized sovereignty are to be addressed by a return to "the biblical and Platonic-Aristotelian metaphysical legacy common to Judaism, Christianity and Islám,"[59] Keller asserts, in contrast, that this "common vision" would "trust that human wisdom can imitate, imperfectly but truly, something of the eternal order of justice."[60] For Keller, Milbank's vision of a single changeless order of timeless origin which humanity should harmoniously imitate is challenged as a Eurocentric and historical, rather than "eternal" order. Her authority for this challenge is derived from the postcolonialist or postmodern theories of difference, so readily dismissed by Milbank as secular and thus antagonistic to the Christian *mythos*.

This difference of view about politics is itself political. Where Milbank argues for a theological linguistic turn, wherein logos is inscribed as central to an orthodoxy that "presses against substance,"[61] Keller may be read as offering a distinctive theological *ecriture feminine*, poetically imaging a scripturally informed created order in becoming, the work "of the unpredictable, uncontrollable, and uncontrolling *wisdom* of the whirlwind."[62] She speaks of a possible, and therefore imperative, theopolitical vision of justice and mercy, common to the Abrahamic faiths, wherein "the creative Wisdom of the universe holds her human stewards responsible for the state of their world and its mutually vulnerable bodies."[63]

In her articulation of a *creatio ex profundis*, Keller is careful to say she offers this as a complementary hermeneutic to the long-standing *creatio ex*

---

58. Burrus, "Radical Orthodoxy and the Heresiological Habit," 36–53.
59. Milbank, "Sovereignty," 75.
60. Keller, *God and Power*, 124.
61. Milbank, *The Word Made Strange*, 110.
62. Keller, *God and Power*, 31 [my italics].
63. Ibid., 51.

nihilo theological interpretation of scripture.[64] She also refers to "God as *Elohim*, as Word or Wisdom,"[65] thus heading off any unavoidable stand-off between logos and Sophia. In contrast, in his discussion of Old Testament poetics, Milbank comments on the "particularly extreme situation" where Wisdom sometimes approximates to divine *Logos* and sometimes "to a kind of *anima mundi*, . . .which man [sic] after his own mode of freedom, must body forth."[66] Although Milbank offers his poetics as the resolution of this extremity, it is a resolution in which logos is sufficient without recourse to any sapiential approximation.

In juxtaposing the work of these two creative and innovative theologians, both of whom ground their work within a scripturally-informed deposit of faith, and both of whom turn to poetics, the parallel traditions of logos and Wisdom/Sophia are revealed as being respectively pivotal within their poetics. Is this the predicament of theology in the century to come, that boy and girl theologians develop parallel oeuvres, in disconnection, each attempting to invalidate the other?[67] Or is there a different possibility, evident in Keller's offering of her theological insights as complementary— but resolutely absent from Milbank's pristine Christian *mythos* and his apparent delight in the "heresiological habit"?

In the context of a different kind of argument, Wonhee Anne Joh speaks of the "heart of the cross."[68] Making a poetic image of this, the poetics of Milbank and Keller may be conceived as meeting at the heart of the cross, where Milbank's vertical gothic vision[69] intersects with Keller's multidimensional horizontalism. At the heart of the cross, Milbank's horizontal vulnerability, in terms of his always unacknowledged situatedness by gender and Eurocentrism, meets with Keller's poetic renderings of vertical glimpses of the eternal Christian mythos. The heart of the cross is a meeting point for orthodox and contextual theologies, wherein, perhaps, Sophia might continue her work of wisdom, infusing logocentrism and restoring Christian theology to a pre-lapsarian and both post-patriarchal and post-Eurocentric possibility within the economy of salvation. The heart of the cross is thus a

---

64. Ibid., 146.

65. Ibid., 147.

66. Milbank, *The Word Made Strange*, 132 (drawing on von Rad).

67. As Keller might put it, "voicing doctrinal certainties only by silencing competitors." Keller, *God and Power*, 72.

68. Joh, *The Heart of the Cross*.

69. Milbank, "On Complex Space." In *The Word Made Strange*, 268–85.

place where, with the goodwill of the girls and boys on the street, feminist theology and Radical Orthodoxy may be put into play together.

Interval

It will be helpful to pause for a moment between our first and second encounters. In her response to the Radical Orthodoxy of Daniel Bell, Lisa Isherwood refers to his work as "a dangerous and seductive conservative theology," in that, while he offers an analysis of how Christianity has become co-opted into the service of capitalism,[70] he then espouses the failure of liberation theology. As Steven Shakespeare puts it, for Bell, liberation theology has forsaken specifically Christian stories and practices in favour of [secular] ideas of justice and human rights;[71] it must therefore fail. Isherwood is unequivocal in her resistance to this dangerous seduction; it is not liberation theology that has fallen short, rather: ". . . our [traditional] theology has failed us . . . the basic technologies of traditional theology have delivered us up [to the Imperial monster] through their assumption of hierarchical power and their fleeing from passion."[72]

With so much at stake, is the very notion of bringing feminist theology into play with Radical Orthodoxy evidence of a further dangerous seduction? Through our second encounter, I hope to show that feminist theological commitment to the struggle for justice within the immanent "horizontal" need not rely on a refusal of the "vertical": rather, something of the riches of Christian orthodoxy can infuse and inform the co-creative projects of women's redemptive communities. In the other direction of the encounter, a serious deficit within radical orthodoxy may be addressed in its encounter with feminist theology. I refer to the radical orthodox relegation of the struggle for justice to mere secular immanentism, with the corollary that the will to power exercised within Christianity is ignored. Thinking with feminist theology invites radical orthodoxy towards a different praxis.

---

70. Isherwood, "Embodying and Emboldening Our Desires," 161.
71. Shakespeare, *Radical Orthodoxy*, 16.
72. Isherwood, "Embodying," 163.

Mayra Rivera's Touch of Transcendence Meets Catherine Pickstock's Liturgical Consummation

TIME AS MOVING IMAGE OF ETERNITY

In her book, *After Writing*, Catherine Pickstock makes a substantial contribution to Radical Orthodoxy.[73] True to the radical orthodox genre, Pickstock offers a sophisticated philosophical argument in making her case. Repudiating modern and postmodern thought alike,[74] she conceives of the oral and written words of the medieval mass as an opening wherein time may be restored as "the moving image of eternity."[75] Her choice rests on her view that "time can only be affirmed through the liturgical gesture which receives time from eternity as a gift and offers it back to eternity as a sacrifice." Her project is offered over against the "polity of death"—the valorizing of spatial immanence in the modern *necropolis*, with its "refusal of liturgical life."[76]

Pickstock evokes the medieval perception of the community flowing from eternity through the sacraments.[77] The rationale for her return to the medieval Roman Rite lies in its constant repetitions and recommencements—which she perceives as undone by the Council of Trent well before the rationalizing effects of modernizing Vatican II reforms. The value of this "haphazard structure" is that it "betokens our constitutive, positive, and analogical distance from God, rather than our sinfulness and humiliation."[78] Her surprising turn to the medieval rite seeks to retrieve the liturgy as "embedded within ecstatic temporality," where life and liturgy merge in the celebration of the gifts of the varied fruits reflective of local differences; Pickstock goes in search of this temporality in the rite as

---

73. Pickstock, *After Writing: On the Liturgical Consummation of Philosophy*.

74. Her critique of Derrida contrasts with the work of other significant radical orthodox theologians, notably Graham Ward, who was a significant voice in the early years of the project, albeit he now charts a more independent course. See Ellen T. Armour, "Beyond Belief?: Sexual Difference and Religion after Ontotheology" for a critique of Pickstock's reading of Derrida.

75. Pickstock, *After Writing*, 116.

76. Ibid., 118.

77. Ibid., 171.

78. Ibid., 173.

celebrated before the centralizing impetus of the Council of Trent reduced liturgy to spectacle and sundered it from life.[79]

Pickstock sets out to rejoin the "mystical" and the "real," so reinstating the traditional configuration of transubstantiation in the Eucharist, and restoring the lost diachronic aspect, wherein the sacramental signifier participates ontologically in the signified: the Eucharistic body participates in the historical body of Christ.[80] Her move counters the synchronic tendencies emerging in the later middle ages, as confirmed in Tridentine forms, with their subsequent emphasis on Eucharist as symbol; here the focus is on Eucharistic presence at the moment of the elevation of the host, rather than on sacred action connecting past event with ecclesial present and future.[81] Pickstock's retrieved understanding of transubstantiation assumes continuity between the real and the mysterious, so that knowing the real involves "a whole bodily contact including person, desire, will, faith, and memory."[82]

Whereas the Reformers corrected an imbalance by stressing the link between the Eucharist and everyday life as a shared common feast, for Pickstock, it is more important that the dynamic work in reverse: every meal should occur as a ritual feast, drawing everyday life towards a ritual mode.[83] Despite her refusal of Derrida, Pickstock asserts the "impossibility" of liturgy, due to a process of supplementations and deferrals. She writes: "this impossibility does not, as with postmodernism, indicate a suspension over the abyss, but rather the *occurrence* of the impossible through Christological mediation, which reveals the void as a plenitude, impossibly manifest in the very course of deferral and substitution."[84]

---

79. Ibid., 165.

80. Ibid., 164. See 158–66 for an appreciation of Pickstock's reliance on de Lubac's analysis in his *Corpus Mysticum* of a shift in the punctuation of the three dimensions of the theological "body": the historical body of Jesus, the sacramental body, and the ecclesial body. De Lubac argues the traditional *caesura* between the first and second foci connected the sacramental and ecclesial bodies, connecting apostolic origins to the present ecclesial event, in the sacrament, and to the future, and assumed the continuity of the categories of the "mystical" and "real." However, in the late Middle Ages, the *caesura* had shifted so that the historical and sacramental bodies were now connected, and separated from the ecclesial body, so transposing the *temporal* distribution of the sacrament to a *spatial* one. Pickstock's retrieval aims to reverse this shift in punctuation.

81. Pickstock, *After Writing*, 165–66.

82. Ibid., 164.

83. Ibid., 174.

84. Ibid., 178.

She asserts the coincidence of identity and journey: "doxological humility" characterizes the apostrophic subject formed through liturgy, where apostrophe—invocation of the absent other—replaces the "nominalization" through which the post-Cartesian subject is formed.[85] One who calls upon God becomes one to whom God speaks, in contrast to the apparent autonomy, but actual disempowerment, of the subject formed through immanentist manipulation.[86] Further, ". . . our doxological expressions are not distinct from God's epiphany." In the Creed, the reciprocally constituted relations between Father, Son, and Holy Spirit are performed and repeated.[87] The transcendent God overflows into immanence; God *preoccupies* space, as the excessive structure of divine space overflows into that of our liturgical journey.[88] Our outward journey towards the altar of God involves a concomitant journey into ourselves, body and spirit, which "serves to intensify the physicality of our bodies, reminding us that we eat and drink, and are situated within a community."[89]

THE TOUCH OF TRANSCENDENCE

Where Pickstock is concerned to reinstate eternity, Mayra Rivera crafts an elegant reflection on divine transcendence as otherness. Rivera is clear that notions of transcendence that emphasise God's aloofness, separation and immateriality have been used to validate hierarchical rule, including legitimation of the subordination of women and the devastation of creation: many feminist theologians have therefore emphasized the immanence of God.[90] Rivera's rehabilitation of transcendence is thus an interesting move for a feminist theologian, made in the conviction that transcendence has the potential to promote ethical relations. She envisions ethical human relations by offering a "relational transcendence," which privileges touch "within creation and between creatures." Transcendence thus needs to be in respectful touch with the concrete realities of our world: for the good of interhuman relations, associations with "otherworldliness" must be resisted.[91]

---

85. Ibid., 196 and 193.
86. Ibid., 196.
87. Ibid., 205.
88. Ibid., 211 and 229.
89. Ibid., 230 and 231.
90. Rivera, *The Touch of Transcendence*, 1.
91. Ibid., 2–3.

Rivera engages with Milbank and Pickstock, and with the liberation theologian, Ignacio Ellacuria, to craft a theology of "intracosmic transcendence," wherein interhuman relations, and relations between humanity and the wider creation repeat our relations "to the intimate but ineffable God."[92] Rivera supplements her critical reading of these theologies by turning to substantial theorists of "the other"—Levinas, Irigaray, and Spivak—to develop her notion of transcendence over against the traditional positing of transcendence over against immanence.

This is a "transcendence-within" immanent creation, moving in the world like sap through the branches of a tree:[93] it counters the power-plays which invade from without to dominate and control, by insisting that the other lies beyond this grasp, though always within touch. Rivera offers a richly embodied and earthy conception of creation as the place of relational transcendence, through face-to-face and fleshly ethical encounters. Her work is alert to fleeting traces of the divine and responsive to "the unsettling caress of an indescribable God."[94] Rivera resolutely opposes orthodox cosmologies that open a gap between divine and human, so decoupling divine transcendence from ethical concern with social processes, human needs, and the project of liberation.[95]

The Question of Transcendence

Rivera meets Pickstock when engaging with Radical Orthodoxy in her first excursus in *The Touch of Transcendence*. Milbank's work is firmly in the frame of Rivera's investigations, though this is not my main concern in staging my second encounter between radical orthodoxy and feminist theology. As Milbank draws on Pickstock's *After Writing* in his *Being Reconciled*, Pickstock's work is vulnerable to interpretation through the lens he offers.[96] In my re-staged encounter between Rivera and Pickstock, it will be helpful to bring Pickstock's work out of Milbank's shadow. My argument is that it is possible to read Pickstock *with* feminist theology, as open to an embrace of embodied materiality that resonates with Rivera's gentle touch of transcendence; in parallel with this rendition, it is also possible to read

92. Ibid., 54.
93. Ibid., 53.
94. Ibid., 17.
95. Ibid., 132.
96. Milbank, *Being Reconciled*.

Rivera's "transcendence-within" as capable of resonating with Pickstock's restored sense of community flowing from eternity through the sacraments. These readings in parallel allow a reconnection of feminist ethical commitment with the riches of Christian orthodoxy, while maintaining the hermeneutic of suspicion towards the will to power in which Christian orthodoxy has long been implicated. The poverty of Radical Orthodoxy lies in its reinscription of Christian orthodoxy's failure to acknowledge its own situatedness and its own implication in continuing Eurocentrism. Reading Pickstock with Rivera allows Radical Orthodoxy to borrow from the riches of *The Touch of Transcendence*.

I begin with Rivera's critique of the notion of transcendence in terms of suspension of embodied life "*over-against-the void.*"[97] At this point, Rivera cites the text, *Radical Orthodoxy*, of which Pickstock is certainly coeditor, along with Milbank and Graham Ward. However, while Milbank clearly maintains this position, I suggest Pickstock views the void otherwise. In her consideration of the impossibility of liturgy, discussed above, Pickstock argues it is postmodern nihilism that perceives reality as suspended over the abyss: in contrast, Christological mediation reveals the void as plenitude, albeit impossibly manifest in the not-yet of temporality. This sounds more promising, and more akin to the work of Keller than to that of Milbank. Pickstock's rendering of the void eludes Rivera's depiction of Radical Orthodoxy as fundamentally pitting divine transcendence against the void.

Secondly, Pickstock needs to stand clear of the "universal totem" that Milbank crafts, using her rendering of the medieval Roman rite as a prime example. No surprising, Rivera is disquieted by Milbank's phallic erection, commenting that his proposal "should alert us to the subtle ways in which the privilege of masculinity is inscribed in discourses that are not explicitly about gender."[98] But this is Milbank's reading of Pickstock, who, mercifully, writes more like a girl. I suggest Rivera's reading of Pickstock's account of the rite remains within the shadow of Milbank's universal totem. Rivera highlights the worshipper's repetitive movement "towards an ever-receding divine reality," when Pickstock is discussing the *altar* of God as "ever-receding" at this point; as both supplementary destination and beginning for the worshipper offering a sacrifice of praise.[99] Rivera pinpoints, in Pickstock's discussion of transubstantiation, her "leaping over" the stage of indication

97. Ibid., 22.
98. Ibid., 29.
99. Pickstock, *After Writing*, 183.

or reference: however, Pickstock refers to the words "This is my Body" applied to the referent, bread, as allowing things to exceed their appearance.[100] Rivera asks whether such a leaping over, rather than enmeshing of signs within, the material realities of language does not "suggest a direct path toward divine transcendence that sidesteps the ties of our incarnate existence...?"; but Pickstock can be read differently.

There is a quiet attention to embodiment in Pickstock's book, from her affirmation of orality as linked with embodiment, to her close attention to the coincidence of body and sign in the Eucharist. Albeit she seeks to rescue embodiment from the spatialized living play of bodies she sees in Irigaray, in that paradoxical journey to the ever-receding altar, which is also a journey into ourselves, she finds intensified the physicality of our bodies as we eat and drink in community.[101] Where Rivera is uneasy with the temporal deferral expressed by Pickstock's statement that the "apophatic reserve" of language "betokens our constitutive, positive and analogical distance from God," this statement can also be read in terms of Pickstock's apostrophic subject: this (vertical) distance does not necessarily invite imperial power relations, rather the distance is always traversed as the transcendent God overflows into immanence.[102]

When Pickstock refers to the triple names of Father, Son, and Spirit as one "essential name commensurate with the existential space of the Trinitarian journey," she refers to the "journeying of the generation of the Son from which the Spirit proceeds" in which the liturgical speaker is ambiguously situated.[103] Drawing on the work of Virginia Burrus, Rivera locates these words as a replay of the fourth-century fixing of the Trinity in strictly patriarchal terms.[104] It is beyond the scope of this chapter to argue this point in full, but it is possible to retrieve classical Trinitarian formulations from their long-standing annexation to patriarchy, by troubling assumptions of a gender binary, which necessarily reinscribe the Trinitarian God as resolutely male.[105] Such retrieval creates a different context for the reception of Pickstock's orthodox Trinitarian journeying by feminist theology.

---

100. Rivera, *Touch*, 31; Pickstock *After Writing*, 262.

101. Pickstock, *After Writing*, xviii, xv, 116,

102. Rivera, *Touch*, 30; Pickstock *After Writing*, 173, 211.

103. Pickstock, *After Writing*, 181–82.

104. Rivera, *Touch*, 133.

105. Examples of such gender troubling include: Sarah Coakley, *Powers and Submissions: Spirituality, Philosophy and Gender*; Janet Martin Soskice, "Blood and Defilement."

In her discussion of Milbank's critique of liberation theology, Rivera resists his assertion that Liberation Theology depends on autonomous [secular] social ethics; rather, she insists that Liberation Theology upholds all spheres of society, Christian or not, as potential sites of divine action.[106] This will be fruitful ground on which to close this encounter between Rivera and Pickstock. Rivera's assertion that "all existence is *existence in God*"[107] turns the Radical Orthodox critique of the secular on its head, in her insistence that there is no secular outside the touch of the transcendent God: Radical Orthodoxy's reinscription of theology is already assumed by Liberation Theology. When Pickstock's Radical Orthodoxy and Rivera's feminist theology touch at the heart of the cross, the vertical opens, to reveal the transcendent God overflowing (Pickstock) into the transcendence-within of all existence that is in God (Rivera). The horizontal struggle for justice also opens to the apostrophic liturgical subject, whose doxological *Gloria in Excelsis* requires justice to flow like a river and righteousness like a mighty stream.

Bibliography

Alchin, L.K. "Boys and Girls Come Out to Play: Nursery Rhyme Lyrics, Origins, and History." http://www.rhymes.org.uk/a114-boys-and-girls.htm

Armour, Ellen T. "Beyond Belief?: Sexual Difference and Religion after Ontotheology." In *The Religious*, edited by John D. Caputo. Blackwell Readings in Continental Thought. Oxford: Blackwell, 2002.

Bell Daniel. *Liberation Theology after the End of History: The Refusal to Cease Suffering*. London: Routledge, 2001.

Burrus, Virginia. "Radical Orthodoxy and the Heresiological Habit." In *Interpreting the Postmodern: Responses to "Radical Orthodoxy,"* edited by Rosemary Radford Ruether and Marion Grau. London: T. & T. Clark, 2006.

Coakley, Sarah. *Powers and Submissions: Spirituality, Philosophy and Gender*. Oxford: Blackwell, 2002.

Cupitt, Don. *The Sea of Faith*. London: British Broadcasting Corporation, 1984.

Heath, Malcolm. "Introduction." In *Poetics*, by Aristotle, x–xi. New York: Penguin, 1996.

Harvey SJ, James. "Conclusion: Continuing the Conversation." In *Radical Orthodoxy: A Catholic Enquiry*, edited by Laurence Paul Hemming. Aldershot: Ashgate, 2000.

Hoffmeyer, John F. "Charitable Interpretation." In *Interpreting the Postmodern: Responses to "Radical Orthodoxy,"* edited by Rosemary Radford Ruether and Marion Grau, 3–17. London: T. & T. Clark, 2006.

Hyman, Gavin. *The Predicament of Postmodern Theology: Radical Orthodoxy or Nihilist Textualism*. Louisville: Westminster John Knox, 2001.

---

106. Rivera, *Touch*, 50–51.

107. Ibid., 51.

Isherwood, Lisa. "Embodying and Emboldening Our Desires." In *Interpreting the Postmodern: Responses to "Radical Orthodoxy,"* edited by Rosemary Radford Ruether and Marion Grau. London: T. & T. Clark, 2006.

Joh, Wonhee Anne. *The Heart of the Cross: A Postcolonial Christology.* London: Westminster John Knox, 2006.

Keller, Catherine. *God and Power: Counter-Apocalyptic Journeys.* Augsburg: Fortress, 2005.

Long, Stephen. *Divine Economy: Theology and the Market.* London: Routledge, 2000.

Milbank, John et al. *Radical Orthodoxy: A New Theology.* London: Routledge, 1999.

Milbank, John. *Being Reconciled: Ontology and Pardon.* London: Routledge, 2003.

———. "A Christological Poetics." *The Word Made Strange: Theology, Language and Culture.* Oxford: Blackwell, 1997.

———. "Sovereignty, Empire, Capital and Terror." In *Strike Terror No More: Theology, Ethics and the New War,* edited by Jon Berquist. St. Louis: Chalice, 2002.

———. *Theology and Social Theory: Beyond Secular Reason.* Cambridge: Blackwell, 1991.

Pickstock, Catherine. *After Writing: On the Liturgical Consummation of Philosophy.* Challenges in Contemporary Theology. Oxford: Blackwell, 1998.

Rivera, Mayra. *The Touch of Transcendence: A Postcolonial Theology of God.* Louisville: Westminster John Knox, 2007.

Ruether, Rosemary Radford and Marion Grau. *Interpreting the Postmodern: Responses to "Radical Orthodoxy."* London: T. & T. Clark, 2006.

Shakespeare, Steven. *Radical Orthodoxy: A Critical Introduction.* London: SPCK, 2007.

Sobrino, Jon, and Ignacio Ellacuría. *Systematic Theology: Perspectives from Liberation Theology.* London: SCM, 1996.

Soskice, Janet Martin. "Blood and Defilement." In *Feminism and Theology,* edited by Janet Martin Soskice and Diana Lipton, 333–43. Oxford Reading in Feminism. Oxford: Oxford University Press, 2003.

6

Radical Orthodoxy and the Closed Western Theological Mind

The Poverty of Radical Orthodoxy in Intercultural and Interreligious Perspective

Paul Hedges

Introduction

In this essay, I will be forwarding two distinct but inter-related critiques of Radical Orthodoxy. One is the failure to engage with, or to be able to engage with, the global theological scene, using Intercultural Theology as a means of critique. The other is its approach to other religious traditions. Before examining each of these in turn, it would be useful to address two preliminary issues: my particular focus on John Milbank, and a brief meditation on open and closed theological minds which will set a context for my critiques.

First, Radical Orthodoxy is not a monolithic movement or disposition. However, the work of John Milbank is seen as foundational, and he, in many ways, stands as a spokesperson for Radical Orthodoxy in a way few others can. Therefore, I will focus upon the work of John Milbank, making reference to the work of other writers associated with Radical Orthodoxy mainly as it helps elucidate my argument on Milbank. However, in as far as

The Poverty of Radical Orthodoxy

Milbank's work, to some degree, sets the stage for Radical Orthodoxy, I see the analysis here as applicable, in a broad sense, to many others associated with the movement.[1]

It will be useful to briefly outline a number of key factors that, it has been argued, represent Milbank's theological system.[2] Space does not permit extrapolation of them here, but I will make reference to those pertinent below. The factors are:

1. Chalcedonian Orthodoxy and tradition
2. Reliance upon "pure" Christian resources
3. Overcoming the genealogy of modernity and secularism
4. Not being a movement but a disposition
5. Return to the Via Negativa and a Neoplatonic Augustinianism
6. Nonviolent ontology
7. Rethinking tradition in contemporary form

Second, my argument concerns Radical Orthodoxy's engagement, or, more precisely, its failure to engage, with other religious worlds and cultures. This, I will argue, runs counter not only to certain essential imperatives in theology today, but also the Christian tradition, something to which Radical Orthodoxy lays claim. As such, I will argue that Radical Orthodoxy fails to offer an authentic or compelling (though one that is, undeniably, very attractive to many) approach to Christian theology. Further, I would suggest that Christian theology tends to see itself, along a continuum, as either engaged in relation to the world or in antithetical opposition to it.[3] Especially, it may seek to engage and learn from the religious, and/or philosophical/cultural, Other, or it may repudiate any such encounter. At least as far back as the time Tertullian uttered his (in)famous words, "What has Athens to do with Jerusalem?," there has been a Christian theological approach marked by a closed attitude to the religious (and cultural) Other. In more recent times, this tendency has seen its best known and most influential proponent in Karl Barth, whose Neo-Orthodoxy set out a radical distinc-

---

1. It is debatable whether it is a movement or a disposition. While it often proclaims itself as the latter (as noted in factor 4 just below in the text), I would argue the former as it has an identifiable corpus of works and figures associated with it (see Hedges, "John Milbank's," 797–98).

2. Hedges, "John Milbank's," 796–99.

3. This suggestion may be seen as analogous to Hans Frei's typology of theological styles (*Types of Christian*, 28–55).

tion between God and man, or Revelation and all other forms of human knowledge, beliefs and ways of being. The term Dialectical Theology well exemplifies its stance of oppositional thinking. I would argue that it is this Tertullianist tendency that Radical Orthodoxy has inherited—although it has been suggested that Tertullian's views are "mild" compared with Milbank's! I am not, however, arguing here for any direct correlative link between these figures, rather suggesting that they represent a similar closed tendency of theological thought. How such a closed theology is manifest in Radical Orthodoxy I will elaborate shortly. However, before I do so, I would like to outline a more inclusive, or "open" line of Christian thinking, one which sees God's presence, and the possibility of divine inspiration, beyond narrow confessional borders.

Within the early church, what I will term an "open" theological stance is found in numerous writers. Perhaps the most often cited example is Justin Martyr, who interpreted the early Greek philosophers as conduits of the *logos spermatikos*.[4] However, here it is better to focus on two figures, Augustine of Hippo and Thomas Aquinas, who are central to Milbank's own theological endeavours.[5] Augustine spoke of "mining" the treasures of pagan philosophies for "nuggets of gold"—the truths they held.[6] Aquinas, meanwhile, borrowed freely not just from Aristotle but also from Jewish and Islamic thinkers.[7] Both have been seen amongst the many figures in Christian history who have adopted an "inclusivist" attitude to religious Others which does not mean "selling out to a particular culture's agenda" but rather where "prevailing philosophies have been essentially 'baptized' and have helped to sharpen the articulation of Christian thought and shape its systematic development."[8] Such an "open" attitude to religious Others is then something we find in the very heart of the Christian tradition that Milbank appeals to, yet it is not what we find in his theology. Moreover, as I have argued elsewhere, an openness, or what I term a "radical openness," to religious Others is intrinsic in the message of Jesus, and, as such, has a place at the heart of any authentic Christian theology.[9]

---

4. Justin Martyr, *Apology* I, XLVI and *Apology* II, X and XIII.

5. See for instance: on Aquinas, Pickstock, "Radical Orthodoxy" and Milbank and Pickstock, "Truth"; on Augustine, Milbank, "Postmodern Critical."

6. Carruthers, *Craft of Thought*, 126.

7. Aminrazavi, "Medieval Philosophical," 384.

8. Cheetham, "Inclusivisms," 66–67.

9. See Hedges, *Controversies*, chapter 3.

Such an open attitude is not simply about contrasting "liberal" and "conservative" approaches to Christian theology in naive ways, but about a broader approach to theology and its engagement with the world.[10] Moreover, as I will argue below, it is about seeking to develop and maintain a theology which has credibility within the contemporary theological landscape.

Milbank and Intercultural Theology

Radical Orthodoxy has proved to be an incredibly popular phenomenon, being arguably the world's most widely discussed theological system and attaining a considerable following amongst theologians from many different countries and denominations. It can be seen as allied, and possessing many similarities, to other Anglo-American post-liberal theologies.[11] My argument that it fails as a contemporary theological style may then seem to fly in the face of the evidence, however, such a view, I would suggest, looks at a very partial evidence base—and one based in an out-dated, parochial, and even imperialist or colonial attitude. To explore this, I will introduce the contemporary theological style known as Intercultural Theology, before moving on to show how Radical Orthodoxy fails to measure up to its demands.

INTERCULTURAL THEOLOGY

Intercultural Theology is used in a variety of ways. For some, it is merely an updated term for missiology that lacks the negative connotations this can carry; however, it has a more radical meaning, which is about the contextual nature of all theology, and the need for theology to be continually in dialog with its cultural context. In a global setting, this may mean Hindu, Buddhist, Islamic, Chinese, or other settings.[12] Robert Schreiter explains it in the following way: "The universal [Western] theologies . . . were in fact *universalizing* theologies; that is to say, they extended the results of their own reflections beyond their own contexts to other settings, usually

---

10. For a discussion on the problematic essentialism of contrasting "liberal" and "conservative" theologies see Hedges, "John Milbank's," 799–802, 810.

11. See Reader, *Beyond All Reason*, 70ff., and Hunsinger, "Postliberal theology."

12. A fuller discussion of Intercultural Theology can be found in Hedges, *Controversies*, 44–52.

without an awareness of the rootedness of their theologies within their own contexts . . ."[13]

What Schreiter highlights is that every theology is, at heart, a contextual theology: we can never have access to some pure and unmediated notion of what Christianity is. In particular, the Western theological heritage is but one way to tell the Christian story, and one which is rooted within a particular context, time, and place. The result of this is that there must also be other ways to narrate the Christian story in other times and places. One upshot of this is that, inherently, multiple forms of Christianity exist: "This 'different' view on the history of Christianity . . . exposes the inescapable plurality of its discursive, conflictive and hybrid identities . . ."[14] The implication of Intercultural Theology is the contextual nature of all theology, which means it must be continually rethought and re-imagined in new contexts.

The idea that Christianity must escape the shackles of its Western form to become inculturated into new contexts, whether they be the contemporary Asian or African, or other (not forgetting, of course, that Christianity has a long history in these places, though one largely forgotten, ignored, or subjugated by the mainstream discourse of European-American theology). The phrase, "the Latin Captivity of the Church" is one that has long, and well, been used.[15] Largely ignored within much mainstream European-American theology, Third World Theologies, often classed as "contextual theology," represent not only the majority of the world's Christians, but are also becoming dominant in an increasingly globalized world, where, it can be argued, the kind of postcolonial theology done by figures such as Mercy Amba Oduyoye represent the theological future.[16] As such we know that Intercultural Theology represents a complex and sophisticated theological style: "Inter-cultural theology explores the inter-confessional, inter-cultural and inter-religious dimensions of the Christian faith. An interdisciplinary approach and the use of multimedia are significant."[17]

---

13. Schreiter, *New Catholicity*, 2.

14. Gruber, "Christian Identities," 34.

15. The phrase is perhaps best known from its usage in the title of Boyd, *India*, but the concept predates this by at least a century, with calls for Christianity in India to assume an inculturated form going back well into the nineteenth century. For some of the theological issues in this, see Hedges, *Preparation and Fulfilment*.

16. Kwok, "Mercy Amba Oduyoye," 485.

17. Küster, "Project," 429.

The Poverty of Radical Orthodoxy

This highlights a key issue, which is that in being intercultural, any future theologies must also be interreligious, because it is simply meaningless to suggest that, for instance, Christianity could adopt an Indian form without appealing to aspects of the pervasive Hindu religious worldview. For instance, in India, the use of indigenous philosophical motifs, such as the term/concept *sat-cit-ananda* (being-consciousness-bliss), have been argued to be more suitable than Trinitarian formulation based in fourth century Mediterranean, Greco-Roman Neoplatonic formulations.[18] Moreover, this is not just to argue that Intercultural Theology is something that happens in Third World Theologies, because such issues must also impact on how we understand theology as a whole. In a world where the majority of the world's Christians come from the global south, and in a context where the perceived mainstream of European-American theology has long ignored the writings and work of theologians from elsewhere, the only sustainable theological option is, and must be, to embrace and adapt in relation to the demands of Intercultural Theology. As a variety of postcolonial theologians have argued, the kind of stance that ignores or takes token appreciation of the broader theological and Christian world must change.[19]

To sum up this account of Intercultural Theology, it may be said that within our contemporary global context, any authentic and responsive theology must accept three things: 1) engaging with the various world Christianities; 2) recognizing that our identity and theology changes when faced with religious Others; and, 3) accepting that every theology is "contextual."[20]

MILBANK'S THEOLOGY IN INTERCULTURAL PERSPECTIVE

To assess how Milbank's theology can be assessed in the light of the imperatives of Intercultural Theology we will take a look at a number of the key factors which we have suggested represent his thought. In particular, we will discuss the following: 1) Chalcedonian Orthodoxy and tradition; 2) reliance upon "pure" Christian resources; and, 7) rethinking tradition in contemporary form.

---

18. See Hedges, *Preparation and Fulfilment*, and Aleaz, "Pluralisms," 216–17 and 223–24. The usage is, however, problematic for those from Dalit communities and so is not universally applicable throughout India.

19. See, for instance, Kwok, *Postcolonial Imagination*; and Sugirtharajah, *Postcolonial Reconfigurations*.

20. See Hedges, *Controversies*, 46.

First, one claim advanced strongly by Radical Orthodoxy is that it upholds a Chalcedonian Orthodoxy as its bottom line. However, any theology that claims to be Chalcedonian but rejects an intercultural framework for its current manifestation is utterly uncontextualized and ahistorical. The victory within the Roman Empire of this branch of Christianity (we must not forget that it was far from uncontested, and for centuries following its "victory" as "orthodoxy" it was but a minority Christian movement as Nestorian and other churches spread with immense vigor Eastwards across Asia—mere historical accident has led to its current worldwide dominance). Moreover, Chalcedonian Orthodoxy represents the culmination of the Christian church's inculturation into the Greco-Roman world. Centuries of expression through the terms and thought patterns of Greek philosophy had led to the manifestation of statements of belief that we see in the creeds. They are far from Hebraic formulae in either terminology or worldview. More than this, the ideology that shaped the emergence and victory of such monolithic belief statements (the creeds), alongside the state-sponsored repression that allowed it to become dominant, represents the early church's adaptation to certain mores of Roman rule alongside the adoption of an imperial ideology. Leaving aside arguments of whether the church was compromised in this association, what is clear is that the Church and its theological formulations became inculturated from an early period. As we have seen above, in relation to the issues raised by Intercultural Theology, while, for centuries, much of the Christian world has come to consider this version of Christianity as normative, it is, like all other theologies, simply one contextual version of Christianity. There cannot be a Church, or a theology, which is not enmeshed within the worldview of its own day. In particular, we would ask how Radical Orthodoxy would address the calls for an inculturated Trinitarian formulation in places such as India. It would seem that, from its standpoint, it could only view this as unorthodox and outside the framework it sees as the basis of Christian belief. However, such an attitude, as we have suggested, smacks of a colonial arrogance that reads its own contextual tradition as a universal tradition.

Second, the reliance on tradition raises problematic questions. One is which bits of the tradition are used? It has been argued that there is an arbitrary adoption of those bits congenial to Milbank.[21] Another question is how are they employed? To answer this, I will return to an issue raised above, that the Christian theological tradition has often veered between

---

21. Hedges, "John Milbank's," 805–6.

the poles of "open" and "closed" approaches to other cultures and religions. Milbank, and Radical Orthodoxy generally, stand within what may be termed the "closed" approach, whereas both Augustine and Aquinas, to whom they claim to appeal, stand within the "open" approach. Briefly, I may explain the situation in this way. Both Augustine and Aquinas believed that outside of Christianity, in other religio-culturo-philosophic traditions, were treasures of great value and worth. To this end they sought to integrate, respectively, Neoplatonic and Aristotelian (the latter through Islamic and Jewish sources and interpretations) insights into their work. That is to say, in these non-Christian, or pagan, philosophies and religious worldviews, they believed the Christian worldview could be better expressed or explained. We may therefore argue that both Augustine and Aquinas stand within the framework of Intercultural Theology (recognizing, though, the anachronistic terminology). Both of them are "open" to that which lies beyond Christianity, whereas, by way of contrast, Milbank finds outside of the Christian sphere nothing of value, and in as far as he uses other philosophical systems (specifically postmodernism) he does so only to expose, as he sees it, their ultimate valuelessness and inadequacy (however, it may be argued that he actually does reinterpret Christianity through a postmodern lens, yet denies that he is doing so[22]). Indeed, for Milbank, it seems that the only way in which the Neoplatonism and Aristotelianism of Augustine and Aquinas can be used is because they have, in all essential qualities, become "Christianized," however, this involves a problematic we will explore below.

It is a tenet of Milbank that only "pure" Christian resources should be employed. The groundwork for this idea was laid in his *magnum opus*, *Theology and Social Theory*, which argued that our worldview was pervaded by a secular standpoint. Radical Orthodoxy, as a whole, argues that this straightjacket of secular thought be rejected. This, it is argued, is especially true of theology, which should employ "pure" Christian resources. According to Milbank, theology should speak "directly out of the Biblical tradition, without any recourse to external supplementation," and should be using "the resources of revelation alone."[23] In relation to what we have said above about Intercultural Theology it is apparent that there never can be a "pure" Christian language or tradition, it always exists in mediation with the cultural forms that give it contextual shape, as such, it may be considered surprising that a theologian of Milbank's calibre should make such a

---

22. See Hedges "John Milbank's," 808–9; and Reader, *Beyond All Reason*, 74.
23. Milbank, *Theology and Social*, 389; and Milbank, *Word Made*, 36.

claim. It does though appear, as Gavin Hyman observes, to be a rhetorical claim on Milbank's part, who realizes its impossibility.[24] That he should see it as an aim is, however, in itself quite telling, linking into a whole discourse in neo-orthodox, post-liberal and other theologies. Many of these theological styles have a tendency to relate to other religions from a parochial Western viewpoint, which cannot, and does not wish to, engage meaningfully with the broader world (amongst those associated with the post-liberal nexus, Stanley Hauerwas and John Howard Yoder may be classed as exceptions who have something to contribute to interreligious thinking[25]). It is notable that one of the originators of Radical Orthodoxy, Graham Ward, has argued strongly against the idea of a pure Christian position in more recent works, which is a sign, it may be argued, of his recent attempts to distance himself from Radical Orthodoxy.[26] (It is worthwhile mentioning that the only attempt I am aware of to use Radical Orthodoxy's thought in some "positive" sense in relation to religious Others involves the use of Ward's thought).[27] Moreover, because of Milbank's use of Augustine and Aquinas, who are indebted to Neoplatonism and the Islamic transmission of Aristotle, his theology is already intercultural and so cannot measure up to his own standards of purity! Far from having "pure" Christian resources upon which he can build, his tradition is already embedded in interreligious contacts, encounters, and contexts. In the second section of this essay, we will explore Milbank's discussion of the religious Other, which asserts mastery and enacts epistemological violence against them; his claim that any sources are "Christianized" should be read in this light.

It can be seen that Radical Orthodoxy cannot free itself from the intercultural context that grounds its theology. The theology Milbank wishes to assert as the true, authentic, and genuine Christian tradition is already one inculturated into particular backgrounds and contexts, and therefore inherently partaking in the problem that Intercultural Theology has located at the heart of all theology: its involvement with philosophico-religio-socio-culturo systems.

We turn now to the way that Milbank's theology rethinks tradition in a contemporary context. Here, we need to bring together two arguments.

---

24. See Hyman, *The Predicament*, 82, referencing Milbank, J., "Programme," 37.

25. This is discussed in Gaston, "Christian Peace," with particular attention to Yoder's essay, "Disavowal of Constantine."

26. Ward, *Cultural Transformation*, chapter 1.

27. See Rashkover, "Semiotics and Embodiment."

One, and which is quite clear from the context of Radical Orthodoxy, is that Milbank regards orthodoxy itself as an unfinished enterprise and therefore ever in need of new expression.[28] As such, it must respond to our contemporary context, and indeed, in this respect we may say that Milbank is actually, even if not acknowledging it, inspired by the contemporary notion of contextual theology.[29] The other is the pressing multicultural world and globalized context we find ourselves in, where, it may be argued, to be responsive to our world situation we must have an Intercultural Theology. With the majority of the world's Christians now in the global south, and vast numbers living in situations where Christianity is far from being the normative tradition, it is imperative that inculturation and new expressions are found. From this context, in failing to respond, Radical Orthodoxy fails utterly in its attempt to forge a contemporary expression of Christian thought. Being wedded to a Western discourse and an imagined monolithic version of Christian truth, it is incapable of responding to the demands of the world's Christians, and the pressing needs to find ways to create a credible Christianity in, for instance, India, where the religious and philosophical background of native traditions can be used to provide a contextualized expression of Christianity in that country, which will make sense to those living there.[30]

Milbank and the Religious Other

Milbank has written very little about other religions. This, in itself, is not untypical of many Western theologians, but something which is increasingly problematic in our multicultural and globalized world. He has, however, addressed the theology of religions directly in at least one place, where he suggested that the only Christian approach to other religions is one based on "mutual suspicion" with any encounter being intended to convert the religious Other.[31] We should spend some time examining

---

28. Milbank, "Programme," 44; for comment on this see Hedges, "John Milbank's," 799 and 807.

29. I have argued elsewhere that Milbank's theology can be understood as a "liberal" theology, understood in relation to Tillich's concept of mediating theology (see Hedges, "John Milbank's," 802 and 809–10.

30. There are numerous sources which discuss these issues, but for a general overview see Parratt, *Introduction*, as well as works cited already such as Schreiter, *New Catholicity*; Hedges, *Controversies*; and Sugirtharajah, *Postcolonial Reconfigurations*.

31. Milbank, "End," 190.

Milbank's arguments, which, as we will see, are surrounded by a veil of misunderstanding and, it seems, hostility. First, though it would be useful to consider the theological style within the theology of religions which he represents, while, afterwards, we will explore an aspect of his theology which is integral to relating to religious Others, his claims about Christianity's peaceful ontology, which plays out very problematically in relation to non-Christian traditions.

MILBANK AND THE PARTICULARIST MODEL IN THE THEOLOGY OF RELIGIONS

Within the theology of religions, the classical typology of exclusivisms, inclusivisms and pluralisms, first introduced by Alan Race, has become a normative touchstone, however, increasingly, a fourth position labelled "particularities" has been added.[32] Milbank's work can be seen as an expression of this fourth paradigm, which is closely linked to post-liberal theological positions.[33] The following has been offered as an assessment of what is meant by the broad term particularities, which nevertheless holds a variety of different standpoints under this broad umbrella term:

> 1) each faith is unique, alterity[34] is stressed over similarity, as seemingly common elements in religious experience or doctrine are regarded as superficial; 2) it is only possible to speak from a specific tradition, there can be no pluralistic interpretation; 3) the Holy Spirit may be at work in other faiths, requiring them to be regarded with respect and dignity; 4) no salvific potency resides in other faiths, though they are somehow involved in God's plans for humanity but in ways we cannot know; 5) particularity is based in a post-modern and post-liberal worldview; 6) the orthodox doctrines of Trinity and Christ are grounding points from which to approach other faiths.[35]

Within the broader particularist framework it has been argued that Milbank's style is more exclusivist in tone than that of many others, being characterized by a missionary and "suspicious" approach to the religious

---

32. On the background to this and debates see Hedges, "Reflection on Typologies."

33. On particularities in general see Hedges, "Particularities."

34. A word frequently used in postmodern discourse, which may simply be read as difference—though various postmodern writers might give various sub-layers of meaning to it.

35. Hedges, "Particularities," 112–13.

Other.[36] Despite the wide appeal of the particularist approach in the theology of religions, a number of recent works have argued quite cogently that it ultimately fails as a way to engage with religious Others, and, indeed, in what it sets out to be, which is a Christian approach to the theology of religions.[37] This is not the place to rehearse the general critique of this approach; however, it is important to note that the style of theology Milbank represents in relation to the theology of religions is not unique, and while finding much support is nevertheless subject to a considerable amount of devastating critique. Aspects of this will become apparent as we discuss specific aspects of Milbank's thought below.

MILBANK ON THE RELIGIOUS OTHER

Milbank tends not to engage with other religious traditions, nor with the theology of religions. As an area it is something which tends to fall outside the Radical Orthodoxy conceptualization, concerned as it is with internal Christian narratives; we have already noted why, in relation to Intercultural Theology this is a problem, while Paul Lakeland finds Milbank's tendency to "silence on other religious traditions disturbing."[38] He is not, however, completely silent, and in his comments people have found "something seriously worrying."[39] Indeed, his principle foray into the theology of religions is perhaps most notable for its misunderstanding and dogmatism, while he adopts a problematic supercessionism in relation to Judaism.[40]

---

36. Hedges, "Particularities," 120.

37. Besides my own analysis of such issues (Hedges, "Particularities" and, *Controversies*) we can notably mention the work of two of the most prominent figures in the field, Perry Schmidt-Leukel who explicitly positions himself against such views (*Transformation by Integration*, 2–3) and Gavin D'Costa, who in his most recent work has moved from a particularist position to a rather different one and who explicitly attacks certain particularist style approaches (*Christianity and World*, 30–31 and 45–54). It may be noted, though, that both Schmidt-Leukel and D'Costa continue to use Race's three-fold typology.

38. Lakeland, *Postmodernity*, 73–74.

39. Brown, "Radical Orthodoxy," 47. One paper I am aware of suggests a rather different reading to that I will offer here, that Milbank actually does not "stereotype" others and wants to "engage with an extremely wide range of parties"; however, it offers no examples of his engagement with religious Others, and its basic argument is that Christians may speak to, rather than engage meaningfully with, Others in the public arena in relation to religious diversity rather than be wholly isolated (Herbert, "Getting by in Babylon").

40. Brown, "Radical Orthodoxy," 49–50.

Milbank's principle discussion around issues relating to the religious Other is a single essay, whose title "The End of Dialogue" well encapsulates his position, which takes aim at many of the terms or "categories of encounter" such as "dialog," "pluralism" and "religion."[41] Basic to his thesis is a well-rehearsed critique that the contemporary categorization of religion is a modern Western liberal invention and is not one that has any basis in reality and, moreover, distorts the subject matter under consideration.[42] This attitude is common place in particularist writers,[43] and at least one other particularist uses Milbank's ideas as a support for his own espousal of this position.[44] Certainly, such a critique is well established amongst many deconstructive postmodern inclined scholars of religion who wish to dispute the metatheory of how we understand the basic subject matter commonly termed "religion." However, the arguments are far from conclusive and many scholars would argue that "religion" remains a viable category for consideration. We cannot rehearse the arguments here, suffice it to say that, as employed within the particularist standpoint as a whole, the critique against "religion" is highly problematic. For instance, it runs counter to certain historical realities—in particular it is not simply the modern "liberal" Western academy or theologians who have seen interconnections between the world's religious traditions.[45]

The critique that religions are different and diverse phenomenon with different conceptualizations, is related to Milbank's discussion of Trinity, which, for Radical Orthodoxy and all particularists, should be understood in traditional formulae. Importantly, if every religion is distinct and, therefore unrelatable, it must be argued that the Christian understanding of the Trinity is distinct (even, radically different) from other religions' Triadic formulae. Milbank has to claim that Christianity is unique, distinct, and self-contained, so he makes this case by arguing that while certain aspects of the Christian worldview may have roots in a generic Indo-European theism, even a Triadic theism, the Christian Trinitarian formulae is unique.[46]

41. Milbank, "End," 175ff.
42. Ibid.,176–81.
43. Hedges, "Particularities," 115–16.
44. McGrath, "Particularist View," 154–55, citing Milbank, "End," 176.
45. Hedges, "Particularities," 122–26, an argument further explored in Hedges, *Controversies*, chapter 4. For a more extended analysis of critiques of the concept of "religion" and a defense of its viability against its detractors, see Hedges, *Controversies*, chapter 2 and Hedges, "Can We Still."
46. Milbank, "End," 188.

However, we must ask certain questions about this. First, without making a deep study of other religious traditions, how is Milbank to judge that his own preferred triadic theism is unique? As we will see below, he shows a rather shallow and superficial understanding of aspects of Hinduism based on sectarian sources. Second, there are many versions of Christian Trinitarianism, and, indeed, quite a number of Christianities which are not Trinitarian, so how does he decide which one to adopt as his basis for comparison? Third, what are the grounds for deciding what is a "unique" system: does everything that is slightly different constitute a "unique" system, in which case we are left with hundreds, if not more, "unique" Christian systems, and the same holds true for the vast variety of things labelled under the term "Hinduism." Finally, a significant part of Milbank's claim is not only that Christian triadism is unique, but that it is superior, and so the issue comes how does he know, especially as his knowledge of other systems is very limited? We will further question this claim below as it has resonances with other aspects of his theology which need to be explored. What is clear, though, is that although suggesting that "dialog" and "pluralism" are flawed because they try to speak from some space outside of the box, i.e. have a unique bird's eye meta-narrative, Milbank here is guilty of exactly the same charge. Indeed, it has been argued that Milbank is explicitly guilty of making Christianity the general standard by which to read all religion; which both means he still operates with a Western (imperialist?) assumption about what religion is, as read through a theological lens (one of the fundamental critiques), and of imposing his own monolithic meta-narrative about true religion.[47]

Milbank's knowledge of Hindu thought is based upon what seems to be a superficial understanding, yet, on this limited basis, he is judgmental enough to be quite dismissive of a major aspect of it. This is the *bhakti* tradition, often referred to into English as the Hindu devotional tradition. Using a dated and sectarian source, Milbank dismisses the idea that *bhakti* can equate to worship, stating "it is mainly concerned with a systematic appeasement of, and seeking favours from, the various deities."[48] However, Milbank's source for this, a Hindu scholar of the Advaita Vedanta school, Nirad Chaudhuri, is here engaging in a polemical dismissal of an opposing school, Dvaita Vedanta, upon which most *bhkati* is based. For those not

---

47. Brown, "Radical Orthodoxy," 48.

48. Milbank, "End," 176, citing, Nirad Chaudhuri. *Hinduism*, 90–95, and 188–89 (but see throughout on his "West" "East" "schematic contrast").

familiar with the variety of Hindu traditions, Advaita Vedanta is a monistic tradition which believes that God and man are ultimately the same, while Dvaita Vedanta believes God and man are distinct. The former therefore dismisses personal devotion to an individual deity as a lower form of religious belief, hence Chaudhuri's rhetorical dismissal looking back to supposed "primitive" origins, which ignores the reality that Dvaita and *bhakti* is the mainstream Hindu tradition which, as countless scholars have shown, is clearly a devotional scholar, possessing many similarities to Christian devotional practice.[49] Therefore, without reference to mainstream scholarship (theologians may imagine it being similar to the use of nineteenth century Protestant tracts being used to gain an understanding of Roman Catholicism), he presents a misunderstanding of the *bhakti* tradition, which is clearly a devotional path. Moreover, the idea that "seeking favours" or "appeasement" distances this from Christian devotion ignores the way many actual Christians approach God, with much of this being scripturally founded in examples found throughout the Hebrew Bible. Indeed, Milbank's whole approach of looking for what he sees as the best in the Christian tradition and then seeking for examples of what could be the worst to say about the religious Other is something which, as far back as the nineteenth century, was recognized as unfair and unhelpful in missionary circles.

Milbank's dismissal of *bhakti* could be seen as an attempt to deny any similarities between religions, which, as we have seen, is one part of his overall aim. In relation to this, he also launches an assault specifically on pluralist-style theologies which have sought to develop what they see as areas of contact. In particular, he attacks the basis of a liberative theology of religious pluralism, as exemplified by such figures as Paul Knitter, arguing that it is based upon a solely Western, and therefore colonial, set of assumptions.[50] Milbank contends that the idea of justice, liberation, or interfaith praxis seen in such figures as Knitter or Marjorie Suchocki work on the basis of a secular, liberal normativism, which insists upon its own position over and against that of religious discourses. Indeed, a further claim is that

---

49. On *bhakti* see, for instance, the work of some contemporary noted scholars of Hinduism: Lipner, Julius, *Hindus*, 305ff.; Flood, *Introduction to Hinduism*, ch. 6; or, for a good guide to a native appreciation of *bhakti* and its relations to Christian thought see, Appasamy, *Christianity as Bhakti*. See also, *Bhakti, Karuna, Agape*, edited by Marko Zlomislić, David Goicoechea, Suzanne Tebbutt, (Binghamton, Global, 2003).

50. Milbank, "End," 181ff. A sympathetic commentary on Milbank's arguments can be found in Heim, *Salvations*, 200–207, who shows how his thought here ties in with much of Milbank's theological system with particular reference to *Theology and Social*.

it is actually in the social arena where many religions come into dispute, and so we simply cannot bracket out "religious/doctrinal" questions and work on "social/ethical" ones because there is no clear dividing line. There is certainly some substance to Milbank's arguments here, a lot of discourse associated with justice and liberation does assume a problematic Western norm. However, it is the case that within the broader framework of interreligious dialog and the theology of religions what is termed the Dialog of Action is just one part, which often takes place alongside other forms of encounter.[51] In this sense, the kind of criticism that Milbank raises, that he doesn't think it is possible to do it authentically, is disproved by the actual practice of people engaging in interreligious or multi-religious action for social justice, ecology, etc., who understand that a basis for this lies within their own tradition. As an example, many Islamic scholars argue that the kind of justice exemplified in Human Rights can actually be found most authentically in their own tradition, while a lot of discourse in Engaged Buddhism is not based upon the notion that Buddhist thought must be modernized/Westernized but by an appeal to examples from the two and a half thousand year history of their own tradition, and even back to the historical Buddha himself. While critiques exist, it is clearly still possible to viably maintain that similar calls for actions exist between religions, and, if presented carefully, a pluralist call for this is not illegitimate. It is also simply incorrect to argue that pluralists are unaware of the dangers of imposing what is currently a dominant Western discourse in relation to other religious traditions.[52]

Before tying this section together there is one further part of Milbank's argument we need to consider. Milbank argues that it is impossible for us to be in any meaningful or real conversation with the Hindu tradition (and, by extension from this, any religious Others). He claims that any contemporary Hindu view is illegitimate having been contaminated by contact with Western modernism, and any Hinduism we could dialog with would be our own reading of "dead" texts "pre-dating Western intrusion and practices relatively uncontaminated by Western influence."[53] D'Costa takes issue

---

51. On the different forms of encounter and interreligious dialog, see Race, "Interfaith Dialogue," 155–72.

52. Examples of tradition specific discourse related to these issues can be found in such works as Hassan, "Rights of Women"; Zhang, "Idea of Human"; Bloom, "Fundamental Intuitions"; Eppsteiner, *Path of Compassion*. For a discussion of various issues discussed above, see Hedges, *Controversies*, 94–102, 129–33, 254–70.

53. Milbank, "End," 178, see also 176–81.

with this claim, rightly criticizing Milbank for assuming he has the right to adjudicate what is a "legitimate" Hindu development.[54] If Milbank's own claim is right, that these are incompatible systems of belief, then he has utterly no standpoint from which to judge any internal Hindu question. Moreover, this claim helps clarify that behind Milbank's insistence on the difference of religious systems there is not, as he claims, a better way to respect the authentic voice of the religious Other, but rather a domineering and imperialist agenda.[55]

Two further lines of critique which can be levelled against Milbank's claims also help uncover their subtext. First, Milbank's ploy of an appeal to a pristine past as the truth of Hinduism has much in common with many colonialist discourses which make reference to pristine pasts undefiled by colonialism.[56] This negates any legitimate critique they may have of the colonizer's system (the dominant elite Western Christian discourse in this case) by making it an antiquated or untouchable ideal without real consequences. As has been argued of the particularist system as a whole, and is especially true of Milbank, setting up a dichotomy between self and other serves the purpose of simply denying that any legitimate criticism can be directed at you from other sources, and it is associated with a parochial Western insularity.[57] Second, while he accuses others, such as Knitter, of making monolithic separations, he himself does this with reference to idealized standards.[58] In particular, Milbank relies upon deeply unsound monolithic accounts of "East" and "West," placing Indic, European, Middle Eastern, African, Chinese, Central Asian, etc. traditions in undifferentiated blocks, without reference to the reality of historical nuances and interactions; this only, in Sara Suleri's words, "reinforces the old binary essentialism of East and West."[59] An example of this is the way he says the vast diversity of Buddhist traditions all relate to his own imagined monolithic category of "Eastern goals of power and freedom":[60] such profound essentialism speaks of a lack of understanding of the religious Other that could be remedied by a first year university course in world religions. These two

54. D'Costa, *Christianity and World Religions*, 51.
55. Milbank, "End," 187.
56. Kwok, *Postcolonial Imagination*, 41.
57. Hedges, "Particularities," 127–30 and Sargent, "Proceeding Beyond," 822.
58. Barnes, *Theology*, 19.
59. Suleri, *Rhetoric of English*, 13, see also Hedges, "Particularities," 128.
60. Milbank, "End," 190.

points show that Milbank's rhetoric of the religious Other is one that seeks not only to sideline or dismiss, but also homogenize them, so that they are placed in relation to his own claims. The same kind of comment could also be made of Milbank's generalized comments about "paganism."[61]

NONVIOLENT ONTOLOGY

We turn now to a particular theme which is of central importance in Milbank's theology as a whole. In part, this will show why Milbankism deals inadequately with the intercultural context of Christian theology, while it will also develop some themes explored above. This theme is his notion of a nonviolent ontology, which we will relate to his advocacy of an aggressive missionary imperative.

A nonviolent ontology is a key feature in Milbank's thought, and of Radical Orthodoxy generally, and we should take a while to explore what is meant by this.[62] Like much post-liberal theology, Radical Orthodoxy wishes to assert "Christian supremacy," although it is aware that charges of asserting a meta-narrative or advocating a dominant or imperialist/colonialist agenda could be levelled at it. The way it seeks to avoid this is through a quasi-metaphysical belief that all other systems of thought seek "mastery" over the Other. That is to say, they wish to define and control the subject of their enquiry, in an act of epistemological and/or ontological violence. This may be linked into a general postmodern philosophical critique of modernity, associated with such figures as Emmanuel Levinas and Michel Foucault, that knowledge and systems of thought tend to define and thereby control their subject of enquiry, and violate the Other. By way of contrast, it is claimed, that by grounding being in God, Christianity recognizes that all things are not subject to mastery but ultimately participate in divine unknowability.[63] Moreover, it is suggested Christianity as a system, is nonviolent, because it does not assert its own point of view over and against others, whereas all other forms of thought do.[64]

In term of interreligious relations, Milbank asserts that other religions offer a controlling narrative of the way things are, which contrasts with

61. See, for instance, Milbank, *Theology and Social*, 280.
62. See Hyman, *Predicament*, 73–77 and 111–14.
63. A central theme in Radical Orthodoxy's system; see Milbank, "Knowledge."
64. See Hyman, *Predicament*, 73–77 and 111–14. Mary Doakin has also asked how Milbank's exclusive approach can be a foundation for a peaceful community ("Politics of Radical").

Christianity. Here, Milbank suggests that everything from the *Bhagavad-Gita* to Neo-Hinduism is actually based on a violent ontology, and the latter, in particular, he reads as akin to his understanding of postmodern nihilism, one of his main bugbears, in his attempt to narrate a nonviolent ontology. We find here, though, a number of problems we have seen in Milbank's thought already: his assertion of what the nature of other traditions is regardless of whether he has studied them in any depth or actually has a comprehensive understanding; and, his fervent desire to assert a narrative of difference.

We must also address the actuality of Milbank's nonviolent ontology. Gavin Hyman has argued cogently and persuasively that by looking to a transcendent truth, rather than bypassing violent ontology, Milbank simply transfers it to another level.[65] It has also been termed an "an inaccurate, or at least highly selective claim," which highlights that it is an idealized assertion.[66] Addressing interreligious contexts, Michael Barnes suggesting his thought contains "a covert violence," something others concur with: his discourse has been argued to concern "who controls the table," or that they "surely do violence to the religions (and philosophies) of others," or "vilify the religious and secular Other unnecessarily."[67] We therefore find an array of critics cogently highlighting the violent ontology inherent in Milbank's work, especially in an interreligious context. Particularly in relation to how he violates and misunderstands the religious Other it could even lead us to argue that any Christian theologian who does not have at least a working knowledge of some of the world's other religions is not even capable of doing theology in our contemporary context; to speak from an isolated position is enviable in many ways, something Lakeland highlights: "But what of all the religious traditions of the world that are quite unaffected by the secular reason of Western culture, that have their own metanarrative and which . . . could make at least a good case from their renarration of practice for embodying a harmonious community? Milbank's postmodern gambit secures him from the need to engage in an apologetic or polemic in the

---

65. Hyman, *The Predicament*, 73–77; Insole, "Against Radical Orthodoxy," 221–27, especially 224.

66. Sargent, "Proceeding Beyond," 823.

67. Barnes, *Theology*, 19; Reader, *Beyond All Reason*, 72; Brown, "Radical Orthodoxy," 53, and McMahon, "Theology and the Redemptive," 791. See also Sargent, "Proceeding Beyond," 823.

The Poverty of Radical Orthodoxy

face of these other options, but—and this he does not seem to see—it also makes the claim to superiority one that he cannot justify."[68]

I have argued a similar case, suggesting that Milbank's thought exemplifies a will-to-power in relation to the Other.[69] Indeed, it is not just something we find in Milbank but in many post-liberal and Neo-Orthodox theologies, which insists that just by sitting within its own borders and insisting that its own revelation/tradition is unique and special, it regards itself as in no need, or even incapable of, speaking to other traditions.[70] However, this seeks to bypass the very question which needs answering: what is the relationship of Christianity to other religions; Milbank addresses Christianity's relationship to the religious Other in an utterly inadequate way, which is unhistorical, theologically flawed, and, I would suggest, morally suspect. In particular, we should face the fact that any claim that Christianity is unique will flounder when faced with issues of religious history, especially the fact that its notions share much in common with its two Abrahamic brothers, Judaism and Islám. This is especially the case when, as with Milbank and Radical Orthodoxy as a whole, claims are made to such things as ontological non-violence, as all traditions claim belief in the same deity, the God of Abraham, while their notions of Revelation are entwined. Therefore, similar notions to that which is used to suggest that Christianity resists mastery can be found in them—indeed, it could even be argued that Islám is better placed to make such claims.[71] This, of course, merely addresses the Abrahamic traditions, but what about "how Radical Orthodoxy's claims to have the ontological trump card play out against Hindu, Buddhist, Daoist or other claims," especially as "James Byrne rightly notes that any neo-orthodox theology must present a view of revelation that 'responds to the challenge of religious pluralism,' by being 'more than another case of special pleading wrapped up in a sugarcoating of postmodern nonfoundationalism.'"[72]

It seems clear that the nonviolent ontology that Milbank upholds as a central part of his system is based on extremely shaky foundations,

---

68. Lakeland, *Postmodernity*, 74.
69. Hedges, "John Milbank's," 807–8.
70. See Hedges, "John Milbank's," 807, especially note 96 (816).
71. For a commentary on how a Radical Orthodox claims to transcend mastery, and my comments on how Islam may be better placed to make such claims, see Hedges, "John Milbank's," 807–8. A similar point is argued in Brown, "Radical Orthodoxy," 52.
72. Hedges, "John Milbank's," 807, citing Byrne, James, "A Reasonable Passion," 9.

especially in interreligious perspective, it cannot bear the weight he wishes to place upon it. Moreover, it is another instance of where the claims of respect we find in figures like Milbank, as well as more broadly others associated with Radical Orthodox, post-liberal, or Neo-Orthodox positions, are found to be lacking. Milbank claims: "With an extreme degree of paradox, one must claim that it is only through insisting on the finality of the Christian reading of 'what there is' that one can both fulfill respect for the other and complete and secure this otherness as pure neighbourly difference."[73]

However, the claim of respect can be nothing of the sort because by claiming to hold all the trump cards, disguised as peaceful ontological nonviolence, it undercuts, thereby violating the claims of, the other discourses. Indeed, in some ways this is more pronounced in Milbank than in many other particularists, who, as have seen, interposes his own denigrating interpretations upon other systems, while denying that they can possibly even comment on his own. This kind of assertion of supremacy and mastery is announced in Milbank's own words, that "Christian theology must continue to subvert" the discourses of these other religions, and approach them with "mutual suspicion."[74] As such, his thought partakes in the false claims to respect of all particularist thinking.[75] As Reader has argued, by taking post-modern claims too far, Milbank shuts himself off in his own corner claiming that he should have the ultimate power in any discussion, and as a result refuses discourse with the Other.[76] We must therefore agree with Reader's assessment that Milbank is entirely "positioned by a secular culture" that has led him to refuse the resources of the Christian tradition he claims as his own, of figures like Augustine and Aquinas, who willingly and freely adapted, drew inspiration from, and engaged with the surrounding intercultural and interreligious landscape of their day.

---

73. Milbank, "End," 189.
74. Ibid., 190.
75. For an extrapolation of these themes, see Hedges, "Particularities," 121 and 127–30.
76. Reader, *Beyond All Reason*, 72–73.

Inauthentic Theology: The Failings of Radical Orthodoxy

If Christian theology has always veered between twin poles of "open" and "closed" approaches to other traditions and cultures, then Radical Orthodoxy's closed/ Tertullianist, position could be said to represent a valid stance within the tradition. However, I would argue that this is not so. Intercultural Theology clearly demonstrates that there never has been a "pure" and untouched Christian tradition; Tertullian himself, of course, freely, and seemingly unconsciously, adapted Christianity to the North African Roman worldview that was his own. His cry of "What has Athens to do with Jerusalem?" was not then a stand against Intercultural Theology (and, of course, the Roman legalism he helped build into Western Christianity was not simply a "secular" part of the culture but bound up with a whole social and religious worldview), but a claim that his own parochial vision was different, and (crucially) better, to that of others. Such localism is now impossible to maintain, as our historical consciousness has shown us that every position is culturally embedded. Therefore, to stand, today, with a Karl Barth, George Lindbeck, or John Milbank and insist that we must follow some "pure" prototype or isolated island of revelation or tradition is utterly untenable. While it may be a comforting position for those who do not wish to be challenged or discomforted in what they find to be secure beliefs—and hence the long and influential shadow cast over theology by these figures—their theology is, I would argue, an offense against the Christian tradition as well as the spirit of Jesus and his teachings.[77] A theology that refuses discourse with surrounding cultures, religions, philosophies, or worldviews is one that is in poverty. Radical Orthodoxy fails utterly to respond to the contemporary situation of global theology, while impoverishing itself and the whole Christian tradition in its influence. I believe we have no choice but to find the title of this volume very fitting, perhaps it could stand as an epitaph for this particular tradition?

Bibliography

Aleaz, K. P. "Pluralisms: We are No Longer 'Frogs in the Well.'" In *Christian Approaches to Other Faiths*, edited by Paul Hedges and Alan Race, 212–33. Core Textbook Series. London: SCM, 2008.

77. I argue this strongly in Hedges, *Controversies*, chapters 1, 3, and 6.

Aminrazavi, Mehdi. "Medieval Philosophical Discourse and Muslim-Christian Dialogue." *The American Journal of Islamic Social Sciences* 13:3 (1996) 382–88.

Appasamy, A. J. *Christianity as Bhakti Marga*. Madras: The Christian Literature Society for India, 1930.

Barnes, Michael. *Theology and the Dialogue of Religions*. Cambridge: Cambridge University Press, 2002.

Bloom, Irene. "Fundamental Intuitions and Consensus Statements: Mencian Confucianism and Human Rights." In *Confucianism and Human Rights*, edited by Weiming Tu and Wm. Theodore de Bary, 94–116. New York: Columbia University Press, 1998.

Boyd, Robert. *India and the Latin Captivity of the Church: The Cultural Context of the Gospel*. London: Cambridge University Press, 1974.

Brown, Frank Burch. "Radical Orthodoxy and the Religions of Others." *Encounter* 63:1–2 (2002) 45–53.

Carruthers, Mary. *The Craft of Thought: Meditation, Rhetoric, and the Making of Images, 400–1200*. Cambridge: Cambridge University Press, 1998.

Cheetham, David. "Inclusivisms: Honouring Faithfulness and Openness." In *Christian Approaches to Other Faiths*, edited by Paul Hedges and Alan Race, 63–84. London: SCM, 2008.

Doakin, Mary. "The Politics of Radical Orthodoxy: A Catholic Critique." *Theological Studies* 68 (2007) 368–93.

D'Costa, Gavin. *Christianity and World Religions: Disputed Questions in the Theology of Religions*. Chichester: Wiley-Blackwell, 2009.

Eppsteiner, Fred, ed. *The Path of Compassion: Writings on Socially Engaged Buddhism*. Berkeley, CA: Parallax, 1988.

Flood, Gavin. *An Introduction to Hinduism*. Cambridge: Cambridge University Press, 2007.

Frei, Hans W. *Types of Christian Theology*. London: Yale University Press, 1992.

Gaston, Ray. "Christian Peace Witness as Dialogical Encounter." Conference paper delivered at Interfaith Encounter and Social Change: Encounters from the Margins Conference, University of Winchester, September 7 2010.

Gruber, Judith. "Christian Identities: An Imaginative and Innovative Quest for Heterogeneous Unity." *eSharp* 14 (2009) 23–38.

Hassan, Riffat. "Rights of Women Within Islamic Communities." In *Religious Human Rights in Global Perspective: Religious Perspectives*, edited by John Witte and Johan D. van der Vyver, 361–86. The Hague: Martinus Nijhoff, 1996.

Hedges, Paul. "Can We Still Teach 'Religions'?: Towards an Understanding of Religion as Culture and Orientation in Contemporary Pedagogy and Metatheory." In *International Handbook for Inter-Religious Education*, edited by G. Durka et al. New York: Springer Academic, 2010.

———. *Controversies in Interreligious Dialogue and the Theology of Religions*, London: SCM, 2010.

———. "Is John Milbank's Radical Orthodoxy a Form of Liberal Theology? A Rhetorical Counter." *The Heythrop Journal* 51:5 (2010) 795–818.

———. "Particularities: Tradition-specific Post-modern Perspectives." In *Christian Approaches to Other Faiths*, edited by Paul Hedges and Alan Race, 112–35. Core Textbook Series. London: SCM, 2008.

———. *Preparation and Fulfilment: A History and Study of Fulfilment Theology in Modern British Thought in the Indian Context*. Studies in the Intercultural History of Christianity. Bern: Peter Lang, 2001.

———. "A Reflection on Typologies: Negotiating a Fast Moving Discussion." In *Christian Approaches to Other Faiths*, edited by Paul Hedges and Alan Race, 17–33. Core Textbook Series. London: SCM, 2008.

Heim, S. Mark. *Salvations: Truth and Difference in Religion*. Maryknoll, NY: Orbis, 1995.

Herbert, David. "Getting by in Babylon: Macintyre, Milbank and a Christian Response to Religious Diversity in the Public Arena." *Studies in Christian Ethics* 10:1 (1997) 61–81.

Hunsinger, George. "Postliberal Theology." In *The Cambridge Companion to Postmodern Theology*, edited by Kevin J. Vanhoozer, 42–57. Cambridge: Cambridge University Press, 2003.

Hyman, Gavin. *The Predicament of Postmodern Theology: Radical Orthodoxy or Nihilist Textualism*. London: Westminster John Knox, 2001.

Insole, C. J. "Against Radical Orthodoxy: On the Dangers of Overcoming Political Liberalism." *Modern Theology* 20: 2 (2004) 213–41.

Justin Martyr. "The Apostolic Fathers, Justin Martyr, Irenaeus." In vol. I of *The Ante-Nicene Fathers*, edited and translated by Alexander Roberts and James Donaldson, revised by A. Cleveland Coxe. Edinburgh: T. & T. Clark, 1996.

Küster, Volker. "The Project of an Intercultural Theology." *Swedish Missiological Themes*, 93:3 (2005) 417–32.

Kwok, Pui-lan. "Mercy Amba Oduyoye." In *Empire and the Christian Tradition: New Readings of Classical Theologians*, edited by Kwok Pui-lan, Joerg Rieger, and Don H. Compier, 471–86. Minneapolis: Fortress, 2007.

———. *Postcolonial Imagination and Feminist Theology*. London: SCM, 2005.

Lakeland, Paul. *Postmodernity: Christian Identity in a Fragmented Age*. Minneapolis: Fortress, 1997.

Lipner, Julius. *Hindus: Their Religious Beliefs and Practices*. London: Routledge, 1994.

McGrath, Alister. "A Particularist View: A Post-Enlightenment Approach." In *Four Views on Salvation in a Pluralistic World*, edited by Dennis L. Okholm and Timothy R. Phillips, 151–80. Grand Rapids: Zondervan, 1995.

McMahon, Christopher. "Theology and the Redemptive Mission of the Church: A Catholic Response to Milbank's Challenge." *The Heythrop Journal* 51:5 (2010) 781–94.

Milbank, John. "The End of Dialogue." In *Christian Uniqueness Reconsidered: The Myth of a Pluralistic Theology of Religions*, edited by Gavin D'Costa, 174–90. Faith Meets Faith Series. Maryknoll: Orbis, 1990.

———. "Knowledge: The Theological critique of Philosophy in Hamann and Jacobi." In *Radical Orthodoxy: A New Theology*, edited by John Milbank et. al. London: Routledge, 1998.

———. "Postmodern Critical Augustinianism: A Short 'Summa' in Forty-Two Responses to Unasked Questions." In *The Postmodern God: A Theological Reader* edited by Graham Ward, 265–78. Oxford: Blackwell, 1997.

———. "The Programme of Radical Orthodoxy." In *Radical Orthodoxy?—A Catholic Enquiry* edited by Laurence Paul Hemming. Aldershot: Ashgate, 2000.

———. *Theology and Social Theory*. Oxford: Blackwell, 1989.

———. *The Word Made Strange*. Oxford: Blackwell, 1997.

Milbank, John, and Catherine Pickstock. *Truth in Aquinas*. Radical Orthodoxy Series. London: Routledge, 2001.

Pickstock, Catherine. "Radical Orthodoxy and the Meditations of Time." In *Radical Orthodoxy?—A Catholic Enquiry*, edited by Laurence Paul Hemming. Aldershot: Ashgate, 2000.

Race, Alan. "Interfaith Dialogue: Religious Accountability between Strangeness and Resonance." In *Christian Approaches to Other Faiths,* edited by Paul Hedges and Alan Race, 155–72. Core Textbook Series. London: SCM, 2008.

Rashkover, Randi. "The Semiotics of Embodiment: Radical Orthodoxy and Jewish-Christian Relations." *Journal for Cultural and Religious Theory* 3:3 (2002).

Reader, John. *Beyond All Reason: The Limits of Post-Modern Theology.* Cardiff: Aureus, 1997.

Sargent, Benjamin. "Proceeding Beyond Isolation: Bringing Milbank, Habermas and Ockham to the Interfaith Table." *The Heythrop Journal* 51:5 (2010) 819–30.

Schmidt-Leukel, Perry. *Transformation by Integration: How Inter-faith Encounter Changes Christianity.* London: SCM, 2009.

Schreiter, Robert J. *The New Catholicity: Theology between the Global and the Local.* Maryknoll, NY: Orbis, 2004.

Sugirtharajah, R. S. *Postcolonial Reconfigurations: An Alternative Way of Reading the Bible and Doing Theology.* London: SCM, 2003.

Suleri, Sara. *The Rhetoric of English India.* Chicago: University of Chicago Press, 1992.

Ward, Graham. *Cultural Transformation and Religious Practice.* Cambridge: Cambridge University Press, 2005.

Yoder, John Howard. "The Disavowal of Constantine: An Alternative Perpsective in Interfaith Dialogue." In *The Royal Priesthood—Essays Ecclesiological and Ecumenical.* edited by Michael G. Cartwright, 242–61. Grand Rapids: Eerdmans, 1994.

Zhang, Qianfan. "The Idea of Human Dignity in Classical Chinese Philosophy: A Reconstruction of Confucianism." *Journal of Chinese Philosophy* 27:3 (2000) 299–330.

7

Reading Yoder against Milbank

A Yoderian Critique of Radical Orthodoxy

Angus Paddison

Introduction

"Radical Orthodoxy" is not alone in claiming a return to the "roots" of the Christian faith. This essay shall engage critically the work of John Milbank, a Radical *Orthodox* theologian, through the work and output of a Radical *Reformation* theologian, John Howard Yoder. Thus, in this volume of critical essays on Radical Orthodoxy, I recognize the diversity of the movement by focusing on one of its (key) figures. In essence, the guiding question of this essay is What happens when you read Milbank and Yoder together? In addition, subtitling this response "A Yoderian Critique" is a way of saying that in this essay, I am attempting to think in the ways that Yoder would have us think, following the direction of his pacifist imagination. After briefly outlining the common ground these two different theologians share I shall then put Yoder's insights to work in demonstrating the misconstruals of Milbank's project.

Common Ground

Bringing John Milbank and John Howard Yoder in critical interaction might seem a little idiosyncratic.[1] After all, despite the fact that Milbank's *Theology and Social Theory* was first published in 1990 (seven years before Yoder's death), I can find no reference to Milbank in Yoder's work, notwithstanding his parsimonious referencing to other people's work generally. Likewise, there are very few references to Yoder in Milbank's work. So, what common ground could this Anglo-Catholic socialist and Mennonite share? It needs to be said at the outset: quite a lot. Both place a heavy emphasis on the church as the locus of salvation, the people who perform and embody the new life God has made possible for humans in his Son, and in the fellowship of the Spirit. Both presume they are writing, not theology for their own denominations, but ecumenical theology in which all Christians can have a share. Their theologies are *moods* or *stances*, which other Christian theologians can replicate in their own confessional contexts.[2] Both are critical of liberal theologies (though there is a difference in tone) that reduce the cosmically significant life of Jesus to "values" which society is presumed to share or already know. Both are unimpressed by attempts to make theology "relevant" to society at large and impressed by the conviction that the faith of the church is *necessary* to understanding the world.[3] Both are therefore committed (though in rather divergent ways) to ontological descriptions, with tracing how the Gospel is a telling "of the way things really are."[4] And both hold that the course of the church is in need of correction—although where they locate this false turn differs.[5]

Despite these significant points of convergence there remain three keys misconstruals of Milbank's project which we can identify with the help of Yoder's theology. Indeed, were Milbank to attend to these three aspects and take Yoder more seriously it would, I venture to suggest, serve *to strengthen* those points of convergence he already enjoys with Yoder. Milbank's theology, it seems, finds it hard to carry the burden of its best intentions. Were there to be a greater attention to Yoder, Milbank might

---

1. Though, see now Huebner and York, *The Gift of Difference*, which brings Radical Orthodox and Radical Reformation impulses together.
2. Yoder, "Thinking Theologically," 251.
3. See Holcomb, "Being Bound to God," 246.
4. Yoder, "Politics," 164.
5. For Milbank, it is the Catholicism of the late Middle Ages; for Yoder it is the turn to Christendom in the fourth century.

find resources to help him imagine the church as a community without borders, "that paradox: a nomad city."[6]

Three Yoderian inspired questions can be raised in critical response to Milbank's work:

1. Does he attend with enough rigor to the vulnerability of the particular Jesus?
2. Is the kind of church Milbank speaks of willing to not be in control?
3. And what might he learn from attending to the Christian pacifism of Yoder?

The Vulnerability of the Particular Jesus

There is no doubt that for Yoder Jesus is the eternal Son of God, a member of the triune fellowship that is Father, Son, and Holy Spirit. Indeed, it is precisely the origins of Jesus in the recesses of eternity that secures his authority in our time. Yet, consistently resisting the lure of metaphysics (contra Milbank), Yoder fastens onto the incarnation of Jesus in a way that more radically re-orientates history than Milbank manages to achieve. The incarnation is not a metaphysical riddle but, as a measure of how seriously God takes history, an invitation to re-imagine history and our place within it.[7]

The radical demands of Jesus on how we are to live our lives is, for Yoder, bound up with his particularity, the one who in this particularity is non-negotiably "the Lord of History."[8] The Word becoming flesh is not a baptism of humanity without conversion, but a direct challenge from God within our humanity to re-imagine the cosmos and our action within this world. The entry of this Jew into history fundamentally re-aligns history and so our agency within history. Revelation—God revealing himself in his own Son—is therefore bound to the particular historicity of Jesus of Nazareth.[9] It is this emphasis on the particularity of Jesus which resources works like *The Politics of Jesus* with its renewed attention to the political *life* of Jesus. Meticulous metaphysical explorations of Jesus's person or endless historical explorations into the "real" Jesus are therefore exposed by Yoder as attempts to release the pressure of Jesus's particular life and teachings on

6. Milbank, *Future of Love*, 342.
7. Yoder, "Prophetic Task of the Pastoral Ministry," 98.
8. Yoder, *He Came Preaching Peace*, 52.
9. Yoder, *Discipleship as Political Responsibility*, 53–54.

our behavior. "The real issue is not whether Jesus can make sense in a world far from Galilee, but whether—when he meets us in our world, as he does in fact—we want to follow him,"[10] Yoder writes with characteristic perspicuity. Yoder's persistent reminder is that any evasion of the particularity of Jesus is merely a flight from "the risk of particular allegiance . . . the cost of following his way."[11]

Jesus's particularity is of one piece with his vulnerability. The God of Jesus Christ saves within history precisely by taking on "the risks of enfleshment."[12] Reflecting on John 1:14, Yoder wittily notes that the Word dwells "in a tent, not in a castle."[13] This vulnerability extended even to the risk that Jesus's message might be rejected, as indeed it was. "Incarnation" means for Yoder God's willingness to entrust his mission and work to "the hands of ordinary people."[14] The scandal of the gospel is God coming in flesh in Jesus Christ, submitting to our mercy, and so letting his whole mission brew, since creation depends on us. The truth of creation and the truth of God as he eternally is—to use the most universal terms we can muster—are revealed therefore in the most particular and vulnerable of ways. It is this tension which Yoder consistently resists releasing: "The eternal *Word* condescending to put himself at our mercy, the creative power behind the universe emptying itself, pouring itself into the frail mold of humanity, has the same shape as Jesus. God has the same shape as Jesus, and he always has had. The cross is what creation is all about. What Jesus did was local of course, because that is how serious and real our history is to God. But what the cross was locally is universally and always the divine nature."[15]

The life of Jesus reveals then the nature of the God that Christians worship. Another way of binding revelation to Jesus is to say that for Yoder the life, death, and resurrection of Jesus taken together is apocalyptic—this life reveals "the grain of the universe."[16] It is this apocalyptic invasion of Jesus into our time and history that enables Christians "to participate in history differently—in hope."[17] Yoder is a strikingly consistent thinker. From his

---

10. Yoder, *Priestly Kingdom*, 62.
11. Yoder, *Royal Priesthood*, 111.
12. Yoder, "Free Church Syndrome," 174.
13. Yoder, "On Not Being Ashamed," 291.
14. Yoder, *He Came Preaching Peace*, 72.
15. Ibid., 85.
16. Yoder, "Armaments and Eschatology," 58.
17. Yoder, *He Came Preaching Peace*, 45.

1972 publication of *The Politics of Jesus* through to his 1988 essay, "Armaments and Eschatology," Yoder emphasized apocalyptic as a feature of the New Testament that bids us to see history as now cracked open and bearing new possibilities of action. On this basis, Yoder attacks consequentialist ethical reasoning, which neglects how the order of the world has been destabilized. We simply cannot justify violent action on the basis of presumed results if we are people who confess that time has been invaded by the one who non-violently defeated death. Yoder thus refuses to be embarrassed by the particularity of Jesus. Indeed, it is precisely attention to the particular Jesus that pushes us to see that all of history has been transfigured. Salvation has been lodged in our human history. Or, put another way, the particularity of Jesus's entry into history deconstructs consequentialist modes of ethical reasoning deemed universal, yet captive ultimately to a particular cosmology that sees the world as a closed system.[18] We can say, therefore, a resolute maintenance of theology's apocalyptic mood is a faithful response to the historical particularity of Jesus—the decisive entry of God into the world—and the cosmic re-ordering this interruption initiated.

Apocalyptic, as defined in this essay and informed by Yoder, responds to God's decisive, particular entry into history in his Son, an entrance around which all time is ordered and now can find its meaning. Apocalyptic is revelation (if the tautology can be excused). Apocalyptic is not chiefly concerned with the "end things" or timetables for the judgment of the world, rather apocalyptic marks the insertion of God's action within our world and so disrupts the view that our world is "one massive causal nexus with no loopholes."[19] Such an account of apocalyptic maintains a determinedly theological grasp on history, denying history any autonomy apart from God's agency and saving purposes. Without sufficient attention to "apocalyptic" the risk is that we court a self-enclosed account of history explicable without any reference to God. "The whole point of an apocalyptic style," states one recent writer on apocalyptic theology, "is precisely an unwillingness to grant history a status apart from God: It is God's story."[20] Toole's binding of apocalyptic to God's story is a reminder of Yoder's plea that apocalyptic is not a style reserved to the more exotic fringes of the Bible. Rather, it infuses the whole of Scripture.[21]

---

18. Kerr, *Christ, History and Apocalyptic*, 131. I am much indebted to this book at a number of points in my argument.

19. Yoder, "Ethics and Eschatology," 120.

20. Toole, *Waiting for Godot in Sarajevo*, 301 n. 16.

21. Yoder, "Ethics and Eschatology," 127.

A careful reader of Milbank will find precious few references to "apocalyptic." To be sure, Milbank talks of the "'interruption' of history by Christ and his bride, the Church, [as] the most fundamental of events, interpreting all other events."[22] But Milbank does not consistently deploy either the language or the mood of apocalyptic, and so it is not clear that his theology as a whole can either carry this sentence just quoted or chase all its implications. There are numerous reasons why we should not be surprised that Milbank is insufficiently seized by apocalyptic as a resource for theology. First, there is in Milbank's work a lack of sustained attention to biblical texts. We are unlikely to see anything as scriptural as *The Politics of Jesus* from Milbank's pen. If the Bible is the chief source for apocalyptic thinking this lack of scriptural reasoning is ultimately problematic. Second, I suspect that Milbank's inattention to the apocalyptic re-ordering of history is related in some way to his battles with extrinsicism and his desire to overcome any dualism between grace and nature. Linked here too is his unease with neo-orthodox accounts of revelation and a preference for revelation as the elevation of our reason rather than an interruption from without.[23] The very style of Milbank's theology is not one looking to be interrupted. Third, Milbank's inattention to apocalyptic is of a piece, I submit, with his neglect of the singular historicity of Jesus (more on which will be said below). It is apocalyptic that secures the historicity of Jesus as God's revelation in our time. The particularity of Jesus is not in competition with his universality. Just the opposite. The universality of Jesus is secured only by his particularity: the way to the universal is through the particular, and this universality at no point displaces his particularity. All of time and all of history can "be said to have its origin and content in the particular history of God's relation with humanity" revealed in the life, death, and resurrection of Christ.[24] Thus, Yoder writes, "[t]he particularity of incarnation is the universality of the good."[25]

Milbank risks displacing the particular contingency of Jesus by quickly moving from Christology to ecclesiology, occluding the former by his fascination with the latter. For Milbank, there is no chink of light between Christology and ecclesiology: the emphasis that Jesus's character "will entirely coincide in its representation with the new categories of the

---

22. Milbank, *Theology and Social Theory*, 388.
23. Milbank, "Knowledge," 24.
24. Kerr, *Christ, History and Apocalyptic*, 96.
25. Yoder, "'But We Do See Jesus,'" 39.

new ecclesial society" imperils the particular independence of Jesus.[26] What one finds in Milbank is what Nathan Kerr has recently diagnosed in Hauerwas: a prioritizing of ecclesiology ahead of Christology in a manner that encroaches upon the invasive and "*ongoing*" independence of Jesus.[27] About this move Milbank is quite candid: "there is a priority to ecclesiology" and "a primarily Christological context for Christology cannot take us very far."[28]

The direction of Milbank's theology therefore leaves him pointing to the particularity of Jesus standing "almost, as a mere cipher" to his universality.[29] If Jesus had what Milbank calls a radical "specificity" it seems now absorbed by the church.[30] Thus, in his essay "The Name of Jesus," Milbank argues that the gospels are best read not as the story of Jesus, but of the foundation of a new community. The problem here from a Yoderian perspective is that given the church's peccability, the authority of the earthly Jesus is likely always to be displaced in evolutionary understandings of the church's life.[31] Moreover, the Cyrilline insight that "[i]n this particular person, in this particular life, in this particular story, divine and human, God's reality and our reality are indissolubly and redemptively one" (from which Yoder would not demur) is imperilled by seeing the Word as any kind of draining energy upon the flesh of Jesus.[32] Worryingly, Milbank says "the effect of implying that a person situated within the world is also, in himself, our total situation . . . is to evacuate that person of any particular, specifiable context."[33] In contrast to Yoder who charges history with significance through his emphasis on Jesus's apocalyptic appearance, Milbank's Jesus remains elusively abstract, the particular and the historic always being subsumed by the larger metaphysical picture he presumes to sketch. One suspects with Stanley Hauerwas "that sometimes Milbank does ontology when he ought to be listening to Jesus."[34] For Milbank Christology melts into ecclesiology. For Yoder, the strength of a high Christology—*God* becoming

26. Milbank, *Future of Love*, 349.

27. Kerr, *Christ, History and Apocalyptic*, 104 (emphasis added). See also Milbank, *Future of Love*, 341, "God's self-disclosure does not precede liturgy."

28. Milbank, *Word Made Strange*, 148. See also Milbank, *Theology and Social Theory*, 387.

29. Milbank, *Word Made Strange*, 149.

30. Milbank, *Being Reconciled*, 103.

31. Yoder, *Jewish-Christian Schism Revisited*, 139.

32. Yeago, "Crucified Also for Us under Pontius Pilate." 92.

33. Milbank, *Word Made Strange*, 150.

34. Hauerwas, "Explaining Christian Nonviolence," 176.

flesh in this world—is measured by the force with which it pushes us to the concrete demands of Jesus. Abstraction from the humanity of Jesus, in the manner of Milbank, risks de-politicizing his life and ministry precisely in the ways that Yoder's *The Politics of Jesus* was designed to counter. In riveting his attention to the teaching and life of Jesus, Yoder insists that he is only being more Chalcedonian than those who dwell over long on the two-natures debate.[35]

We need to be clear what we are saying here. Yoder writes that for those attracted to ontologically-driven Christology there is a tendency for their writing to imply that the incarnation had "to happen somewhere and sometime, but to attend to that particularity would be a distraction from the ontological mystery of the majesty."[36] In line with this, Milbank speaks of the importance of the concreteness of Jesus's practice yet his ultimate interest is more in casting a panoptical vision than attending to the particularities of the Gospel stories.[37] Again, Yoder writes of the Alexandrian Christologies Milbank is drawn to, that Jesus had to become human of course but "[i]t does not much matter what kind of human he was."[38] Sidelined here is Jesus's humanity as the locus of communication, the place where God makes known to humans new possibilities of being. Milbank is enthralled by the universalism of the gospel much more than he is its radical particularity, fearing seemingly its "fetishization."[39] The emphasis is on Christ as "the *infinite* particular, the concrete *universal*," rather than "the infinite *particular*, the *concrete* universal."[40] For Milbank, the sheer universalism of Christianity relativizes its necessary particularity.[41]

Theologies that absorb Christology into ecclesiology could reasonably be expected to absorb Israel into the church, denying Israel its particularity. Accordingly, a measure of Milbank's drive towards universalism, short-circuiting the particularity of God's action in Jesus, is his well-documented inattention to Jews and Judaism. Indeed, little of Milbank's project seems

---

35. Yoder would be unmoved by the charge of Horton that Milbank seems close to the Monophysite error. But such a critique is doubtless related to the concern that Milbank seems insufficiently attentive to the particularity of Jesus. See Horton, *Covenant and Salvation*, 171, and Milbank, "Sophiology and Theurgy," 80.
36. Yoder, "Historiography as a Ministry to Renewal," 216.
37. Milbank, *Word Made Strange*, 165.
38. Yoder, *Preface to Theology*, 220.
39. Milbank, *Future of Love*, 286.
40. Milbank, "The Double Glory," 187 (emphasis added).
41. See Milbank, "Materialism and Transcendence," 400.

The Poverty of Radical Orthodoxy

to rely on Jesus being *Jewish* flesh. That Jesus had to become human is clear in Milbank's work. That Jesus was made Jewish flesh is not so clear. Equally, one will not find much reference to the Old Testament in Milbank's writing.[42] Such sustained inattention to the branch that supports Christian faith is in marked contrast to Yoder, whose *The Jewish-Christian Schism Revisited* represents an assertion that attentiveness to the Jewishness of Christianity is not a matter of good inter-faith manners but is historically and theologically justifiable.[43]

Scott Bader-Saye argues that Milbank's "Israel forgetfulness" is the outcome of his binary logic which asks us to choose between Christendom and the nihilism of late modernity. With such a division there seems precious little space for those who Yoder calls "non-non-Christians."[44] Milbank's "inattention to the Jews" and the "compulsive singularity of his rhetoric . . . are correlated and mutually reinforcing."[45] Equally, we can see that Milbank's fixing on Christianity's "absolutely universal claim" is of a piece with his call to "transcend[ing] . . . the Jewish legacy."[46] Echoing our critique above, Bader-Saye diagnoses that Milbank's ontological metanarrative has pushed the Jews out of the story imperilling the permanent difference they are to make to the whole. "Milbank's God turns out to have little in common with the God of Abraham, Isaac, and Jacob."[47] There is accordingly scant recognition in Milbank that Judaism relates to Christianity in a different manner to all other religions, including Islám. Thus, although Milbank is right to point out the mutations of Israel's elect status in the hands of American Evangelicals,[48] he is wrong not to use this opportunity to point out the *continuing* elect status of the Jews (something to be fair, that Yoder could have also said more loudly).

Once again, Yoder reminds us that particularity and universality are neither competitive nor successive, as if the particularity of Jesus or Israel could be sloughed off like old skin. Indeed, the universal thrust of

---

42. See Horton, *Covenant and Salvation*, 162, "It is easy to gain the impression from Milbank's work that anything valuable in the Old Testament mist be salvaged from its Hebraic soil and be transplanted in Hellenic thought."

43. Milbank positively responds to criticisms of his "Israel forgetfulness" (the phrase is Kendall Soulen's) in Milbank, *Future of Love*, 170.

44. Yoder, *Jewish-Christian Schism Revisited*, 147–59.

45. Bader-Saye, "Haunted by the Jews," 203.

46. Milbank, "Materialism and Transcendence," 400.

47. Bader-Saye, *Church and Israel After Christendom*, 19.

48. Milbank, *Future of Love*, 231.

the gospel is secured by a more determined attention to its particularity. Yoder and Milbank are both keen to expose the heralded universalism of modernity as provincial and false. Yet it is Yoder's attention to the Jew Jesus who calls us to a way of seeing how asserting Christianity's concern for the whole need not come at the expense of its historical rootedness: "It was the Jewishness of Jesus, the rootage of his message in the particular heritage of Abraham, Moses, and Jeremiah, which ... made it good news for the whole world ... Only the Jewish claim that the one true God, known to Abraham's children through their history, was also the Creator and sustainer of the other peoples as well, could enable mission without provincialism, cosmopolitan vision without empire."[49]

With the help of Yoder, we can therefore identify a number of shortcomings in Milbank's attention to Jesus. But as the different loci of theology are always interconnected, we should expect any Christological shortcomings to spill over into other aspects of Milbank's work. This is indeed what we can see when we turn to Milbank's articulation of the church and the office of theology.

The Vulnerability of the Church and the Theologian

Yoder and Milbank read the time in which we are now in, and the implications for church and theology, very differently. Given that Yoder dwelt much more on Christianity's apocalyptic nature, this different reading of the times is not surprising. For Yoder, the collapse of trust in universal reason unmasks that which is always true: universal visions must be expressed in particular language. There is no bypassing vulnerable particularity. The church, like Jesus, should embody vulnerability. For Milbank, "the end of a single system of truth based on universal reason" is an opportunity to rediscover the truth that "Christianity *is* Christendom."[50] Where Milbank tries to "out-narrate," Yoder moves the church and theology to learn again, especially from the Jews, what it means to be "not in control."[51] Can a theology that wants to out-narrate take on the risk of not being in control, take on the vulnerability of communicating the good news?

---

49. Yoder, *Jewish-Christian Schism Revisited*, 75.

50. Milbank, *Future of Love*, 337, 273 (italics original).

51. Milbank, *Theology and Social Theory*, 330; Yoder, *Jewish-Christian Schism Revisited*, 168–79.

For Yoder, our post-Christendom context helps expose the deceit and error of what he calls "Constantinianism." This shift in the fourth century fused church and world, single-handedly confusing Christian ethics with ethics for everyone and baptizing a world, which in its freedom, should be accorded the status of unbelief. The one dualism Yoder will allow is between those who confess "Jesus Christ as Lord" and those who do not. The error of Christendom was to blur this distinction, "denying to the non-confessing creation the freedom of unbelief."[52] Pleading that we do not read the signs of the times as "one more chance to state the Constantinian position in new terms," Yoder asks instead that we use our time to let the church be the church.[53] The present time is therefore an opportunity for the church to rediscover its faithfulness. The church needs to be distinct from the world in which it witnesses, for if what we mean by "church" is as wide as what we mean by "society" or "world" then there is little point in talking of the new community as "itself the work of God."[54] Equally, the church needs to wrestle free from notions of being in charge if it is to re-capture the visions of history and faithful action within history brought to view by those who know that are not in charge. Christendom is a *theological* error, one which tempted, and even now tempts, the church to get its handles on history. All habits of Christendom and all habits that seek to be in control are a form of forgetting that the church is most responsive to time, as it now is when it gets its hands off history.

Accordingly, Yoder would likely have little time for Milbank's talk of sacralizing society, of opening society up to a sense of the transcendent and of re-invigorating parish life.[55] Yoder's vision of the church stands as a "suspended middle" between the spiritualizing tendencies of evangelicalism and the theocratic tendencies of baptizing all of society.[56] For Yoder, uniting church and society risks occluding the distinctiveness of the community that is the good news. Thus, Yoder resists the rehabilitation of the parish model, a model which confuses "common commitment" with "geographical contiguity."[57] Such drives towards universalism bypass the question of how God cares for the whole: through election, through the calling of a

---

52. Yoder, *Royal Priesthood*, 109.
53. Ibid., 64.
54. Ibid., 74.
55. See Milbank, *Future of Love*, 273.
56. I am here borrowing from Milbank, *Suspended Middle*.
57. Yoder, *Royal Priesthood*, 99.

particular people, Israel and the church, and allegiance to a particular Jew, Jesus. The church is diasporic before it is territorial.[58] Milbank might suppose that particularity is a way of bypassing the universal implications of the gospel. But as we have seen, a Yoderian perspective highlights this as the wrong kind of dualism, supposing that particularity and universalism are somehow in opposition. The particular demands that flow from the confession of Jesus as Lord are in step with "the way the world really is."[59]

Equally, Yoder would likely be baffled by Milbank speaking of the inevitability of "Christian universalism" breaking out across the world under the steam of providence and of the consequent need to "rethink Christendom."[60] From a Yoderian perspective the church *should expect* to find itself in a minority position, not because of the oddness of its doctrines, but because of the sheer perversity of its behavior. The world is not successfully run along the principles of loving your enemies or refusing to take up arms. Pacifism cannot be anything other than a "minority lifestyle in the midst of a violent world that the Church cannot dominate."[61]

Yoder's minority stance means that he is free from the anxiety that surrounds those whose context over-determines their theology. We have in Yoder, more than we have in Milbank, a theology that carries on as if "nothing has happened,"[62] determinedly attentive to God's revelation in Christ. Mennonites, never having ruled, simply don't have to worry about out-narrating other discourses. But this historical circumstance reveals a theological truth. We can speak of epistemological violence as much as physical violence: there is a kind of foundationalist or apologetic theology that signals an evasion from the God who *risks*, out of love, leaving us free.[63] Just as the incarnation is about the vulnerable revealing of God's self in "the concrete historical reality of the life and death and rising of Jesus" so the manner of the church's communication must be contingent, local, vulnerable, and prone to going awry.[64] The vulnerability of the church and its communication—a task in which theologians have a share—is brought

---

58. Barber, "Epistemological Violence," 288.
59. Yoder, *Royal Priesthood*, 131.
60. Suriano, "Three Questions on Modern Atheism." 66.
61. Yoder, *Jewish-Christian Schism Revisited*, 128.
62. Barth, *Theological Existence Today!*, 9.
63. Yoder, *Preface to Theology*, 310. The phrase "epistemological violence" is used by Barber, "Epistemological Violence."
64. Yoder, "Historiography as a Ministry to Renewal," 217.

The Poverty of Radical Orthodoxy

out much more robustly by Yoder than Milbank.[65] If the truth that has been revealed to us is the vulnerability of a God on a cross then there must be a vulnerability in how we communicate with those around us.[66] Being vulnerable to the language in which one finds oneself is very different from presuming that one must out-narrate it.

The challenge for Christians is to articulate the significance of Jesus from within the particular context in which they find themselves rooted. A search for a foundation, universally accessible, is nothing less than a form of coercion (and so is violent). Just as Jesus becoming flesh entailed a vulnerable submission to the world's freedom to reject or accept the Word, so must the Evangel be similarly vulnerable: "Rejection, according to the 'news' brought by Jesus and his witnesses, is part of the validation. This is where the foundationalists cannot follow. They want to tailor their message for a 'world out there' which they trust will be willing to and will in fact have to listen... The Good News of the Logos, on the other hand, accepts as the price of its communicability that it must suffer at the hands of the addressees."[67]

Yoder would agree with Milbank that in Christian communication there is no such thing as a "pure" Christian language of peace, mercy, love, and so on. Christian language is always to a certain borrowed. It has no choice if it is to communicate in the settings in which it finds itself. Yet at their convergence that "there is no sheerly Christian language," Milbank and Yoder diverge.[68] For where Milbank wants to out-narrate, Yoder wants to convey the news non-coercively. Where one speaks almost of boxing in opponents, the other has considered more deeply what it is to communicate the good news. To out-narrate for Yoder would be coercive and go against the grain of the news, which must be communicated vulnerably and received freely. The attraction towards Christianity as a universal presence occludes in Milbank's work how this universality is always bound to vulnerable particularity. In this kind of universalism, Daniel Barber writes, "a particularity does not explain itself—it does not 'tell' itself—as one particularity among others, it explains itself as the universal horizon of all particularities."[69] In this connection it is not hard to see a certain apologetic

---

65. See Hyman, *Predicament of Postmodern Theology*, 65–94.
66. Yoder, *Jewish-Christian Schism Revisited*, 142.
67. Yoder, "On Not Being Ashamed of the Gospel," 293.
68. Milbank, "Programme of Radical Orthodoxy," 37.
69. Barber, "Epistemological Violence," 283. Barber's essay is key to the point I am making in this paragraph.

thrust to Milbank's omnivorous intellectual appetite. Yoder may not speak much directly of secularism or capitalism, but that does not mean he has nothing to say about these powers. It simply means that his theology is not over-determined by them in a way that polemical theologies like Milbank's tend to be. In not being over-determined by these powers, Yoder ends up outflanking them, in contrast to Milbank who ends up squaring the false universalism of secularism with his own claims to universalism.

How is the theologian to understand her role along these lines? The theologian's language is not for Yoder somehow superior to that of the community of faith. Milbank famously said "the theologian feels almost that the entire ecclesial task falls on his own head,"[70] in one rhetorical flourish imperilling the force of his emphasis on the ecclesia. Such an exalted role clearly contrasts with the more modest role of Yoder as a theologian. Just as God in Christ wills not to be in control, just as the pacifist church trusts that it need not be in control, so too a theologian must strive to not be in control. Theologians should find themselves carried along the ebb and flow of their confessional communities. This contrasts to those theologies of management, which would seek to get a handle on things. In a memorable image Yoder writes that "[t]he task of the theologian is not to impose upon continuing development the deductively ineluctable determinations of his seed idea, after the model of an inertial guidance system whereby a missile knows, when it leaves the silo in Nebraska, which Russian city is to be destroyed."[71] Theology is not something more determinative than the church's faith and the church's task. It is not hard to imagine that upon reading Milbank's work, Yoder would say of Milbank something similar to what he said of Paul Tillich, that "[h]is concern was to demonstrate how his own frame of reference could master and encompass everyone else's, whereby the internal coherence of his system, he claimed, validated itself, standing above communities."[72]

The Vulnerability of Christian Pacifism

From a Yoderian perspective, the shortcomings in Milbank's project come to a head in his reaction against Christian pacifism. Such a response to pacifism might seem surprising given the considerable emphasis given to

70. Milbank, *Word Made Strange*, 1.
71. Yoder, *Royal Priesthood*, 120.
72. Yoder, "Thinking Theologically," 255.

the ontology of peace in the final chapter of *Theology and Social Theory*. Yet, just as for Yoder pacifism is not a "position" one holds in isolation from discipleship and fellowship in the church,[73] so too, for Milbank, we cannot detach his resistance to pacifism from the shortcomings we have identified in his Christology and ecclesiology.

The most extensive critique Milbank launches against pacifism can be found in the chapter "Violence: Double Passivity" in *Being Reconciled*. Following on from his argument that evil is to be seen as the privation of good, Milbank holds that evil and violence are not to be regarded as synonymous terms. Violence is however always vulnerable to conversion to evil and every use of violence must be interrogated with that in mind. What is violent must be *discerned*. Launching his critique of pacifism Milbank states that the pacifist embodies the Western predilection merely to gaze rather than squarely counter violence when it is directed towards evil. At this point it is worth quoting Milbank at length:

> The pacifist elects to gaze at violence, and he maintains this stance even if he turns his face away from a violent spectacle, since it persists in his memory. But in fact, this question of averting one's gaze also points towards the issue which I will return to later concerning the counter-intuitive character of the pacifist outlook . . . For if the pacifist is confronted with an act of violence against the innocent which he is not going to meet with counter-violence . . . then does he stay and watch, or does he shrink quietly away into his prayers? If he does the latter, if he averts his gaze, then how will not the innocent, catching this act out of the corner of their terrified eyes, not perceive here the signifiers of indifference or embarrassment? On the other hand, if he stays to watch, how will they not discern in his gaze of pious sorrow a trace of the non-intervening voyeur?[74]

Accordingly, Milbank argues that pacifism is *more violent* than well-directed acts of counter violence. Pacifism is caught within the gaze of violence, caught in the act of giving violence more than its due rather than combating it.[75]

From a Yoderian perspective, there are a number of ways we could criticize Milbank's limited justification of violence. I highlight four.

First, any "justified" use of violence assumes that we can sight down the line to see the results of deploying violent means. This is the lure of

73. Hauerwas, "Explaining Christian Nonviolence."
74. Milbank, *Being Reconciled*, 28.
75. Ibid., 29.

effectiveness and precisely the failure to see that history is apocalyptically charged. Yoderian pacifism refuses to see a straight line between obedience and effectiveness. Indeed, for those who prioritize obedience above effectiveness, there is no option to "sight down the line of our obedience to the attainment of the ends we seek."[76] The relationship between obedience and effectiveness is to be traced along the way that leads from the cross to the empty tomb.[77] Precisely because of his apocalyptic politics, Yoder has a firm grasp on time as interrupted by the peace of God in Jesus. Action cognizant of time as it now is looks different from those whose action is uninformed by this interruption. In contrast, Milbank sees the peace of Christ as alarmingly deferred, as "primarily . . . eschatological."[78] For Yoder, the church is pacifist precisely because it responds faithfully to the Christ who has re-ordered our time and because it shares now in his reign.[79] The church's responsibilities are not to be confused with what the state sees it as its responsibilities, unless we wish to succumb to the Christendom error. In contrast to the eschatological deferment of peace that we see in Milbank, the church for Yoder "is called now to be what the world is called ultimately to be."[80] Criticizing the tragic note sounded in Milbank's theology over the use of violence, Toole accurately states therefore that "to oppose peaceableness as a virtue to peaceableness as an eschatological goal is to depart from an apocalyptic eschatology and an apocalyptic politics."[81] A rather different account of time is at work in Milbank, caught as it is within (Niebuhrian) terms of responsibility. Thus, Milbank accuses pacifists of failing to protect the fragile, fleeting appearance of good in time, of "trying to leap out of our finitude, embodiment and fragility."[82]

Second, in justifying the use of coercion by the church in earlier centuries, Milbank displays the weakness of his ecclesiology. Milbank mischievously aligns the coercion of the national curriculum with the coercion of premodern churches, justifying "in certain ways" the violence of the church's past.[83] Unresolved here is just in what kind of ways? Was the burning of

76. Yoder, *Original Revolution*, 154.
77. Yoder, *Politics of Jesus*, 238.
78. Hauerwas and Milbank, "Christian Peace." 211.
79. Yoder, *Preface to Theology*, 277.
80. Yoder, "Neither Guerilla nor Conquista." 106.
81. Toole, *Waiting for Godot in Sarajevo*, 83. See Milbank, *Word Made Strange*, 31.
82. Milbank, *Being Reconciled*, 40.
83. Ibid., 37.

The Poverty of Radical Orthodoxy

Servetus correct, but the drowning of women accused of being witches not? For Milbank, the church properly resorts to justified coercion as a matter of "self-belief."[84] Yet the church is not primarily a community that believes in itself in isolation from its trust in God, and nor is the church's endurance something that lies ultimately in the church's hands. Jesus needs no defense, and the truth of his work and person is not something the church possesses, like a treasure to be defended, but a reality which the church *confesses*.[85]

Third, there is a problem with the limits of Milbank's universalism. Although Milbank is, as we have argued, ultimately fascinated with the universalism of Christianity, he does not pursue all of the more radical implications of this confession. Part of the curiosity of Milbank's allergy to pacifism is that although he speaks of Christianity as a universal religion, he does not follow the logic of this conviction when it comes to the use of violence. Arguing that we are justified in the use of violence to defend those most near to us (does he mean those who share the same nationality?), Milbank misses the more radical thrust of Christianity's universalism: that fellowship within the church should trump any justification for killing Christians unfortunate enough not to share our nationality. For all his talk of universalism, Milbank does not reap perhaps one of the most pregnant implications of membership of the worldwide body of Christ and of our fellowship with all those made in the image of God: nonviolence. The implications of confessing belief in the church universal beckons a fundamental suspicion of the determination of our responsibilities around the preserve of the nation-state or a principle like "democracy," a suspicion that for Yoder can only lead to pacifism.[86]

Fourth, in arguing that the defense of the good or protection of the weak justifies the use of force, one notices the shortcomings of not attending to the concrete humanity of Jesus at this point of his argument. According to Yoder, it is not unjust violence that Jesus rejects—that would only limit the scope of his challenge. What Jesus rejects is precisely violence in the pursuit of just ends.[87] It is thus not surprising that in his dismissal of pacifism, Milbank does not at this point think Jesus displays an "exemplary practice which we can imitate."[88]

84. Ibid., 38.
85. Yoder, *Jewish-Christian Schism Revisited*, 142.
86. Yoder, *He Came Preaching Peace*, 23.
87. Yoder, *Original Revolution*, 130–31.
88. Milbank, *Theology and Social Theory*, 396.

Conclusion

With the help of Yoder and the kind of thinking he ignites, we can then identify a number of shortcomings in Milbank's project, in his Christology, his ecclesiology, his account of theology, and his rejection of pacifism. That such a Yoderian critique of Milbank is possible only makes more baffling Gregory Baum's description of Milbank's work as Anabaptist.[89] To be sure, both Yoder and Milbank are radical theologians, in that both seek to return to the roots of the faith. But the point to which Milbank returns is precisely when Christianity was beginning to forget how its universality was bound up with its non-negotiable particularity. The result is that Milbank is left in a staring match with modernity, setting its false universalism against the universalism of Christianity, a universalism bereft, it seems, of much vulnerable particularity. The problem with this is it ends up accepting the terms of the debate as set by modernity. *More* radical still is the haunting challenge Yoder's work leaves us with in our post-secular context: is there not a "a better way to restate the meaning of a truth claim from within particular identity"?[90]

Bibliography

Bader-Saye, Scott. *Church and Israel After Christendom: The Politics of Election*. Eugene, OR: Wipf and Stock, 1999.

———. "Haunted by the Jews: Hauerwas, Milbank, and the Decentred Diaspora Church." In *Unsettling Arguments: A Festschrift on the Occasion of Stanley Hauerwas's 70th Birthday*, edited by Charles R. Pinches, Kelly S. Johnson, and Charles M. Collier, 191–209. Eugene, OR: Cascade, 2010.

Barber, Daniel Colucciello. "Epistemological Violence, Christianity, and the Secular." In *The New Yoder*, edited by Peter Dula and Chris K. Huebner, 271–93. Eugene, OR: Cascade, 2010.

Barth, Karl. *Theological Existence Today! A Plea for Theological Freedom*. Translated by R. Birch Hoyle. London: Hodder and Stoughton, 1933.

Baum, Gregory. "For and Against John Milbank." In *Essays in Critical Theology*, edited by Gregory Baum, 52–76. Kansas City, MO: Sheed & Ward, 1994.

Hauerwas, Stanley. "Explaining Christian Nonviolence." In *Must Christianity Be Violent? Reflections on History, Practice, and Theology*, edited by Kenneth R. Chase and Alan Jacobs, 172–82. Grand Rapids: Brazos, 2003.

89. Baum, "For and Against John Milbank." 54.

90. Yoder, "On Not Being Ashamed of the Gospel," 290. See here the pregnant chapter of Barber, "Epistemological Violence," although I worry over his downplaying of the necessarily cosmic nature of the Christian gospel.

Hauerwas, Stanley, and John Milbank. "Christian Peace." In *Must Christianity Be Violent? Reflections on History, Practice, and Theology*, edited by Kenneth R. Chase and Alan Jacobs, 207–23. Grand Rapids: Brazos, 2003.

Holcomb, Justin S. "Being Bound to God: Participation and Covenant Revisited." In *Radical Orthodoxy and the Reformed Tradition: Creation, Covenant, and Participation*, edited by James K. A. Smith and James H. Olthuis, 243–62. Grand Rapids: Baker Academic, 2005.

Horton, Michael. *Covenant and Salvation: Union with Christ*. Louisville: Westminster John Knox, 2007.

Hyman, Gavin. *The Predicament of Postmodern Theology: Radical Orthodoxy or Nihilist Textualism?* Louisville: Westminster John Knox, 2001.

Huebner, Chris K., and Tripp York. *The Gift of Difference: Radical Orthodoxy, Radical Reformation*. Winnipeg: Canadian Mennonite University Press, 2010.

Kerr, Nathan. *Christ, History and Apocalyptic*. Theopolitical Visions. Eugene, OR: Cascade, 2009.

Milbank, John. "The Double Glory, or Paradox Versus Dialectics: On Not Quite Agreeing with Slavoj Žižek." In *The Monstrosity of Christ: Paradox or Dialectic?*, edited by Creston Davis, 110–233. Cambridge: MIT Press, 2009.

———. *The Future of Love: Essays in Political Theology*. Eugene, OR: Cascade, 2009.

———. "Knowledge: The Theological Critique of Philosophy in Hamann and Jacobi." In *Radical Orthodoxy: A New Theology*, edited by John Milbank, Catherine Pickstock, and Graham Ward, 21–37. London: Routledge, 1999.

———. "Materialism and Transcendence." In *Theology and the Political: The New Debate*, edited by Creston Davis, John Milbank, and Slavoj Žižek, 393–426. Durham, NC: Duke University Press, 2005.

———. "The Programme of Radical Orthodoxy." In *Radical Orthodoxy? A Catholic Enquiry*, edited by Laurence Paul Hemming, 33–45. Aldershot: Ashgate, 2000.

———. *Being Reconciled: Ontology and Pardon*. Radical Orthodoxy Series. London: Routledge, 2003.

———. "Sophiology and Theurgy: The New Theological Horizon." In *Encounter Between Eastern Orthodoxy and Radical Orthodoxy: Transfiguring the World Through the Word*, edited by Adrian Pabst and Christoph Schneider, 45–85. Farnham: Ashgate, 2009.

———. *The Suspended Middle: Henri de Lubac and the Debate Concerning the Supernatural*. London: SCM, 2005.

———. *Theology and Social Theory: Beyond Secular Reason*. Signposts in Theology. London: Blackwell, 1990.

———. *The Word Made Strange: Theology, Language, Culture*. Oxford: Blackwell, 1997.

Suriano, Ben. "Three Questions on Modern Atheism: An Interview with John Milbank." In *"God is Dead" and I Don't Feel So Good Myself: Theological Engagements with the Secular*, edited by Andrew David, Christopher J. Keller, and Jon Stanley, 58–66. Eugene, OR: Cascade, 2010.

Toole, David. *Waiting for Godot in Sarajevo: Theological Reflections on Nihilism, Tragedy, and Apocalypse*. Radical Traditions. London: SCM, 1998.

Yeago, David S. "Crucified Also for Us under Pontius Pilate: Six Propositions on the Preaching of the Cross." In *Nicene Christianity: The Future for a New Ecumenism*, edited by Christopher R. Seitz, 87–105. Grand Rapids: Brazos, 2001.

Yoder, John Howard. "Armaments and Eschatology." *Studies in Christian Ethics* 1 (1988) 43–61.

———. "'But We Do See Jesus': The Particularity of Incarnation and the Universality of Truth." In *A Pacifist Way of Knowing: John Howard Yoder's Nonviolent Epistemology*, edited by Christian E. Early and Ted G. Grimsrud, 22–39. Eugene, OR: Cascade, 2010.

———. *Discipleship as Political Responsibility*. Translated by Timothy J. Geddert. Scottdale, PA: Herald, 2003.

———. "Ethics and Eschatology." *Ex Auditu* 6 (1990) 119–28.

———. "The Free Church Syndrome." In *With the Perfection of Christ: Essays on Pace and the Nature of the Church*, edited by Terry L. Brensinger and E. Morris Sider, 169–76. Nappanee: Evangel, 1990.

———. *He Came Preaching Peace*. Scottdale, PA: Herald, 1985.

———. "Historiography as a Ministry to Renewal." *Brethren Life and Thought* 3 (1997) 216–28.

———. *The Jewish-Christian Schism Revisited*. Edited by Michael G. Cartwright and Peter Ochs. Radical Traditions. London: SCM, 2003.

———. "Neither Guerilla nor Conquista: The Presence of the Kingdom as Social Ethic." In *Peace, Politics, and the People of God*, edited by Paul Peachey, 95–116. Philadelphia: Fortress Press, 1986.

———. "On Not Being Ashamed of the Gospel: Particularity, Pluralism, and Validation." *Faith and Philosophy* 9 (1992) 285–300.

———. *The Original Revolution: Essays on Christian Pacifism*. Scottdale, PA: Herald, 2003.

———. "Politics: Liberating Images of Christ." In *Imaging Christ: Politics, Art, Spirituality*, edited by F. A. Eogo, 149–69. Villanova: Villanova University Publications, 1991.

———. *The Politics of Jesus: Vicit Agnus Noster*. Grand Rapids: Eerdmans, 1972.

———. *Preface to Theology: Christology and Theological Method*. Grand Rapids: Brazos, 2002.

———. *The Priestly Kingdom: Social Ethics as Gospel*. Notre Dame, IN: University of Notre Dame Press, 1984.

———. "The Prophetic Task of Pastoral Ministry: The Gospels." In *The Pastor as Prophet*, edited by Earl E. Shelp and Ronald H. Sutherland, 78–98. New York: Pilgrim, 1985.

———. *The Royal Priesthood: Essays Ecclesiological and Ecumenical*. Edited by Michael G. Cartwright. Scottdale, PA: Herald, 1998.

———. "Thinking Theologically from a Free-Church Perspective." In *Doing Theology in Today's World: Essays in Honor of Kenneth S. Kantzer*, edited by John D. Woodbridge and Thomas Edward McComiskey, 251–65. Grand Rapids: Zondervan, 1991.

8

Touch, Flux, Relation

Feminist Critique of Graham Ward's "The Schizoid Christ"[1]

Sigridur Gudmarsdottir

> *"Who touched me?"*
> MARK 5:30

The crowd comes to a halt.[1] So far, they have traveled with speed to the house of one Jairus, whose daughter is ill. They stop because he stops. He stops because a hand has dared to touch him. Time stands still and so does Jesus. He will not leave until he gets an answer. And hesitantly, she comes forth, telling her story about a touch.

In the essay "The Schizoid Christ," Ward appropriates the story of the hemorrhaging woman in Mark 5:24–35 in order to frame his inquiry into the intricate operations of Christ. Ward writes: "Our thinking-through of central concepts in a doctrine of Christ—incarnation, atonement and

---

1. An earlier version of the article has been published in Icelandic, "Rof-Kristur og konan með blóðlátin: Tengsl Krists og samtíma af sjónarhóli Grahams Ward og kvennaguðfræði."

community—emerges from a participation in which we are responding to representations of this figure. This participation and responding I will call the Christic operation."[2] Ward is emphatically not trying to explain questions about what Jesus really wanted or figure out Jesus's self-consciousness as the Christ. For him, such explorations into selfhood and identity presuppose the old liberal dream of the enlightened, unified self. Proposing not the historical Jesus, but the instances where people participate in Christ, Ward suggests three biblical characteristics of christic operations—touch, flows, and relation—and then uses the story of the hemorrhaging woman in Mark 5:24–34 to underscore those three themes.

Commenting on Paul's statement in Galatians 3:28, "There is neither Jew nor Greek . . ." Ward writes: "For that sentiment is read today in terms of democratizing of differences; Christ the leveler of hierarchies, liberator of the subjugated. And what my reading has sought to point out is how that is not so. The oneness is in Christ and it does not concern the equality of social positions."[3] For the radically orthodox and post-feminist Ward, the woman who bleeds and touches Jesus, becomes a trigger for touch and flow dynamics of relation, which help to bring out the operations of Christ. Like Ward, many feminist biblical scholars and theologians are interested in the interaction between Jesus and the touch and flow of the woman, but from angles more sensitive to social location and gender oppression, which Ward finds irrelevant to oneness in Christ. Mark 5:24–35 often serves as a frame to women's particular probing into oppressions and resistances through which culture and the Christian message are formed.

How schizoid is Ward's schizoid Christ exactly? I am intrigued by Ward's proposal of using Deleuzian/Guattarian schizoanalysis for doing relational Christology. However, I would like the christic schizoid to be able to wander further into "social positions" and "economies of response" than he is allowed in his articulation of the christic schizo. First, I maintain that it would strengthen Ward's argument of the christic operations if the feminist analyzes of patriarchal oppression were taken into account. Probing the unequal interactions between a Jewish rabbi and a ritually impure woman would, in my view, serve to distinguish the social channels of flow and the clots that impede such flows in the body of Christ. I also want to point out Ward's insistence upon the hierarchy between creator and the created, which is reiterated in his interpretation of the relationship between

---

2. See Ward's essay "The Schizoid Christ" in *Christ and Culture*, 61.
3. Ibid., 89.

the male Jesus and the woman. In spite of Ward's poststructuralist inclination and his stress on flow, I argue that his image of Christ the schizo takes on more stable, hierarchical, and one-directional dimensions than the fluid, horizontal, and multidirectional. Thus, in order to explore some of the possibilities left open by Ward's taunting figure of the schizoid Christ, I turn to two sources: the poststructuralist thinkers from whom Ward inherits the figure of the schizo, and the feminist theologians who work with the figure of the hemorrhaging woman.

Christ the Schizo

Ward borrows the figure of the schizo from the psychoanalyst Félix Guattari and the philosopher Gilles Deleuze in order to probe christic operations that he finds flowing from the body of Christ. Instead of psychoanalysis, which for Deleuze and Guattari is yet another example of a philosophical method pervaded with transcendence, they suggest schizoanalysis in order to express multiplicities, flows, and heterogeneities. In *Anti-Oedipus Capitalism and Schizophrenia*, Deleuze and Guattari describe the schizo as the one "who scrambles all the codes and is the transmitter of the decoded flows of desire," someone who crisscrosses and operates at the binaries of the metaphysical processes of nature and the historical processes of culture: "As for the schizo, continually wandering about, migrating here, there, and everywhere as best he can, he plunges further and further into the realm of deterritorialization, reaching the furthest limits of the decomposition of the socius on the surface of his own body without organs. It may well be that these peregrinations are the schizo's own particular way of rediscovering the earth."[4]

For Deleuze and Guattari schizophrenia does not only appear as a mental illness, suffered by individuals and treated by psychiatrists, but rather functions as the "the malady of our era," a cultural production of contemporary social stratification, namely capitalism.[5] If the free flow of money and labor serves as the hallmark of capitalism, schizophrenia becomes for Deleuze and Guattari the surplus flow that does not fit into the channels of the twofold flows of capitalism, money, and workforce. As such, schizophrenia is a production of capitalism, but also the element that limits and threatens that very economic structure.

---

4. Deleuze and Guattari, *Anti-Oedipus*, 35.
5. Ibid., 34.

Ward draws similarities between the schizoanalytical ideas of *Anti-Oedipus* and themes and narratives of the Bible to bring out the relational aspect of Christology. Ward proposes to examine the situations where Jesus operates as the Christ, thus treating Christology as a "mobile site for the production of desire and belief, love and hope."[6] Ward points to several themes of flow in Mark 5. He considers the hemorrhaging woman to suffer from two kinds of consumption: biological and economical. Ward also points out that Jesus's body is connected to flows. Like Deleuze and Guattari's schizo, Jesus travels from place to place and often by boat; he has no place to stay, he has intimate connections to watery flows, blood and saliva (Mark 8:23), and healing power (*dynamis*) flows from him. Ward maintains that Jesus is usually in control over these powers. "This is why this encounter with the woman is so remarkable. For it is the woman's touch that initiates the healing that is discharged through the body of Jesus."[7]

Ward examines the way in which knowledge and physicality are interconnected in the story. The woman "knew in herself" that she was cured and Jesus likewise became "aware that power had gone out from him" (Mark 5:30). In Ward's interpretation this knowing desire, intimately felt in one's own body gives the woman power to step forth and tell the truth. Ward points out that the transformation where one flood stops and another one rechanneled is effected through touch. He writes: "Touch initiates transference, involving each in an economy of response that is rooted in the body and calls forth somatic knowledges of recognition . . . Touch gives particular direction to a body continually being situated relationally; it orientates and focuses the various fluid operations. Touch triggers a divine operation, an eschatological operation. It is an operation in which the messianic is performed."[8]

Ward evades the pit of allocating Jesus and the woman to the traditional binary of the dry and the fluid, the stable and the chaotic, the spiritual and the carnal, where the first concept of the binary would symbolically be linked in relation to the male in the Western theo/philosophical tradition and the latter one to the female. Instead, he stresses the fluidity, physicality, and instability of both bodies.

Ward's eschatological Christology of touch echoes in some ways the last words of *Anti-Oedipus,* in which Deleuze and Guattari invoke Nietzsche's

---

6. Ward, "The Schizoid Christ," 61.

7. Ibid., 50.

8. Ibid., 65.

Zarathustra. "We will never go too far with the deterritorialization, the decoding of flows. For the new earth ("In truth, the earth will one day become a place of healing") is not to be found in the neurotic or perverse reterritorializations that arrest the process or assign it goals; it is no more behind than ahead."[9] Deleuze and Guattari have no room for a new heaven in their schizoanalytical philosophy, but the new earth, as a place of healing, is a place of future hope in freedom, touch, flow, and relation that disturb, shift and decode political and libidinal economy. Ward's article, "The Schizoid Christ," is one of the articles grouped under the heading "The Economy of Response." If Ward is willing to use schizoanalysis to emphasize the christic operations of touch, flow, and relation for the eschatological community, the difference between his approach and Deleuze and Guattari's is also evident. If Deleuze and Guattari argue "it is no more behind than ahead," then Ward invokes John Milbank's "asymmetrical reciprocity" in his economy of response, and sets forth to safeguard the hierarchy between God and creation by insisting on a distinction between two levels of reality, the economic and immanent Trinity: "Christ, as the mediator of God to humankind and humankind to God, makes possible both the asymmetrical and symmetrical reciprocity, for the movements of Christ are both participations in the *perichoresis* that constitutes the impassable triune Godhead and the economic operations of that *perichoresis* with respect to creation itself."[10]

For Ward, insofar as the hemorrhaging woman speaks to God who has become human, she is able to trigger and participate in a new flow, which becomes a salvific christic operation. However, insofar as God is impassable in God's triune life, Ward argues that the relationship between the Creator and the created is necessarily asymmetrical and that humans can only respond to God. Ward writes: "In this reciprocity we must always observe a difference . . . The divine reaches out to the human, first and foremost; the human responds and, cooperating with the divine, glorifies God. The reciprocal relation issues from and is sustained by God. There is a priority here and that means there is a politics."[11] Ward's stance works on two levels. He argues that insofar as all social relationships are culturally mediated, hierarchies and social positions are bound to be upheld. However, insofar as all social relationships are supposed to succumb to Christ, they also point towards another kind of polity, which is a participation in

---

9. Deleuze and Guattari, *Anti-Oedipus*, 382.
10. Ward, "The Schizoid Christ," 83.
11. Ibid., 87.

oneness. Not surprisingly, Ward links his theo/political approach to the apophatic stroke of mystical theology, "knowing by unknowing, grasping by surrendering, fuelling a passion that is apathetic."[12]

By linking political theology to such a double plane of existence, according to human society or according to the kingdom of God, Ward manages to squeeze his Schizoid Christ into a familiar ontological pattern of mystical theology. He points out how Augustine uses the hemorrhaging woman as a symbol for the non-Jewish church.[13] In Augustine's interpretation the woman functions to bring out Jesus's mission as being a divine body to the Jewish people but absent to other nations. Augustine's Jesus is present to Jairus's daughter (synagogue) to whom he has been sent, but absent into the bleeding woman in the crowd (church), linking Jesus with the paradox of a historical, local body and "a power among all nations."[14] However, Augustine also wrote another sermon on the hemorrhaging woman. Her example becomes for Augustine the means through which the believer can enter into the sacred presence, move from the pressing throng to healing by touch. He writes: "Be ye than the Body of Christ, not the pressure of his Body. Ye have the border of his garment to touch, that ye may be healed of the issue of blood, that is, of *carnal pleasures* . . . Touch then if you are suffering from a bloody flux."[15] According to Augustine, excluded body becomes included body by touching the border and the woman becomes the body of Christ. Interestingly, one type of boundary in the Augustinian imagery is glaringly dry and concrete, the human body, denotes absence, affliction, pressing. Perhaps not coincidentally, that is left behind in the effort of becoming one with the body of Christ is a bleeding vagina. The divine presence will not be increased or changed by the woman's action, It stays the same, will only move her from one state to another, rearrange the fences in a known and mapped territory.

Ward's Christ is more fluid than Augustine's Christ. However, if humans can trigger the christic flows, the healing flow is one dimensional. Therefore I argue that Ward's political ontology in "The Schizoid Christ" is both Augustinian and Neoplatonic, but has little in common with Deleuzian/Guattarian schizoanalysis, which operates on one plane of immanence only. Deleuze and Guattari emphasize an ontology that is reciprocal and

12. Ibid., 89.
13. Ibid., 63.
14. Sermon XXVII, Philip Schaff, *Nicene and Post-Nicene Fathers VI*, 344f.
15. Sermon XII, Schaff, *Nicene and Post-Nicene Fathers VI*, 300.

multidimensional, non-hierarchical, and has no common origin. Ward's political ontology, however, presumes a flow from God to humans, which humans can trigger, but not share with the God-man. Ultimately, they receive, not him.

I have elsewhere discussed the possibility of poststructuralist Deleuzian kind of mystical ontology,[16] but the point I want to make in relation to Ward's position is this: Who gains by political ontology such as the one Ward is proposing? Kari Elisabeth Børresen has explored in depth the way in which two leveled doctrines of *imago dei* both served to give women access to full humanity and to secure a sanctified, submissive role for them within social hierarchies. According to this view, insofar as men and women lived according to their traditional social positions in the world, *femina* should be submissive to *vir*, a sub-male as it were. Only insofar as they take part in Christ, they are reckoned as fully human, *homo*, and created in the image of God.[17] If Børresen's analysis is correct, the ontological framework to which Ward so lovingly adheres, may bring less glad tidings to those on the lower end of the social ladder that those at the top. I am not suggesting that feminism and apophatic ontology have nothing in common and have written articles to the contrary.[18] As Ward points out, Christology is never apolitical. Therefore, if the Christ symbol does not function as the leveler of social hierarchies and transformer of social oppressive structures, it will function as the preserver of such hierarchies and oppressions. If anything good can come out of the traditional framework of Neoplatonic mystical theology in Christianity for the oppressed of the *polis*, such ontological proposition must, in my view, go hand-in-hand with careful analyses of social oppression.

Feminist Flows

Thus, since I am intrigued by Ward's idea of the fluid Christ (if not his ontological premises), I would like to dig deeper into the possibilities of a fluid Christology. I argue that analyses such as feminist readings of the biblical story would help bring out interesting ways which the schizoid, fluid Christ functions in the story of the bleeding woman. The hemorrhaging

16. See Gudmarsdottir, "God is a Lobster."

17. See Børresen, *Subordination and Equivalence*; and Børresen "God's Image, Man's Image?"

18. See Gudmarsdottir "The Sensible Unsaying of Mysticism"; Gudmarsdottir, "Feminist Apophasis."

woman appears in all three of the Synoptic gospels (Matthew 9:20–22, Mark 5:25–34, Luke 8:43–48). In all three accounts the story is framed by the account of Jairus's daughter; they all indicate the length of the woman's suffering (twelve years) and the age of Jairus's daughter (likewise twelve years). In all three stories Jesus calls the woman a daughter and the woman sneaks at Jesus from behind. The cause of illness ailing Jairus's daughter is never mentioned; however, her age of puberty is mentioned carefully in every story. Sexual organs, female illnesses, and filial relations link the two females as well as their sandwiching stories. Mark's account of the hemorrhaging woman is the most thorough of the three Synoptic Gospels. Luke follows Mark, but makes the account shorter. Luke softens Mark's negative view of the doctors who had made the woman worse, and in some Lukan manuscripts the references to doctors is eliminated altogether. Matthew's version of the story is the shortest and the role of the woman in the healing process is drastically reduced. Matthew keeps Mark's account of the woman talking to herself about touching Jesus (which Luke omitted). However, instead of the instant healing the woman felt after touching Jesus in Mark and Luke, (Mark mentions explicitly her feeling in her body), Matthew's healing does not occur until Jesus has turned and made the woman well. The Matthean word has superseded the Markan/Lukan touch of healing. In Mark, the woman tells Jesus the whole truth. Mark also uses the same word for the scourging of the woman in 5:29, 34 and the scourging of Jesus in 8:31 and 9:12.[19] Mark thus underscores certain likeness between the bleeding of Jesus and the woman, the testimony of Jesus and the testimony of the woman, which further supports Ward's argument of flow between bodies in the narrative of Mark 5.

Jesus's inquiry of the touch has traditionally been considered a rhetorical question. Thus, Jesus is seen as knowing all along who has touched him, but he wants the woman to make a public confession, to exclude any indication of magic or possible manipulation of divine powers by the bleeding woman.[20] The encounter of Jesus and the hemorrhaging woman has been of considerable interest to feminist commentators who usually interpret the question to indicate a genuine confusion of Jesus.[21] Instead

---

19. Reid, *Choosing the Better Part?*, 142.

20. Swete, *The Gospel According to St. Mark*, 104–5; Turlington, *The Broadman Bible Commentary Vol. 8*, 310; Perkins, "The Gospel of Mark," 588.

21. For further feminist commentaries on the story see for example, Tolbert, "Mark," 355; Dewey, "The Gospel of Mark," 481.

of Jesus as omniscient and forever in control, these commentators stress the rupture of the story, created by the initiative of the woman in her own healing, her own touch, her own boldness and faith.

The woman has been ill for a long time and has spent all her money going between doctors to find a cure. Her flow is draining her resources, both physically and economically. Ward depicts the woman as bent in on herself, thus in some ways suggesting her misery and estrangement are her own fault. He writes: "The woman's spring of blood (that has caged her in concern of herself, with her health, with spending all she has on the care of that self and trying to restore that self) dries up—because she enters into the flows of God's power. Participating now in a new dynamic economy—living out that appetitive and creative kenosis and *pleroma*—issues new asymmetrical and symmetrical reciprocities: the relationship that constitutes the body of Christ."[22] Ward is distrustful of an overemphasis of kenosis and points to the hemorrhaging woman as an example of an emptying out that is not productive. Feminist theologians such as Rebecca Parker and Joanne Carlson Brown have taken Ward's distrust of certain kenotic practices even further and argued against atonement theories in Christian theology.[23]

If Ward thus blames the woman's illness on her, Musa W. Dube envisions the hemorrhaging woman as Africa and her healing as "a persons's entire well-being: economic, political, social, spiritual, the physical body."[24] Dube uses feminist practices of reading from location in her focus on the suffering of the woman; her Africa is bleeding from economic and political exploitation. "In the year 1939, Africa woke up severely ill. She felt walls had entered into all of her body. She felt fenced, bound. Africa cried out saying, 'Take this thorn of suffering away from my flesh! Take it away!' And as she spoke, she began to bleed non-stop." [25] She has drained her financial resources in trying to find a cure to her illness, moving from one doctor to another. "Dr. Colonial Master," "Dr. Struggle-for-Independence," "Dr. Independence," have all provided her with bad and short-sighted remedies. Africa is still bleeding and has just been visiting "Dr. Neocolonialism" and "Dr. Global Village." She has AIDS and her children die in infancy. Then she hears of the healer Jesus, who is coming her way to heal a child already dead. Refusing to leave the open future, Dube writes: "Mama Africa

22. Ward, "The Schizoid Christ," 84.
23. Brown and Parker, "For God so Loved the World?," 36–59.
24. Dube, "Fifty Years of Bleeding," 60.
25. Ibid., 52.

is standing up. She is not talking. She is not asking. She is not offering any money—for none is left. Mama Africa is coming behind Jesus. She is pushing through a strong human barricade. Weak and still bleeding but determined, she is stretching out her hand. If only she can touch the garments of Jesus Christ."[26]

Dube has thus chosen to portray the hemorrhaging woman to express the situation of many women and other poor people in general, people suffering from the lack of healthcare rather than Ward's assumed upper-class ennui and hypochondria, "that has caged her in concern of herself."

Elaine Wainwright draws attention to the importance of female bodies for the gospel of Matthew: "Women bodies . . . configure the divine healing power, mediated through Jesus."[27] Is it a coincidence that in the encounters with these "sites" or "configurations" of divine healing powers, where female bodies and uterine blood frame the excesses of the story, Jesus gets confused, touchy, bereft of power? Interestingly, the traditional exegetical reaction to the story, starting with the interpretations of Matthew, works hard on retrieving for Jesus some respectability, some initiative, knowingness, and control over the situation? What kind of "magic" has taken place in those fleeting moments of uncertainty, when Jesus is touched from the rear?

Hemorrhage was not only considered to be a physical illness, but a social one as well. Any discharge from the body, albeit male or female, was considered unclean according to Leviticus 15:25–30: "If a woman has a discharge of blood for many days, not at the time of her impurity, or if she has a discharge beyond the time of her impurity, all the days of the discharge she shall continue in uncleanness . . . Every bed on which she lies during all the days her discharge shall be treated as the bed of her impurity; and everything on which she sits shall be unclean . . . Whoever touches these things shall be unclean" (Lev. 15:25–27). Both women and men had to obey the purity laws and both genders needed to offer two turtledoves or pigeons after their recovery (Lev. 15:14:29). Judith Romney Wegner points out that even though the offering is the same, there is a difference in the religious practice of women and men. While the male was supposed to bring their offering before YHWH, the female needed a priest as mediator between her sacrifice and her God. Her cultic relationship to YHWH was indirect.[28] Early feminist scholarship in the hemorrhaging woman usually emphasized

---

26. Ibid., 60.
27. Wainwright, "The Matthean Jesus and the Healing of Women," 91.
28 Wegner, "Leviticus," 47.

strongly the cultic ostracization of the woman, while Mary Rose D'Angelo argues that cultic impurity plays no role in the story.[29] However, Susan Haber convincingly maintains that a third stance is needed. Haber concurs with early feminist readings of the story on the point that the woman is impure according to Leviticus. She also concurs with D'Angelo when she criticizes the supersessionist opposition to Jewish law, but argues that the Jewish purity laws may still offer a valuable insight into what is going on in the story. Haber writes: "Her hemorrhage carries with it an impurity that could not have been ignored either by Mark's audience, or the society in which she lived. Her illness is explicit; her impurity is implicit."[30] Elisabeth Schüssler Fiorenza emphasizes the marginality of the woman, and her healing as redemptive socially as well as physiologically. She argues that the Jesus movement redefined "the *basilea*" or the kingdom of God as "wholeness" instead of ritual.[31] The story of the woman who had issues with blood signifies for Schüssler Fiorenza a radical change of social order, taboos, insides and outsides of culture, where Jesus has led the woman back into the social order by accepting her and calling her daughter.[32] However, Barbara Reid argues that the filiations of the woman as "daughter" of Jesus does not necessarily bring good news to women. For her, the evangelist "tames the woman's initial boldness with a final portrait of her trembling and prostrate before Jesus. Full incorporation into the religious and social community for woman today is not achieved when women fall back into a submissive stance as 'daughters' to dominant 'fathers.'"[33]

For Rita Nakashima Brock, the specific ailment of the woman makes her an outcast of society, which is restored and healed in the gospel. Brock maintains that Jesus cannot see the woman in the crowd, because he is unable to help someone who "suffers from her very femaleness," as defined by her culture.[34] She elaborates social concept of wholeness, which she refers to as "erotic power." Brock defines psychological barriers which prevent erotic power flowing freely between individuals as "brokenheartedness." She interprets the story of the hemorrhaging woman as a tale of twofold brokenheartedness, the woman's because of her illness and social alienation, but

29. D'Angelo, "(Re)presentations of Women in the Gospels," 141.
30. Haber, *They Shall Purify Themselves*, 125.
31. Schüssler Fiorenza, *In Memory of Her*, 113.
32. Ibid., 124.
33. Reid, "Choosing the Better Part?," 143.
34. Brock, *Journeys by Heart*, 83; Schüssler Fiorenza, *In Memory of Her*, 124.

also the brokenheartedness of Jesus, who is unable to help her as a Jewish man who cannot overcome the sexual boundaries of his culture. For her, the boldness of the woman, her "erotic power," heals Jesus's brokenheartedness, by breaking his boundaries between male and female territories. Because of the healing of patriarchal wounds, Jesus is able to heal both the bleeding woman and Jairus's daughter. She writes: "Erotic power creates life in the midst of the ambiguity of existence by making heart possible. Passion and compassion are alive in the touching of hearts."[35] I find Brock's interpretation of the healing of the hemorrhaging woman insightful in three important ways. First, she defines the difficulty of the woman's situation precisely as a gender issue, since she is suffering from "her very femaleness." Secondly, she describes the scene in the crowd as an erotic power at work in human relations and gendered bodies. Thirdly, Brock illustrates this reciprocal sharing of sacred power as a revelation of the sacred.

Brock's aim by reading the story is to use it to reveal remedies to patriarchy: "I am seeking to turn patriarchy inside out, to reveal its ravaged, faint, fearful, broken heart, and to illuminate the power that heals heart. It is a power that allows the touching of heart to heart, a healing and touching that guide toward a greater experience of the sacred in life."[36] While Ward admits in a footnote to the article that "there is also the crossing of sexual difference (man-woman) and cultic difference (clean-unclean)," but social taboos and this "crossing of sexual difference" plays no role in his treatment of the biblical fluids in Mark 5.[37] If Ward thus pays little attention to the woman's "very femaleness," Ward and Brock both emphasize the flowing *dynamis* between the bodies of the hemorrhaging woman and Jesus, Brock through process notions of erotic power, Ward through schizoanalysis. They also have in common the insistence of a revelation of the sacred in human relations. This revelation is not static, but rather emerges through the narrative. Brock writes: "The function of the healer is not to gain power, but to facilitate the recreation of it. In the sharing process heart reveals the sacred."[38]

And then—back to the crowd to witness what is happening in their midst, where a woman has touched the fringes of Christ's coat and the moment has been frozen. As already indicated, many feminists are unhappy with traditional interpretations of the story of the hemorrhaging woman.

---

35. Brock, *Journeys by Heart*, 88.
36. Ibid., xv.
37. Ward, "The Schizoid Christ," 66.
38. Brock, *Journeys by Heart*, 82.

Reid criticizes the traditional interpretations that force the woman out of concealment, yielding her coerced truth, and appropriate into the order of patriarchy as the "daughter" of Jesus. Dube's narration of Mama Africa brings out the way in which the idea the woman is herself to be blamed for her ailments erases the political element of the story. Many of the feminist readings I have mentioned point out how quickly this moment of uncertainty is glossed over when power goes out of Jesus's body. The leaking gap in an intercalated story is dried up in the economy of daughters and truths.

Instead of Ward's one-dimensional framework, Brock proposes a feminist Christology of brokenheartedness and shared healing. In my view, such an approach could open up new ventures for the schizoid operations of Christ through reciprocal healing of touch, flow and relation.

Bibliography

Augustine, Saint. "Sermon XXVII." In *Nicene and Post-Nicene Fathers VI*, edited by Philip Schaff. Cosimo Classics. Peabody: Hendrickson, 1995.

———. "Sermon XII." In *Nicene and Post-Nicene Fathers VI*, edited by Philip Schaff. Cosimo Classics. Peabody: Hendrickson, 1995.

Børresen, Kari Elisabeth, ed. "God's Image, Man's Image? Patristic Interpretation of Gen. 1, 27 and I Cor. 11,7." In *The Image of God: Gender Models in Judaeo-Christian Tradition*, edited by Kari Elisabeth Børresen, 187–209. Minneapolis: Fortress, 1995.

———. *Subordination and Equivalence: The Nature and Role of Woman in Augustine and Thomas Aquinas*. Washington: University Press of America, 1981.

Brock, Rita Nakashima. *Journeys by Heart: A Christology of Erotic Power*. New York: Crossroad, 1991.

Brown, Joanne Carlson, and Rebecca Parker. "For God so Loved the World?" In *Violence Against Women and Children: A Christian Theological Sourcebook*, edited by Carol J. Adams and Marie M. Fortune, 36–59. New York: Continuum, 1995.

D'Angelo, Mary Rose. "(Re)presentations of Women in the Gospels: John and Mark." In *Women and Christian Origins*, edited by Ross Shephard Kraemer and Mary Rose D'Angelo, 171–198. New York: Oxford University Press, 1999.

Deleuze, Gilles, and Felix Guattari. *Anti-Oedipus: Capitalism and Schizophrenia*. Translated by Robert Hurley, Mark Seem, and Helen R. Lane. Minneapolis: University of Minneapolis Press, 1983.

Dewey, Joanna. "The Gospel of Mark." In *Searching the Scriptures, Volume 2: A Feminist Commentary*, edited by Elisabeth Schüssler-Fiorenza. New York: Crossroads, 1994.

Dube, Musa W. "Fifty Years of Bleeding." In *Other Ways of Reading: African Women and the Bible*, edited by Musa W. Dube, 60–66. Atlanta: Society of Biblical Literature, 2001.

Gudmarsdottir, Sigridur. "Feminist Apophasis: Beverly J. Lanzetta and Trinh Min-ha in Dialogue." *Feminist Theology* (January 2008) 157–68.

———. "God Is a Lobster: Whitehead's Receptacle Meets the Deleuzian Sieve." In *Secrets of Becoming: Negotiating Whitehead, Deleuze and Butler*, edited by Roland Faber and Andrea Stephenson, 191–200. New York: Fordham University Press, 2010.

———. "Rof-Kristur og konan með blóðlátin: Tengsl Krists og samtíma af sjónarhóli Grahams Ward og kvennaguðfræði." In *Studia Theologica Islandica*, edited by Pétur Pétursson, 45–65. Reykjavík: Skálholtsútgáfan, 2007.

———. "The Sensible Unsaying of Mysticism." In *Apophatic Bodies: Negative Theology, Incarnation and Relationality*, edited by Catherine Keller and Christopher Boesel, 273–85. New York: Fordham University Press, 2009.

Haber, Susan. *"They Shall Purify Themselves": Essays on Purity in Early Judaism*. Edited by Adele Reinhartz. Atlanta: Society of Biblical Literature, 2008.

Perkins, Pheme. "The Gospel of Mark: Introduction, Commentary, and Reflections." In *The New Interpreter's Bible: Matthew–Mark (Volume 8)*, edited by Leander E. Keck. Nashville: Abingdon, 1995.

Reid, Barbara. *Choosing the Better Part? Women in the Gospel of Luke*. Collegeville, Minnesota: Liturgical, 1996.

Schüssler Fiorenza, Elisabeth. *In Memory of Her: A Feminist Theological Reconstruction of Christian Origins*. New York: Crossroads, 1986.

Swete, Henry Barclay. *The Gospel According to St. Mark: The Greek Text with Introduction, Notes and Indices*. London: Macmillan 1909.

Tolbert, Mary Ann. "Mark." In *Women's Bible Commentary*, edited by Carol A. Newsom and Sharon H. Ringe. Louisville: Westminster John Knox, 1998.

Turlington, Henry E. *The Broadman Bible Commentary Vol. 8*. Nashville: Broadman, 1946.

Ward, Graham. *Christ and Culture*. Challenges in Contemporary Theology. London: Blackwell, 2009.

Wainwright, Elaine. "The Matthean Jesus and the Healing of Women." In *The Gospel of Matthew in Current Study*, edited by David E. Aune, 74–85. Grand Rapids: Eerdmans, 2001.

Wegner, Judith Romney. "Leviticus." In *Women's Bible Commentary*, edited by Carol A. Newsom and Sharon H. Ringe. Louisville: Westminster John Knox, 1998.

9

Communities of Faith, Desire, and Resistance

A Response To Radical Orthodoxy's Ecclesia

Christopher Newell

Introduction

I must acknowledge from the outset of this essay that these musings and reflections come from an applied and experiential theological perspective. In a moment I shall list some of the most significant places and contexts where I "reside" and by which my theological perspective continues to grow, contract, and expand. I can proudly say, however, that I regard myself as an applied theologian alongside those whose faces, bodies, lives, and contexts generously ask of my attention. They, in many cases, would not in a million years describe themselves as applied theologians; perhaps I am being rather too presumptuous in placing them in a space of reflective experience and contemporary engagement, but that is who they are, from my partial and contingent narrative, so shall we agree to leave us all there for a while and see where such presumption takes us. Indeed, one of the related critiques of Radical Orthodoxy to their ideas of *Ecclesia* and its members, is who the theologians regard as theology-makers, whether this activity is exclusively an activity of the church and whether it is a secondary activity as reflective practice, always privileging human experience, particularly from the perspective of the poor, the excluded, and the transgressors. John Milbank, in writing about where one might find and locate true Christian practice, on the very first page of *The Word Made Strange* says this: "In his or her uncertainty as to where to find this, the theologian feels almost that the entire ecclesial task falls on his own head: in the meagre mode of reflective words he must seek to imagine what a true practical repetition would be like. Or at least he must hope that his merely theoretical continuation of the tradition will open up a space for wider transformation."[1]

Here the she or he theologian (but notice, only for a sentence, then we return to the solitary he, for textual reasons, I am sure) and the "ecclesial task," whatever that may be, are intimately connected; indeed the great theologian must feel a great headache as "he," in his solitary study, creates a space without context, human or divine presence, caution or contingency, bodies, gender, earth, or text for transformation. The Fathers of the Church would be proud of him.

But I too am being rather presumptuous. This argument is for later in the essay. I promised this introduction would enable you to understand where my context and experience resides, where my subjectivity lies, and where, if I ever fall into the trap of being too objective, you can haul me before the courts of my own experience.

So, who am I and from where do I come and where do I think I reside in my narrative, from which my theology speak and from which theology emerges:

> Father of daughters (one a brainy theologian, the other a gorgeous, autistic child with anger and passion veiled and unveiled, beyond the text); mysterious fatherhood really as the theory and act of penetration is deeply problematic to me (virgin father, perhaps?); friend to partner; survivor of nasty things and nasty men; bisexual (the desirer of men's bodies whilst remaining committed to one woman's); Anglican priest (of sorts!); Christian by nature and inclination; privileged member and guest of many communities of faith, desire, and resistance; hanging on to the creedal notion of *ecclesia* (not really sure about that); beer drinker; wine imbiber; hearer of voices; see-er of angels; adorer of books and quiet; quiet libraries; damascene theologian for whom in the midst of madness and recovery only feminism and queerness would do; lover

1. Milbank, *The Word Made Strange*, 1.

The Poverty of Radical Orthodoxy

of cricket; walker of mountains; swimmer of quiet and angry seas; deep, deep lover of friends; wonderful chef of a limited menu; hater of washing clothes; respecter of washing dishes; chaplain to a great institution and to those who find themselves within and without its embracing walls and ethic; defender of a national health provider, yet wondering all the while what "health" might be; chaotic diabetic (habitual consumer of giant chocolate buttons); lover of film, of ridiculous fantasy and dream, *Pan's Labyrinth*, *Lord of the Rings*; typical middle-class customer of the National Trust and English Heritage (sticker on car!); finder of lost socks behind the sofa; bad poet; lover of knowledge, of study, of other's stories and journeys; sadly bad chess player, even worse scrabble player; white, grey male in the process of being un-phallused (de-phallused?); in the process of dialoguing in the process; client and friend of wonderful therapist; dreamer of "psychotic" dreams; habitual survivor of suicide; sectioned by the "system"; cradled by the ward; diagnosed and evangelical about it; charismatic speaker; angry, old man; disconnected and forever deconstructed . . . [2]

So, that, is part of my story so far, and I haven't even mentioned the very current "fact" that I am writing this in a university library, overlooking a wet courtyard, drinking a cold cup of tea . . .

Within these contexts, communities, and relationships reside many and diverse expressions of faith, desire, and resistance. More of this later.

I think this is enough of my introduction, except to say this essay seeks to find alternative narratives of experiential theological communities that may be seen as a natural progression from the Jesus story and entirely consistent with a Christian narrative of radical mutuality, while also contrasting with a seemingly exclusive and disembodied idea of church, totally theoretical and dualistic, and even in its supposedly radical response to secular rationality, denying the diversity of human voices and bodies.

---

2. Inspired by Jyl Lynn Felman, "Nurturing the Soul" *Tikkun* vol 11:4 (July–August 1996), 50. "I am a Jewish lesbian vegetarian chicken writer; attorney at law, performance artist, silky smooth dancer, high femme, soft butch, adjunct gender-bender Brandeis professor, racquetball player, wild child, wild beast, grilled salmon lover, Portobello mushroom gorger; loving friend, would-be rabbi, cultural worker, postmodern Zionist, deconstruction activist, five-mile-a-day jogger, U Conn women's basketball aficionado, French food connoisseur; Scrabble fanatic, budding rollerblader; hot bath soaker, snorkeler supreme, and coalition builder between Blacks and Whites; Jews and Gentiles; gays and straights; men and women; nuclear families and none. I am unsolidly middle class, upwardly mobile, highly educated, politically astute, and intellectually gifted. And I have been severely depressed, hospitalized, aspirin overdosed, stomach excruciatingly pumped, and therapized since my Bat Mitzvah in Dayton, Ohio, thirty years ago."

Some Paradoxes and Consistencies

It is clear from much of what Radical Orthodox writers say, with the possible exception of Graham Ward, there is an undeniable split between the nature of church and the nature of secularism. Emanating from the disastrous Western Enlightenment project—namely the triumph of rationalism and the defeat of all other modes of textual and linguistic engagement, especially the religious and theological—Radical Orthodoxy attempts to reify the idea and practice of church as the means of restoring story, narrative, and subjectivity at the heart of theological truth. Indeed, much of this project seems to resonate with the ideas of feminist theology, although it is interesting that, apart from Graham Ward, Radical Orthodoxy hardly acknowledges the contribution of feminist theologians who were addressing and challenging the nature of the post-enlightenment theological subject over 20 years before anyone heard of Radical Orthodoxy. Radical Orthodoxy rarely acknowledges the gender-body contexts on which patriarchal orthodoxy has established fixed, unchanging notions of the hierarchy of religious experience, and it categorically denies the insights of feminist theologies with the possible exception of Graham Ward. As Mary Grey has commented: "It is ironic the feminist theology shares some of the agenda of Radical Orthodoxy: both are critical of the Enlightenment and the subsequent privileging of an excessive rationality. This is not only because of the inferior place given by Enlightenment thinking to emotion and a non-dualistic form of human personhood but because by this—together with the progressive autonomy of the secular world—the way was paved for that form of competitive individualism so characteristic of the contemporary age of 'capitalism triumphant.'"[3]

Mary Grey's essay was written and published in 2006. Since then the march of "contemporary capitalism" has been painfully halted and the green agenda of challenging the very philosophy of excessive consumption and exchange has come right to the fore of the political and theological agenda. The idea of earth as gift and the subsequent consequences for human relationships and community has come principally from the "secular" world, with the actual and real institution of the church lagging someway behind, despite the contributions of theologians such as Sallie McFague, Matthew Fox, and Thomas Berry, theologians who have not exactly been seen as coming from the mainstream of Christian theology and practice. Indeed, the best examples of the philosophy of gift and the critique of

---

3. Grey, "My Yearning is for Justice," 175–76.

modernism have come from distinctly non-church thinkers such as Derrida, Levinas, Kristeva, and Deleuze—hardly paragons of the Anglican or even Christian mainstream. Though Radical Orthodoxy has attempted to impose its own "metanarrative" of meaning and truth, where the exclusive Jesus text resides despite continuing to deny there is any such thing anymore as the grand narrative, the subsequent description of the church as the exclusive place of the sacred and the sacred future denies the reality of the institution and its very human manifestations. One wonders where one is to find this "church," except, perhaps, beyond the orthodox boundaries. This is the paradox of Radical Orthodoxy: it seeks to challenge the overarching, overwhelming, grand narrative of rationalism and the capitalist endeavour of consumption, and yet replaces it with a theology of church that is as equally overarching and exclusive of all other communities and narratives. As Rosemary Ruether has commented: "There are many who find things worth pondering in some of radical orthodoxy's critiques but who are disturbed by the superficial application of often flat and reductionist notions of what modernism or secularism is rather than a deep, sustained rethinking of what it might mean to move beyond modernism."[4]

Much of the inspiration for Radical Orthodoxy's theology of the church and the nature of the secular come as much from St. Augustine as it does from a rather bland critique of western enlightenment. In *City of God* Augustine equates in absolute terms the relationship of Jesus and the church, the Heavenly City. In effect, the church is Christ and those outside the confines of the church are outside any possibility of salvation or relationship with Christ. And the contrast between those "outside" and those "inside" will be absolute. Here we see not only individual salvation but the salvation of the community in contrast to the "other" City. "For everything that is here said about those human beings who are not citizens of that City is said with this purpose, that the City may show up to advantage, may be thrown into relief, by contrast with its opposite."[5]

And what is the opposite? How may it be described? "This City which was called "Confusion" is none other than Babylon."[6]

The church equals the Heavenly City and secularism—Babylon? In Radical Orthodoxy it as clearcut as that, except yet again for the contribution of Graham Ward. Just as for St. Augustine the being and activity of the

---

4. Ruether, "Introduction," ix.
5. Augustine, *City of God*, 652–53.
6. Ibid.

church and the being activity of Christ are one and the same thing; so for John Milbank, if there is a grand narrative, it is the intimately, inextricably linked narrative of Jesus and the developing life and witness of the Church. As Steven Shakespeare has written: "The metanarrative—the big overarching Christian story—is a story of everything, centred on Christ. But it seems to depend entirely on the Church . . . is it based on anything more than the arbitrary authority of a flawed human institution which claims to be divine? Does it put the Church in the place of Christ?"[7]

Indeed, Mary Grey goes further, referring to two theologians who have chosen two other embodiments of *ecclesia* rather than Milbank's Augustinian model: "William Cavanaugh is one of the few theologians of Radical Orthodoxy who has developed a Eucharistic ecclesiology in the context of violence in Chile . . . But, like Daniel Bell, whose chosen embodiment of *ecclesia* is the 12th century of Bernard of Clairvaux, he fails to engage with the realities of the contemporary church-corruption, betrayal of trust through widespread sexual abuse, clerical elitism and absolutist forms of governance—that are estranging thousands of loyal believers today."[8]

In all of these theologies of Radical Orthodoxy, however diverse they may seem, there is one common theme: somewhere, somehow, whether it is in the ecclesiology of Augustine or the contemporary church in Chile, whether it is in the contemplative, monastic tradition of Bernard of Clairvaux or the truth residing in Thomas Aquinas, we shall find an almost certain, unerring template for Christian truth, for the authentic process of the Jesus Story, and for an exclusive claim to storytelling, fixed, stable, and ever present in the contemporary reflections of the great theologians. There seems to be no room in this particular inn for diverse communities of faith, desire, and resistance, whether from inside the Christian story, stories of other faiths, or the stories of those for whom the secular world has freed them the too-rigid creedal paradigms of the faith story itself and transformed them in a real and contingent engagement with the polis of the world: environmental struggle, the continuing stories of liberation from gender and racial discrimination, or the struggle to hear the voices of poverty so often silenced and excluded, stigmatized and marginalized. If there is one consistent theme in the gospel narratives is that Jesus never really appears when he is expected to appear: his parables are about unexpected guests and miracles at wedding feasts; unexpected good Samaritans; unexpected

---

7. Shakespeare, *Radical Orthodoxy: A Critical Introduction*, 61.
8. Grey, "My Yearning for Justice," 183.

welcomes home; unexpected women transgressing unexpected boundaries of blood and touch; unexpected feasts with unexpected, excluded people; unexpected empty tombs. Jesus is never where he is meant to be and he receives as many gifts as he offers, from those who seemingly have nothing to gift but themselves. Radical Orthodoxy, or at least most of their most prestigious representatives, seems to want to fix this unexpected stranger, nail him to the cross of predictability and ensure he doesn't escape our own, unacknowledged, subjective gaze, refusing to welcome the gaze of others, especially outside the confines of our theological limitations, our contingent and partial lives, only completed in relation to the bodies, voices, gazes of others, especially those who unexpectedly give us love.

And then there is Graham Ward!

Here, there seems no consistency and much paradox.

As Shakespeare has written: "Graham Ward . . . offers a much more positive reading of the Church's unstable identity . . . his reflections on the body of Christ suggested that bodies and identities are always in relation to one another. They are not self-contained wholes. This applies to the body of Christ too—to Jesus, to the Eucharist, to the Church. The Church in particular cannot claim to be the only reality, the sole community where God is known, because God 'cannot be housed.'"[9]

And Shakespeare then quotes from Graham Ward's book *The Cities of God*, which he describes as "bold in Radical Orthodoxy's terms":[10] "The institutional churches are necessary, but they are not ends in themselves; they are constantly transgressed by a community of desire, an erotic community, and a spiritual activity."[11]

Desire, *eros* for each other, for the divine immanence at the heart of all mutual relations, for the godding that takes place wherever human flourishing is affirmed and human struggle and resistance is shared, cannot ultimately be contained by any institution, however much that institution seeks to live by the embodied hunger of desire. As Ward himself describes it: "The body of Christ desiring its consummation opens itself to what is outside the institutional church; offers itself to perform in fields of activity far from chancels and cloisters. In doing this certain risks are taken and certain fears can emerge within those who represent the institution."[12]

---

9. Shakespeare, *Radical Orthodoxy*, 108.
10. Ibid.
11. Ibid.
12. Ward, *Cities of God*, 180.

But as Shakespeare points out, the central reference point is still a particular theology of the body of Christ and, as such, the movement out of church, or at least the movement that cannot be contained by human incarnations of church, indicates that every other community of faith, desire, and resistance is always defined by their affinity to Christ-centered-ness and their distance from modernism and secularism in the terms that Radical Orthodoxy describes them. Thus there remains a deep paradox at the heart of Radical Orthodoxy, which Ward represents. Even he, with a much looser and fluid definition of church, through a much more embodied theology, seeks to resist the private, solitary, and depoliticized definition of church by making it the only real alternative to "dead" secularism, even if the definition embraces a much more inclusive imaginary of the body—it is still the body of Christ and non-other. However other and strange Christ is, however uncontainable and mad, however unable to speak any other language but the language of reciprocity and gifting, it is Christ, according to Ward, who defines our humanity, even though, significantly he says: ". . . we cannot simply project our images of being human onto the figure of Christ"[13] as if we have any other images or projections, but our human ones. It is as if Ward ultimately cannot accept the implications of incarnation, the implications of the divine merging absolutely into our human conditions, struggles, faiths, and desires.

Graham Ward, however, of all the Radical Orthodox writers, proclaims the need for describing who we are and where we reside in our theological subjectivity. He is the only one, even though they all seem to describe themselves as contextual theologians, to write about, "what we know, or what we believe we know (and its representations), is always situated—historically, culturally, economically—and sexed."[14] However, he spoils it a little by going on to say our situations are only a means to an end, and that end is a kind of return to ultimate objective rationality, or, in his words, "maximizing objectivity."[15] It is as if the maximizing objectivity is the Christ after all, and that however flexible and fluid Christ-likeness is, it is this maximized objectivity that is our ultimate goal, rather than the place we find ourselves in today and alongside the people amongst whom we reside and the unexpectedness of tomorrow. No, it is established that our

---

13. Ward, "The Schizoid Christ," 250.
14. Ward, "Transcorporeality," 303.
15. Ibid.

The Poverty of Radical Orthodoxy

subjectivity is only a means to the ultimate object—the Christ, the body of Christ, and his church.

And yet, there is a paradox here, and who's afraid of a little paradox? Sometimes the language we use to communicate our theology defeats our theology and leaves us with an open humanity born of experience and context grasping for new words. And out of that experience and context comes something unexpected, which does not quite fit where we thought we were and what we thought we believed. I am sure in the last sentences of "The Schizoid Christ," Ward believes what he says is entirely consistent, rational, and stable with the rest of his theology. I am sure I believe everything I have written here is entirely consistent, rational, and stable with my theology. We shall see! At the end of the essay, Ward speaks like no other Radical Orthodox writer. He speaks of himself and his situatedness; and in that brief moment there is a power in his words that seems to transcend his ultimately exclusive Christian theology of redemption. He tells a story of David and Jon, as David dies of AIDS and Jon is profoundly bereaved. In the midst of the dying, a Presbyterian minister has undertaken the liturgies of marriage and confirmation. Ward argues that only can such liturgies, and the sacred love behind them, enable the dying, AIDS, and the grieving to be redemptive. Ward then describes a body theology where the body bears the burden of its own wondrous uniqueness. It is beautifully told and, for me, demonstrates the ultimate paradox of Radical Orthodoxy for a theologian such as Ward. The story is only complete when, in the final sentences and only near completion, what happens at the bedside of Jon and David is everything they expected it to be; not because it was about holy church or a displaced body of Jesus, but because it was about their bodies, their love, their sanctification of the moment. The next paradox is that the church provides two sacraments in which David and Jon's love created the context for such universal liturgies to provide an embrace. But this is a community of faith and desire and resistance that uses the liturgies of the church in rebellious ways and by transgressing orthodoxy rediscovers meaning and sacrament.

Finally Ward speaks, personally and powerfully, of where he is and the place he resides, and in completing the essay, provides the unstable, contingent place of human living, where theology places itself not in the role of containment and explanation, but of continual liberation and transgression.

He says: "For me, something of that standpoint is composed of the fact that I am a male, Christian theologian who openly advocates same-sex unions, who has friends dying or living with the fear of AIDS, and a family that lives in the shadows, embarrassments and sufferings of a genetic disorder. But we, each, of us, move out from where we are placed and place ourselves, and in doing so we understand that we are also elsewhere."[16]

The Elsewheres' We Might Be

"When did the stories of God become a story of totality, of a closed system, of a One? To what corner of human longing does the story of the One belong? As the motors of fundamentalism in all the religions of the One God race on the fuel of battered bodies and broken hearts, the logic of the One chokes on itself like a stone in the mouth. The story of the One denies fleshiness and the stubborn shiftiness of bodies; it cannot abide ambiguities; it cannot speak syllables of earth."[17]

As a male, white Christian Anglican priest, I have joyously lost the art of defensiveness years ago. Despite hanging on to a theology of church that enables me to remain within a community of faith with some degree of integrity, and despite working within inner-city faith communities, both in London and Manchester, where, to quote Simon Oliver, I encountered "the community of the gifted."[18] The question he poses is one I want to profoundly challenge, using some of my earlier contexts and situatedness.

The question he poses, using the community of the gifted as his template, is this: "Do Christians behave generously because they believe they will receive something in return, namely eternal life? Are we involved in some kind of exchange with God whereby he grants us life *in exchange* for our worship and praise? Or can there be a genuine theology of gift which exceeds all secular understandings in unimagined ways and establishes the Church—the community of the gifted—as a radical alternative polity?"[19]

This is the question that always seems to be at the heart of Radical Orthodoxy. Can the church be established as a closed system, a totality, albeit a "radical" totality (whatever that may be), a place that claims ownership of all the stories of God and where excess is seen as some kind of triumph over secularism, which effectively means communities of experience outside this radical church? The church's excess of gift is in direct conflict with the secular world and its inability to imagine the unimaginable.

16. Ibid.
17. Schneider, *Beyond Monotheism*, ix.
18. Oliver, "Christ and Gift," 200.
19. Ibid.

The Poverty of Radical Orthodoxy

What does all this mean? How is it a theology of church can abandon all possibilities of a theology of creation and therefore all possibilities of the presence of the divine/human encounter anywhere else but the church? What model of the church can describe itself as a radical alternative and then deny the possibility of any other alternative? What model of church offers us one model of itself and therefore one model of God, the one Schneider describes so well. Sallie MacFague, nearly thirty years ago, seems to have challenged the very *raison d'être* of Radical Orthodoxy before it was thought of in the twinkling eyes of Cambridge Dons:

> Our lives, our actions take place in networks of relationships. To the extent that we know ourselves, our world, and our God, that knowledge is profoundly relational and, hence, interdependent, relative, situational and limited. The implication for models of God is obvious: we must use the relationships nearest and dearest to us as metaphors of that which finally cannot be named. Aware that we exist only in relationship and aware, therefore, that all our language about God is but metaphors of experience of relating to God, we are free to use many models of God. Aware, however, that the relationship with God cannot be named, we are prohibited from absolutizing any models of God.[20]

Or, therefore, prohibited from absolutizing any models of church? And by implication, prohibited from absolutizing church itself? The church may be one of many expressions of the diverse, inclusive, and incarnate divine encounter within the relational life of human beings, or it may be one of many that, by absolutizing the boundaries of the church and the secular, however radical its theology looks, seeks to impose a violent totality on the nature and language and expression of relational love. Indeed, in reality, there are churches, not the church, there are communities of faith, not a community of faith, and many of these communities are powerful and living incarnations of unbounded, transgressive love. Many of these communities preach and live a different gospel. There are communities of faith seeking fresh and open alliances with those in the so-called "secular" world in order to begin building at local and global levels, post-capitalist communities of gift, without reference to the nature of structure or creed, but honoring primary experience and unexpected sacred incarnations in the relation between others. As David Jensen has written: "The universal claim of the church is not its position of privilege in relation to all other assemblies

---

20. McFague, *Metaphorical Theology*, 194.

and institutions, its demand that all might be 'saved' through it; rather, its universality is its willingness to be in the midst of that world, its call to be *'ek-klesia,'* the community called out into the world, not into itself."[21]

This turns the mainstream Radical Orthodox view of church in relation to the secular upside down. But I would need to go further than Jensen and say all communities of faith, desire, and resistance are called out from idea to practice, from theory to engagement, from the place of stability to the place of instability and possibility, open welcome, and continuing transgression. The language we use about such communities is as important as the theology implicit within them. These communities are not established as Radical Orthodoxy seeks ecclesia to be established as the one and the only voice, however diverse, which drowns with its scream all other voices, especially those deafened by the scream, whose whispers of resistance to totality and violence painfully need to be heard. I shall offer one such community of faith, desire, and resistance with which I have the privilege of being involved in a moment. No, these communities celebrate the very idea that they seek their place amongst other voices, other narratives, other places where the sacred has become revealed. In those places, if we happen to be Christian, we may detect the shadow of the Galilean passing through, whose body, bones, and earthy voice are now ours. But it is not obligatory; the very moment it becomes so, we lose the very point of our relational understanding with each other; we lose the stories of others and their inspiration; we lose ourselves in seeking to define ourselves so tightly to a notion of the one, the one story, the one creed, the one journey; we lose the risk of hospitality as the heart of our community, a hospitality John Caputo detects in two Lucan and Matthean key biblical passages about welcome and the feast, namely Luke 14:12–13, 15–24, and Matthew 22:1–14. Prefacing his conclusions regarding these passages about the nature of welcome and communities that welcome he says: "We are always put at risk whenever we welcome someone, just as we are put at risk whenever we love or believe in someone, and the greater the love, the hospitality, the greater the risk . . . That means that there is always something slightly mad about hospitality, as indeed there is about the gift in all its forms, for what are forgiveness and hospitality if not versions of the gift, of an expenditure without return? But where indeed would one ever expect to find anything so mad?"[22] Not necessarily in the incarnations of the church as communities of faith I know!

21. Jensen, *In the Company of Others*, 145.
22. Caputo, *What Would Jesus Deconstruct?*, 77.

The Poverty of Radical Orthodoxy

Reflecting upon the feast in the Luke and Matthew passages Caputo goes on to say: "These are parties as mad as any Hatter's party dreamed up by Lewis Carroll, mad with the madness of the Kingdom of God—and the madness of the gift in deconstruction."[23]

Consider a visit from a mental health chaplain to a psychiatric intensive care ward. He has been requested to come to offer the most central rite of sacramental Christianity and Radical Orthodoxy: Holy Communion, the Eucharist, the Lord's Supper. I am exercising that most central office of sacramental Christianity and yet as I walk through the doors of the ward, I have crossed a line where theologies are turned upside down and what is at play is sacred play with transgression at its loving heart. Six of us sit around a makeshift altar and two, apart from me, decide they would like to be the priest, with my help of course. Another speaks of her bones feeling like Jesus must have felt on the cross—the blood from the cross mingling with the blood from her self-injured arms. Can she we wipe the blood of Christ on her arms so he can share her pain and allow some kind of healing to take place? She does not want to drink it. Of course she can; of course they can. Another says he is an atheist but needs to be with his friends around this makeshift altar, that when you are with friends you do not refuse what they receive; that is fine and we all welcome him. Finally, another says he is a Buddhist and a Muslim and a Christian, so in his very self the world is at peace. "Shalom," he says, because he is thinking of converting to Judaism.

What a Eucharist we celebrate, far from any theology of the Eucharist I have read, but a moment of deeply Eucharistic passion and love; a community—perhaps an ecclesia—of resistance, where all those personas and identities are medicalized and pathologized in this circle, for this moment, are sanctified and sacred. This ecclesia, this community of resistance might not last for more than the thirty minutes the liturgy takes to be completed. It might root in the hearts of those who took part for longer, in the relations that have been formed, and in the lives that await them outside the locked hospital doors. We don't know and in this moment, we don't care. The only sadness is that all of them rise from the table saying they will definitely go to church when they leave the hospital. I cannot bear to say they will not find what they are looking for; they will not find what they have just experienced together. Perhaps the task of this mental health chaplain is to discover how they might find such a "mad" community of the kingdom, even if it exists for moments, or for days, or for years.

23. Ibid.

I am brought back by sisters and brothers to the wonder of uncertainty and the needless desire for the spiritual journey to be safe and without risk, for the church to be established. And for the many to be reduced to the one: "Are we not like people following an obscure clue, on the tracks, on the trail, in the trace of something-we-are-not-sure-what? Are not those who write about spiritual journeys sometimes a little too assured about where they are going and how to get there?"[24]

Perhaps, we can replace the word "spiritual" with many other words: theological, ecclesiological, etc.? Perhaps we can also add that the companions with whom we travel, whether for a lifetime, for a moment captured from within the chaos of identity on a psychiatric intensive care ward, will always surprise us with their theological reflections, deeply embodied in seemingly broken bodies and minds, as we surprise them. I am reminded of a passage from Rita Brock's remarkable book, *Journeys by Heart: A Christology of Erotic Power* (New York, 1991) where she reflects upon the gospel as a place of movement and transposition, where Jesus never resides where we expect, indeed never residing at all: "The empty tomb . . . represents the final step before the mediation of all the oppositions that characterize Mark's Gospel. The tomb, a cleft in an opening that emerges deep in the earth—the ultimate symbol of ultimate chaos—is transposed with the holy mountain, the usual symbol of divine revelation and power. The Gospel continually transposes expected relationships of sacred and profane, powerful and weak. Jesus, who has no final location, is always on the move between places."[25]

There is nowhere and no excluded companions where the risk of uncertainty and contingency in the context of our gendered, cultural, "mad" bodies and identities does not exist in the serious playfulness of the human/divine encounter. Graham Ward seems to effectively contradict Radical Orthodoxy's claim of the primacy of a particular theology of church when he writes: "Similarly, that which I exclude from my body, or that which is excluded in my name from the corporations to which I belong, will affect me, for good and ill. The ghettoisations and the segregations of racism, sexism, class, and ageism done in my name, condoned by my silence, injure me."[26]

I, you, we do not belong to those corporations of the "secular" as many of us do not belong to the institutions of the "religious," but we inhabit both.

---

24. Ibid., 39.
25. Brock, *Journeys by Heart: A Christology of Erotic Power*, 102.
26. Ward, "Transcorporeality," 299.

As I leave my particular church on a Sunday morning, as someone else goes to collect the papers, as Jew and Muslim have left their places of worship previously in the week, we inhabit the corporations of the secular that provide us with our work, housing, food, education and the education of our children, transport, parliament, and the needs of our health and many others'. Do not say the vast majority of our week and our work are excluded from theologies of the human and the divine; we are beginning to understand how deeply we belong to each other and in that belonging how we inhabit the divine. We realize we inhabit the same world and recognize, reflect, and are surprised at the faith we share, the desires we have, and the resistance many have to being associated with a fixed place of belonging. However seductive such places might be, however radical they might be seen in the hands of the radical orthodox, our experience pushes us further to a mutual theology of the human/divine.

In Conclusion

Finally, I wish to return to the many and diverse personas I listed at the beginning of the essay. I am not sure I belong to any of them completely and unconditionally, though close relationships with family, friends, and theological companions come very close to defining my reasons for being and living. I think it is good, however, to always leave a little gap in your heart for others; that way your heart seems to continually expand.

There is one community of faith, desire, and resistance I wish to speak of as contradicting Radical Orthodoxy's claim that the secular world cannot imagine what possibilities lay within the nature and polity of the church. In fact, it most often, in practical, embodied terms, is completely the reverse. Real and lasting progress in human rights, women's liberation, racial justice, mental health reform (with the exception of the Quakers), involves hearing the voices of the unheard, who have been in the face of church opposition rather than alliance. And what is the incarnation of the divine revealed in human form unless it is the continuing respect for and love of the body, both personal and communal?

I have the enormous privilege of being a member of the "Respect" Group, a community of adults with learning disabilities, who gather together not only as a means of mutual support, but to raise awareness of their own issues and needs and how they can be more fully met by statutory agencies. Indeed, their life together goes further than that in that they actively challenge those with power in their lives to justify that power by coming to attend meetings where the agenda, the means of communication, and the people invited are all in the hands of the members of "Respect." Of course, they do not and cannot wholly redress the power imbalance, but they make a bloody good attempt at it. I do not come as priest, as pastoral carer, as a kind and inclusive messenger from kind and inclusive Jesus, though I might well be perceived in all those personals in one way or another. I come as friend, as colleague, perhaps as theologian; for the question of what it means to be described as having a learning disability and what people's assumptions might be as a result, are constantly items for discussion. We have even produced the first healthcare leaflet describing learning disabilities from the perspective of those who are described as thus. I do not come with ritual, liturgy, or the baggage of the church, though I implicitly reflect upon my membership as a member of church and as a Christian theologian, and as all the other personas I often wear, especially that of a father of a daughter with disabilities. We have though, produced a leaflet of what kind of things we might talk about in terms of God, with all the words and symbols being written by a small group. Members of the group regularly sit on interview panels for healthcare staff, regularly audit hospitals and other public institutions for disabled-friendly environments.

We are undoubtedly a community of faith, in our abilities and strengths as individuals and as a relational whole; we are clearly a community of desire, a desire for each other's presence and flourishing and a desire for justice for those who may not be able to speak easily for themselves; we are a community of resistance to anything and anybody who denies our right to speak, our right to challenge, our right to all the other rights people may take for granted. We are a community that has begun the process of refusing to be stigmatized and marginalized, by church as much as society. It has, in Simon Oliver's words, been a time of unimagined ideas and unimagined realities, of the incarnation of dreams into embodied truths. It has nothing to do with Radical Orthodoxy's idea of ecclesia as the alternative to a dead secularism; indeed, religious communities of faith are often not even close to addressing the very existence of marginalized and excluded communities—an overarching theology of the church even less so. Oh, yes, there might be a kind and loving pastoral care going on where a Down's Syndrome girl is feted for assisting at the altar, but how about her becoming a member of the church council; how about her being eligible for ordination; how about her becoming whatever she may become? Not quite there yet, I think. It is an insult for Radical Orthodoxy to claim that human liberation lies in one direction, through one narrative, however groundbreaking, through one fantasy of a theology of ecclesia that seems to ignore its partial, incredibly fragmented, and largely exclusive self-definition, seemingly so defensive as to be unable to accept challenge, criticism, and the multiplicity of alternative voices.

I wanted to finish by describing a real, grounded community of faith that challenges the fantasies of the Radical Orthodox project. In the main, Radical Orthodoxy seems to be a theologian's dream of how to restore authority to a discipline that, since the advent of Feminist and Liberation Theology, has opened the doors to theological reflection in the experiential, within all lives, including the lives of the poor, the silenced, the gift-givers, and the transgressors of the fixed and stable. Radical Orthodoxy would like the church as partner, which liberation theologies have enabled to be replaced by church as The One, The Only, leaving the rest of creation to a nihilistic future. This is their fantasy, because there will be communities of faith, desire, and resistance popping up everywhere, possibly made up of many faiths and none. All will bring their story, tools of passage, bodies, and above all, their open and vulnerable hospitality. In these meetings we shall discover the endless waters of the uncontainable Spirit. I would like to conclude with a passage from Catherine Keller:

> The truth of living waters . . . suggests another subtler flow, the way neither of a timeless truth nor of a truthless time: a way of *timely* truth. Beyond the mirror-play of ex-nihilism and nihilism exists a "worship in spirit and truth." This spirit deterritorializes every city, every site, movement, church, or dogma that would confine truth within a boundary—or a bucket . . . Theology could instead remember the path of the *bottomless spring*: infinite flux within creaturely limits. The radical reciprocity of Spirit generates its new subjects precisely at the interfluency of those limits. The truth of this Spirit and the gift of this life, far from offering escape from the creation, *immanates* from its bottomless flux.[27]

Remember, along with the Spirit of endless flux and reciprocity, there remains the wonderful uncontainability of all our gendered and contextual bodies in systems, creeds, and theologies.

---

27. Keller, *Is That All*, 35.

Bibliography

Augustine, Saint. *City of God*. London: Penguin Classics, 1984.
Brock, Rita Nakashima. *Journeys by Heart: A Christology of Erotic Power*. New York: Crossroad, 1991.
Caputo, John D. *What Would Jesus Deconstruct? The Good News of Postmodernity for the Church*. Grand Rapids: Baker Academic, 2007.
Felman, Jyl Lynn. "Nurturing the Soul." *Tikkun* 11:4 (July–August 1996) 23–25.
Grey, Mary. "'My Yearning is for Justice': Moving Beyond Praxis in Feminist Theology." In *Interpreting the Postmodern: Responses to "Radical Orthodoxy,"* edited by Rosemary Ruether and Marion Grau, 175–96. New York: T. & T. Clark, 2006.
Jensen, David H. *In the Company of Others: A Dialogical Christology*. Cleveland: Pilgrim, 2001.
Keller, Catherine. "Is That All? Gift and Reciprocity in Milbank's *Being Reconciled*." In *Interpreting the Postmodern: Responses to "Radical Orthodoxy,"* edited by Rosemary Ruether and Marion Grau, 18–35. New York: T. & T. Clark, 2006.
McFague, Sallie. *Metaphorical Theology: Models of God in Religious Language*. London: SCM, 1983.
Milbank, John. *The Word Made Strange: Theology, Language, Culture*. Oxford: Blackwell, 1997.
Oliver, Simon. "Introduction to Part IV: Christ and Gift." In *The Radical Orthodoxy Reader*, edited by John Milbank and Simon Oliver, 197–99. London: Routledge, 2009.
Ruether, Rosemary. "Introduction." In *Interpreting the Postmodern: Responses to "Radical Orthodoxy,"* edited by Rosemary Ruether and Marion Grau, vii–xv. New York: T. & T. Clark, 2006.
Shakespeare, Steven. *Radical Orthodoxy: A Critical Introduction*. London: SPCK, 2007.
Schneider, Laurel C. *Beyond Monotheism: A Theology of Multiplicity*. London: Routledge, 2008.
Ward, Graham. *Cities of God*. London: Routledge, 2000.
———. "The Schizoid Christ." In *The Radical Orthodoxy Reader*, edited by John Milbank and Simon Oliver. London: Routledge, 2009.
———. "Transcorporeality." In *The Radical Orthodoxy Reader*, edited by John Milbank and Simon Oliver. London: Routledge, 2009.

10

Paper Cut-Outs of Christ in Plato's Cave

Casting Aside Radical Orthodoxy

Marko Zlomislić

> Once while some Israelites were burying a man, suddenly they saw a band of raiders; so they threw the man's body into Elisha's tomb. When the body touched Elisha's bones, the man came to life and stood up on his feet.
>
> 2 Kings 13

> There some people brought to him a man who was deaf and could hardly talk, and they begged Jesus to place his hand on him. After he took him aside, away from the crowd, Jesus put his fingers into the man's ears. Then he spit and touched the man's tongue. He looked up to heaven and with a deep sigh said to him, *"Ephphatha!"* (which means "Be opened!").
>
> Mark 7:32–34

Introduction

In this preliminary study, I want to examine what I find to be some of the shortcomings of the Radical Orthodoxy Movement as it seeks to renarrate reality. I will argue that a rejection of Franciscan nominalism results in the pacification of difference and the unique singularity of persons. In opposition to Milbank, I do not think that theology involves redirecting our loyalties away from the state and market and toward the exemplary human community of the church, but rather putting into practice the radical message that Jesus preached. This radical message was lived by many Franciscans. They displayed the existential sensibility that Christian theology needs to embrace.

Graham Ward argues that Radical Orthodoxy is a theological sensibility . . . shared to a greater or lesser degree with several other contemporary theologians. Nathan Kerr characterizes this sensibility as "a critique of modern liberalism; the articulation of a post-secular theological agenda; an emphasis upon creaturely participation in God; a renewed assessment of the importance of sacramentality; an unswerving commitment to the critique, and transformation of culture." While it will be necessary one day to return to analyze these five symphonic movements, in what follows I want to focus on what I see as the main error perpetuated by the Radical Orthodoxy movement. In reappropriating a premodern tradition by filtering it through a postmodern narrative, Radical Orthodoxy misreads key medieval thinkers such as Scotus, Bonaventure, and Occam. This misstep also results in a misreading of thinkers such as Nietzsche, Kierkegaard, Heidegger,[1] and Derrida who have incorporated key elements from the Franciscan philosophers. The Franciscan philosophers: Bonaventure, Scotus, and Ockham became nominalists in order to safeguard each single individual from the power of totalization.

Nominalism requires a vigilance that calls us to protect the uniqueness of the person. For Scotus, this uniqueness is "that by which something is a this."[2] To protect the uniqueness of persons Derrida will argue that we cannot be satisfied with a neutral and conceptual analysis that reduces the difficulty of our situation, which is ultimately irreducible. Such systems deal with homogenization and calculability, and "close themselves off from this coming of the other."[3] If we take seriously the uniqueness of each Self,

---

1. McGrath argues that "Heidegger's *Seinsvergessenheit* is not the forgetfulness of *esse* but the forgetfulness of *hacecceitas*." in "Heidegger and Duns Scotus on Truth and Language." See also McGrath, "The Forgetting of *Haecceitas*: Heidegger's 1915–1916 *Habilitationsschrift*."

2. Scotus, *Questions on Metaphysics*, Book 7.

3. Derrida, "On the Priceless," 182.

which according to Kierkegaard is "a work of the most faithful love,"[4] then we are necessarily involved in an excessive responsibility of which cannot be absolved; not even in the moment of death where according to Kierkegaard "all ways meet."[5]

I

WHO IS AFRAID OF NOMINALISM?

"Who can know the unlimited number of seeds which exists?"

St. Bonaventure

Radical Orthodoxy claims to "reconfigure theological truth." Yet, one wonders how the retrieval of Platonic and Aristotelian thought through a synthesis of Augustine and Aquinas can accomplish this move. Radical Orthodoxy retrieves the mistakes of the tradition while presenting itself as the answer to the ills of modernity. By critiquing nominalism, the Radical Orthodoxy movement fails to understand the radicality of the Franciscan philosophers whose lineage continues in the writings of existential-postmodern thinkers such as Nietzsche, Kierkegaard, Foucault, Derrida, and Deleuze.[6]

N. Den Bok shows how Scotus proposed a new concept of individuality, "a concept that does not define it as material or accidental feature, but as essential individuality (*haecceitas*)."[7] This essential individuality is understood as "a specific kind of independence."[8] Den Bok explains that for Scotus

---

4. Kierkegaard, *Works of Love*, 317.

5. Ibid.

6. For example, see May, "Philosophy as a Spiritual Exercise in Foucault and Deleuze." May writes, "Doing philosophy as a spiritual exercise, then, is doing philosophy with an eye to how one ought to live rather than with an eye to what will simply be intellectually convincing or stimulating," 224. See also Tonner, "Duns Scotus' Concept of the Univocity of Being: Another Look." Tonner writes, "In Europe a renewed interest in Scotus amongst philosophers influenced by the works of Martin Heidegger and most recently by Gilles Deleuze has resulted in a series of fresh looks tat Scotus' philosophy . . . those readers of Scotus influenced by Heidegger have breathed new life into Scotus' concept of *haecceitas* (thisness) finding in it a principle of individuality and unrepeatability unique of the medieval thinkers that would ultimately prove influential in the very early states of the advent of existential philosophy," 129.

7. Bok, "More Than Just an Individual," 169.

8. Ibid., 196.

human nature cannot exist as a general nature but only as a "this." The distinction between individuality and personhood for Scotus is essential. Den Bok writes, "a human person is not individual in virtue of his personhood, but in virtue of his essentially individual nature."[9] The thisness of the person cannot be reduced. It remains singular and unique. It cannot be framed, boxed in, or reduced to a bland uniformity. Thisness is unrepeatable.

While Catherine Pickstock attempts "to explore the relation of the Scotist legacy to modernity and postmodernity"[10] she misses a very important point. Pickstock writes, "the issue does not involve a contrast between the modern and the postmodern. It is rather that both represent 'a certain Middle age' (with roots which reach back before Duns Scotus in his Franciscan forbearers)."[11] As I see it, the issue does involve a contrast between the modern and the postmodern. The postmodern is a recovery of the Franciscan tradition. Pickstock is incorrect to maintain that postmodernity is "an advanced version of modernity." The Franciscans would be opposed to Luther's reformative modernity that abolished the haecceity of the person.[12]

Pickstock reads Scotus through a Thomistic lens. This perspective is critical of Scotus for his emphasis on the univocity of Being. However, the univocity of being goes beyond the Thomistic notion of analogy. It is the "one voice" of the individual that is important. This one voice is unlike all other voices. The uniqueness of the person cannot be upheld under the shackles of representation and analogy.[13] The person cannot be reduced by being represented in a prior system of reference. The person is incommensurable

---

9. Ibid., 170.

10. Pickstock, "Postmodernism," 568.

11. Ibid., 566.

12. Sluhovsky, in his essay, "Discernment of Difference, the Introspective Subject, and the Birth of Modernity," makes a number of important points. He argues that the modern self was seen as "introspective and unified . . . as opposed to the medieval porous, fragmented, and somewhat slumberous individual." The modernity that the Protestant movement created was "masculine . . . rational, stable . . . as opposed to premodernity that was Catholic, exterior, irrational, unstable, feminine, and corporeal," 174. Sluhovksy shows how "the intersubjectivity and soul-searching of these early modern Catholic women did not necessitate a rejection of the body . . . the portrayal of modern subjectivity as purely cerebral (and therefore masculine), purely intellectual, and Protestant, ignores the origins of discernment and introspection in late medieval Catholic practices," 189. A detailed history of what Luther trashed as a result of his reformation needs to be written, beginning with a rejection of the body and the feminine.

13. For more on why philosophy is univocity see Deleuze and Guattari, *What Is Philosophy?*

The Poverty of Radical Orthodoxy

with any system of reference that seeks to contain what it is. Each person is actualized differently. Each time is new in its singular possibilities.

Scotus does not share the Thomistic perspective because it does not do justice to individual persons. Pickstock, as Ingham shows, criticizes "Scotus on the basis that he is not a Thomist."[14] Scotus is not a Thomist because Aquinas' Aristotelian approach ignores the existential reality of persons. As Scotus argues, "It is impossible to abstract universals from the singular without previous knowledge of the singular."[15] It is the singular that counts. The singular can never be contained by any intellect.[16]

Pickstock argues that analogy "allows more scope to revelation than does univocity."[17] According to Pickstock, "revelata now bear with themselves not just their own historical contingency but also their own logic which reason without revelation cannot fully anticipate."[18] The precise counter point is that reason can never fully anticipate what will happen. Logos itself is guided by the principle of *multiforme theorae*. The revelation that Pickstock favors is already framed. Her position fails to grasp the implications of Scotus's vision. The integral vision is not based on logic, but love. It is the love of thisness that cannot be bound by logical categories. Pickstock argues, "In the long run, this allows the possibility of 'Scotist' nihilism as evidenced by Deleuze."[19]

The opposite is the case. Postmodern theorists, that is, those influenced by the Franciscans such as Foucault, Deleuze, and Derrida see the individual as a complexity that cannot be contained within pre-established forms and categories. Thisness overflows any border to produce rhizomatic events. St. Bonaventure with his concept of *multiforme theorae* had already developed a theory of dissemination upon which Derrida grounded his aporetic ethics.[20] Bonaventure shows the insufficiency of seeing God

---

14. Ingham, "Re-Situating Scotist Thought," 612.

15. Scotus, *De anima* XXII, cap.iii.

16. For a reading of Scotus's concept of *haecceitas* see Wolter, *The Philosophical Theology of John Duns Scotus*.

17. Pickstock, 555.

18. Ibid.

19. Ibid., 557. It is clear that Pickstock has not understood Deleuze or Scotus. Scotus's concept of *haecceity* where every individual is individuated by their differences has new social and political implications, which would take us into the realm of justice.

20. See my *Jacques Derrida's Aporetic Ethics*. I argue that Derrida's ethics can be understood in terms of his four main philosophical concepts: deconstruction, dissemination, difference and undecidability.

as a substance and as the first cause of a chain of causes. Substance is no longer sufficient to account for the complexity of persons, which are more than just subjects who know objects. Bonaventure shows that things are so complex such that there can never be a final accounting that would connect all the dots.

Pickstock and other Radical Orthodox theologians seem to fear the multiplicity in Scotus's thought. Multiplicity remains confined by the moderns within the discipline imposed by institutions. As Ingham writes, Scotus's "labours to make clear that the categories of Being found in Aristotle's metaphysics (or even those present in Platonic thought) do not exhaust the domain of Christian theology." [21] Ingham shows that Pickstock is "unable to see what is truly going on in the Franciscan's thought."[22] While this is true, I would add that Pickstock perhaps does see what the Franciscan philosophers are doing and therefore cannot accept the implications of their message, which is grounded in the life that Jesus lived. In other words, Franciscan thought would be the true root, the radix of Catholic theology, which was already postmodern.

As Ingham writes, "The centrality of creation is no less important to Scotus than to Aquinas; he defends it in a different way. Scotus defends the dignity of creation in his discussion of the principle of individuation (*haecceitas*), the centrality of the human person . . . it is Aquinas who views human nature in an inferior light, not Scotus."[23] Scotus defends the contingency of creation because of his Franciscan spirituality. This spirituality emphasizes love rather than sin. It emphasizes the conception and Incarnation rather than sin and the fall.

Following some of the insights given by Pickstock, James K. A. Smith argues that a paradigm shift began with Scotus. This shift led to modernity and nihilism. In his text, *Introducing Radical Orthodoxy*, Smith argues that the Franciscan Scotus neglects the transcendent. Smith wants to retrieve the transcendent by going back to Augustine. Smith argues for a participatory ontology that links all of creation to the transcendent. This participatory ontology seems to short-circuit the incarnation.

Radical Orthodoxy is a renewal of Christian Platonism rather than a renewal of the good news proclaimed by Jesus and the Franciscans. In other words, Radical Orthodoxy is not radical. It has not gone to the roots

---

21. Ingham, 611.
22. Ibid., 613.
23. Ibid., 614.

of the tradition. It is a deformation of the Catholic tradition as it perpetuates a misreading of Scotus, the Franciscans, and existential-postmodern thought. What is required, I think, is not another treatise showing us how the secular state must be replaced with a church that controls the political and economic space of its domain, but a spirituality that contains a radical love. This radical love is to be found in the sayings of Jesus and in the writings of the Franciscan thinkers who lived a life of theological immanence. [24]

In *The Courage to Be*,[25] Paul Tillich gives his account of the dangers associated with nominalism. He writes, "In connection with the rise of modern individualism, I have mentioned the communalistic splitting of universals into individual things. There is a side in nominalism, which anticipates motifs of recent existentialism. There is for example, its irrationalism rooted in the breakdown of essences under the attacks of Duns Scotus and Ockham. The emphasis on the contingency of everything that exists makes both the will of God and the being man equally contingent. It gives to man the feeling of a definite lack of ultimate necessity, with respect not only to himself but also to his world."[26]

Tillich's theory of participation, much favored by Radical Orthodox theologians paves the way to conformity and the leveling off any unique singularity. Those who favor conformity will see nominalism as a heretical stance. The anxious words of Jesus on the cross confirm the truth of nominalism rather than the harmonious community of Neoplatonism defended by Milbank.[27]

Milbank sees nominalism as nihilism.[28] To overcome this nihilism, Milbank says that he engages in "a deliberate uncompromising and fearless

---

24. It is telling of course, that Milbank turns to the conservative Lutheran theologians Johann Georg Hamann and Franz Heinrich Jacobi who argued for a theory of knowledge by faith alone to overcome the legacy of Scotus. Luther's "Disputation Against Scholastic Theology" can be read as his critique against the Franciscans. For example: "One must concede that the will is not free to strive toward whatever is declared good. This is in opposition to Scotus and Gabriel." Also: "It is absurd to conclude that erring man can love the creature above all things, therefore also God. This is in opposition to Scotus and Gabriel." Luther's theology of sin cannot accept the place of radical love. He writes, "To love God is at the same time to hate oneself and to know nothing but God."

25. Tillich, *The Courage To Be*.

26. Ibid., 129.

27. In an interview with Rachael Kohn, *Radio National*, July 11, 1999, Milbank states, "secular modernity was born in a perverse theology at the end of the late Middle Ages."

28. There is a long and erroneous history that links nominalism with nihilism and skepticism, beginning with Plato's condemnation of Antisthenes. Jacques Maritain and

appeal back to the real center of the western tradition, which is essentially a neo-Platonic, Judaic, and Christian center.[29] He further claims, "the watchword for Radical Orthodoxy is participation in the Platonic sense . . . reason only works through that participation, faith only works through that participation . . . metaphysical participation is the only possible basis for social participation."[30] The stance developed by Milbank has little to do with the root teachings of Jesus. They are in fact, a throw back to the Christian Platonism criticized by Nietzsche in his *Anti-Christ*. As Nietzsche has repeatedly shown us, it is this life that is to be valued, not something beyond life. Milbank's return to Christian Platonism is a rejection of nominalism along with the unique singularity of the individual.[31]

II

TOUCHING FLESH: HEALING THE CORPSE

> But Jesus answered, "No more of this!"
> And he touched the man's ear and healed him.
>
> Luke 22:51

Lisa Isherwood is clear in showing how Radical Orthodoxy has "trouble with allowing the divine to be a truly unfolding process." The God Milbank

---

Etienne Gilson claim nominalism leads to skepticism, without of course seeing that such a move is necessary for the sake of a better ethic. For more on how nominalism has been cast see Crockett, "The Confusion over Nominalism." Crockett writes, ". . . one might simply assert that Durand was a nominalist and not a skeptic, while Nicholas of Autrecourt was a skeptic and not a nominalist."

29. Ibid.

30. Ibid.

31. See for example, Sections 32, 33, and 36 of *The Anti-Christ* where Nietzsche defends a Franciscan vision of the Gospels. He writes, "The 'glad tidings' are precisely that there are no more opposites; the kingdom of Heaven belongs to *children;* the faith which here finds utterance is not a faith which has been won by struggle—it is there, from the beginning, it is as it were a return to childishness in the spiritual domain . . . One could with some freedom of expression, call Jesus a 'free spirit'—he cares nothing for what is fixed: the word *killeth*, everything fixed *killeth* . . . It is not a 'belief' which distinguishes the Christian: the Christian acts, he is distinguished by a different mode of acting . . . A new way of living, *not* a new belief . . . One constructed the *Church* out of the antithesis to the Gospel." I give a sustained reading of *The Anti-Christ* in my *Franciscan Postmodernity* (forthcoming).

advances is fixed and frozen. Any system to come out of such a theology is fixed as well.[32] Jesus reacted to this type of theology when he criticized the Pharisees.

To overcome the limits imposed by Radical Orthodoxy, Isherwood recommends, "engagement with raw/radical incarnation, the vulnerability and bravery to feel and to touch." Isherwood describes such a theology as "a skin-trade." Such a view urges us "to take incarnation much more seriously." Nominalism is the philosophy that takes the implications of the incarnation seriously. I would argue that a rejection of nominalism is a rejection of the radical nature of the incarnation and the promise that "all flesh will be saved." Taking a cue from Isherwood, we can further examine the implications of touch.

What touches us shows where our love is directed.[33] The woman in Matthew's gospel says, "If only I may touch His garment, I shall be made well." Jesus responds by saying, "Be of good cheer, daughter; your faith has made you well."[34] What is needed if we are to believe this event, is a touch of faith. This mustard seed faith that touches, transforms us, and takes our lives along a different tangent, allows us to see the kingdom, here, now.

They wanted to touch the fringe of his cloak, the hem of his garment in order to be healed. Luke's gospel records that "all the people were trying to touch Him, for power was coming from Him and healing them all."[35] His touch makes them whole. His touch heals. He saves by touching them. He touches the coffin of the widow's son. He tells the corpse to arise. It listens. Luke writes, "And the dead man sat up, and began to speak. And he gave him to his mother."[36] The one who saves touches what is untouchable.

After the resurrection he asks Mary not to touch him, that is, not to cling to him, clench him, latch on; in other words, Jesus does not wish to be seized. He teaches about possession. To take possession is to capture. The other must not be captured, seized, or possessed. The touch must be light. It must not grip, grasp, or grab. In short, it must not be Platonic. We understand the power of touch the least because it is so close to us. We

---

32. By fixed I mean castrated, made impotent, and uncreative. Nietzsche saw this as the main work of the priest.

33. For an excellent reading of touch in Derrida and Nancy see Secomb, "Amorous Politics."

34. Matthew 9:21–22.

35. Luke 6:19.

36. Luke 7:13–15.

have fled from the intimacy and proximity of this root and turned toward a Greek tradition that favored sight and distance. Platonic thought carries an aversion to the tactile. Aristotle associated touch with animality.

Can theology teach us to touch what is untouchable, what is impossible to touch, what will always remain excessive, whole, intact, and never damaged? Is this not the "good news" namely, that what we are, at our core is safe and sound, always already intact. It is this being-intact that does not require the tactile. It gives of itself without exhausting its plentitude. This being-intact changes the landscape of the tangible. It untangles the knot that surrounds the heart.

Derrida has written that "touch is finitude." What we seek is not touch but what cannot be touched by death, disease, suffering, and sorrow. This being-intact gives the resurrection, which can be understood as the always new. It cannot be subtracted or framed within a contract.

Luke best displays the Franciscan spirit Nietzsche would make use of in *Thus Spoke Zarathustra*.[37] Luke writes, "People were also bringing babies to Jesus for him to place his hands on them. When the disciples saw this, they rebuked them. But Jesus called the children to him and said, 'Let the little children come to me, and do not hinder them, for the kingdom of God belongs to such as these. Truly I tell you, anyone who will not receive the kingdom of God like a little child will never enter it.'"[38]

Here I think we have located the kernel distinguishing Franciscan thought from Radical Orthodoxy. The child contains the spirit of creativity and innocence. Their presence and exuberance has the power to transform. The child is the event that brings in the radically new. Francis felt the holy surge of God's creative power. It led him to have a radically new outlook on life that took him away from the commercial and capitalistic world of his father.

With its reliance on Neoplatonic thought, Radical Orthodoxy returns us to more of the same. It wants to return us to a conservative status-quo that is anti-life. It seeks the organization and control of the individual. Ultimately, this is what Francis rebelled against as he stripped naked before his father. If one really believes in haecceity, then the universal cannot comprehend the singular. This is what nominalism shows us as it protects the

---

37. I have examined this theme in "The Child's New Love." Goicoechea has written on this theme at length. See his remarkable book, *Zarathustra's Love Beyond Wisdom*.

38. Luke 18:15–17.

unique name of the person and following St. Francis, protects the uniqueness of all flesh.

The difference between Franciscan thought and Radical Orthodoxy can be best illustrated by turning to the well-known children's book, *Scaredy Squirrel*.[39] Scaredy Squirrel is unable to leave his nut tree. He fears the unknown. Watts writes, "He'd rather stay in his safe and familiar tree than risk venturing into the unknown." The unknown is a fearful place full of danger and chance. Scaredy Squirrel suffers from an extreme version of post-traumatic stress disorder. He spends his day assaulted by anxiety, fearful of green Martians, tarantulas, poison ivy, killer bees, germs, and sharks. He stays in his tree protected by the transcendence of its branches. He cherishes predictability, routine, and control. His life is reduced to a liturgy of boredom where the same sacraments are enacted according to a strict schedule. He wakes up, eats a nut, and looks at a view, and goes to sleep. He thinks he is prepared for the unexpected second coming with his hardhat, antibacterial soap, calamine lotion, parachute, mask and rubber gloves, net, Band-Aid, and sardines. He believes that his emergency kit will protect him. One day, his world is shaken by the arrival of a "smiling killer bee." This event traumatizes him. Filled with panic, he loses his emergency kit. Jumping out of the tree to catch the kit he realizes that he is "no ordinary squirrel. He's a flying squirrel." He discovers his "thisness." He becomes, "overjoyed, adventurous, carefree, alive." In short, he becomes a Franciscan. Watts writes, "All this extreme excitement has inspired Scaredy Squirrel to make drastic changes to his life."

There is nothing radical about sin, fear, anxiety, guilt, and shame. The truly radical happens when we discover how love erases these things to

---

39. Watts, *Scaredy Squirrel*. Of course, I am being serious here. This thought occurred to me while I was reading *Scaredy Squirrel* to my daughter Holly just as we finished watching another great Franciscan TV show, namely *Little Bear*. Luke's gospel can be read as a meditation on the words, "Fear Not." The seven passages are: 1) Luke 1:13, "But the angel said unto him, 'Fear not, Zacharias: for thy prayer is heard; and thy wife Elisabeth shall bear thee a son, and thou shalt call his name John.'" 2) Luke 1:30, "And the angel said unto her, 'Fear not, Mary: for thou hast found favor with God.'" 3) Luke 2:10, "And the angel said unto them, 'Fear not: for, behold, I bring you good tidings of great joy, which shall be to all people.'" 4) Luke 5:10, "And so was also James, and John, the sons of Zebedee, which were partners with Simon. And Jesus said unto Simon, 'Fear not; from hence forth thou shalt catch men.'" 5) Luke 8:50. "But when Jesus heard it, he answered him, saying, 'Fear not: believe only, and she shall be made whole.'" 6) Luke 12:7, "But even the very hairs of your head are all numbered. Fear not therefore: ye are of more value than many sparrows." 7) Luke 12:32, "Fear not, little flock; for it is your Father's good pleasure to give you the kingdom."

establish a transformative creativity. This transformative creativity takes flesh and makes it exuberant. It lives and works under the phrases, "Behold I have made all things new." The Neoplatonic framework upon which Radical Orthodoxy wishes to establish itself leads us to a valley of dry bones without hope of resurrection.

Radical Orthodoxy embraces Neoplatonism and its participatory framework. Nominalism challenged this worldview by developing an immanent position. This position demonstrated that the Platonic-Christian synthesis was in need of an uncoupling. Creation is not a frozen Platonic form. It is contingent because of radical freedom. Nominalism rejects Platonism in order to have a better philosophy of love. The so-called stability that Platonism gave to Christian theology positioned it away from the faith demonstrated by Jesus. By appropriating Platonism, Milbank's Radical Theology arrives stillborn. Under this vision, we become screens on which theology—yet another ideology—displays its flattened patterns. Here we are fixed and dehumanized.

III

THE IMMEDIACY OF THE SINGULAR

> It must therefore be in everyone's power to become what he is, a single individual; no one is prevented from being a single individual, no one, unless he prevents himself by becoming many.
>
> Søren Kierkegaard, *The Crowd Is Untruth*

By arguing in favor of nominalism, Franciscan philosophers such as Scotus and Occam embraced a new relationship between the individual and divine nature. The focus was on the primacy of the singular and the immediacy of the singular in relation to God. In 1268 Roger Bacon argued for the preeminence of the individual in *Communia Naturalium*. He shows God created the world for the individual and not for a concept of humanity. The emphasis is on immediacy rather than the mediation of genus and species.

The debate between nominalism and realism concerns not only the question of whether universals are real, but what the real is. If we consider what the word "real" means, the significance of nominalism in defending the singularity of all flesh becomes crucial. *Realis* is the world rich with things. Reality has wealth. Reality is the wealth of creation in all its glory.

The Poverty of Radical Orthodoxy

It was the wealth of created reality, which led St. Francis to a life devoted to joy. St. Francis privileged the singular existing individual. Justice is given to each individual thing. Along these lines, I think that James K. A. Smith is clearly mistaken when he criticizes immanence as "war by another means."[40] The postmoderns, whom Smith claims to have understood so well, argue the opposite position. Analogical participation produces violence in the order of being because justice is not given to each individual. The alternative *mythos* proposed by Milbank and his followers is a return to the violence of metaphysics where peace means the pacification of difference and singularity. Here we would all be seated in Plato's Cave while the so-called Radical Reformists would parade paper cut-outs of Christ onto the screen. It is precisely this hegemonic view that Nietzsche, Kierkegaard, and other existential-postmodernists desired to liberate us. In short, Milbank's theology is a repeat of Plato's noble lie. It is a falsity that has buried the real religion lived and defended by the Franciscans.

When columnists of the Christian right such as Joel Belz writes, "nominalism and its handmaiden relativism are as repugnant to God as is outright denial and maybe more so"[41] it is clear what is at stake for the individual person, namely the loss of freedom, thought, and action. For those in favor of clear-cut centers and stable hierarchies, nominalism is presented as a threat to certainty. Nominalism does undermine foundations for the sake a better ethics, a better love, and a better justice. Nominalism speaks to each singular experience. Peirce argued that nominalism "blocks the road to inquiry."[42] The opposite seems to be the case, namely that nominalism removes roadblocks so that inquiry can freely proceed on its way. The anti-nominalist position found in the works of Milbank, Pickstock, Smith and Peirce favor prediction, control, conformity, predictability, and reliable expectation. I see this as an attempt to impose constraints on what is real.

The dialectic of skepticism does not limit the scope of rationality; it widens its scope. Within the universe proposed by Radical Orthodoxy the individual is reduced to a predictable machine, God becomes an abstraction and society becomes a panopticon driven by disciplines of control. The critics of nominalism stifle individualism in order to maintain a spiritual aristocracy along with a theological elitism.[43]

40. Smith, *Introducing Radical Orthodoxy*. 195.
41. Cited in Marty, "Nominalism," 39.
42. Peirce, *Collected Papers*, vol. 1, 170.
43. In his article, "Radical Orthodoxy and the New Culture of Obscurantism," Janz

IV

LOVE AND GLORY, NOT SIN AND HOMO SACER

> Preach the Gospel at all times and when necessary use words.
>
> St. Francis

The move away from nominalism diminishes the status of personhood. The nominalism upheld by the Franciscan philosophers and the followers of Scotus is precisely what safeguards the irreducibility of the person. Gerard Manley Hopkins best expressed this view in his poem "As Kingfisher's Catch Fire" where he writes, "For Christ plays in ten thousand places / Lovely in limbs and lovely in eyes not his" (lines 12–13). Hopkins's poem echoes the words of Jesus in Matthew's gospel that say, "Every hair on your head is numbered."[44] To believe as Milbank and Pickstock do, that nominalism is a slide into nihilism, is to misread the gospels, late medieval philosophy, and postmodern thought. In short, Milbank constructs a Christ for whom I would not want to be a Christian.

The Franciscan philosophers whom Milbank disapproves of have the best understanding of the incarnation. They see the incarnation as grounded in ultimate love rather than sin. This love embraces the whole of creation. In St. Paul's words, Christ is the fullness "who fills everything in everyway." Milbank takes the plentitude of Christ and reduces it to "our new political life in Christ." Following Agamben, Milbank sees Christ as *homo sacer*; as abandoned and excluded. Milbank writes, "For the church is founded on Christ who was only excluded—by imperial Rome, by tribal-cum-city-state Israel, by modern democracy . . . But Christ as purely excluded is risen: therefore the life he is risen to is the possibility of life after exclusion from life." Here we have located the precise problem of Milbank's theology. He takes insights from Agamben and then contorts the Gospel to fit into the space of Agamben's discourse. Milbank's use of Agamben's narrative is problematic from a Franciscan perspective. Scotus argued that

---

clearly shows how Radical Orthodox theologians have come to rely on a special type of "intellectual intuition that relies "on the prophetic ingenuity of a few." Janz believes that Milbank's thought gives rise to "a new kind of esoteric gnosticism." Such a move Janz contends is anti-philosophical and even "radically anti-rational in outlook."

44. Matthew 10:30.

the Incarnation reflects God's glory.[45] Bonaventure argues, "When God became Man, the works of God were brought to perfection." If the whole of creation is incarnational, then it cannot be the bare life of *homo sacer*, however trendy Agamben has become after Derrida's death.

The Franciscan philosophers with their understanding of the incarnation develop a difference universalism that upholds the unique singularity of all flesh. This outlook led Francis to a radical love that echoed the love of Jesus. Francis developed a love for each individual creature. Scotus takes this position and develops the concept of *haecceity* or "thisness." While persons do share a common form and have equal worth and dignity, their "thisness" makes them irreducible and unique.

Conclusion

Nominalism is a skepticism that is skeptical for the sake of a better ethic. Nominalism shows us we can never have full knowledge of any person and thing. Nominalism protects the complexity of each unique singularity from being reduced and universalized in a Platonic manner. The Radical Orthodox claim that social justice is empty without connection to the transcendent misses the relevance of justice. Recovering the teachings of Augustine and Aquinas by reading them through a Neoplatonic filter may fill the space of specialized journals but it does nothing to live up to the radical message preached by Jesus. Jesus no more requires the help of Augustine and Aquinas than Paul requires the help of Žižek, Badiou, and Agamben.

It is difficult to see how Milbank's movement can overcome the ills of modernity by rereading Augustine and Aquinas. The attempt of Radical Orthodoxy to reclaim the world for theology ignores the kingdom in favor of the church. A theology that fails to follow the teaching and practice of Jesus remains academic rather than existential.

How does Radical Orthodoxy with its renewed concern for worship and liturgy perform the works of love? How does the recovery of the "pre-1300 vision"[46] help to overcome secular culture and preach the good news?

---

45. Chiesa claims that Agamben has a Franciscan Ontology. My reading here indicates otherwise. If the Kingdom is here, now, then messianic time is a waster of time. Chiesa writes, "Agamben's notion of "weak" being, a being characterized by a "presentative poverty" could qualify his ontology as "Franciscan." The Franciscan notion of poverty is an ordering of desire, not private property or worldly goods. See *The Italian Difference*. Agamben's diagnosis of this world was bleak. St. Francis's diagnosis was not.

46. John Milbank, "The last of the last: Theology, Authority and Democracy."

When theologians fail to address the suffering of those cast out, rejected, and overlooked, their theology is neither radical nor orthodox. It remains cut off from its roots; a pseudo-orthodoxy that returns us to a place where contingency and complexity are avoided. In the face of this, Radical Orthodoxy needs to be cast aside for the sake of a better religious and spiritual practice.

For my daughter, Holly Anne Bliss

Bibliography

Bok, N. Den. "More Than Just an Individual: Scotus's Concept of the Person." *Franciscan Studies* 66 (2008).
Chiesa, Lorenzo. *The Italian Difference: Between Nihilism and BioPolitics*. Melbourne: Repress, 2009.
Crockett. Campbell. "The Confusion over Nominalism." *The Journal of Philosophy* 47:25 (December 1950) 752–58.
Deleuze, Gilles, and Félix Guattari. *What Is Philosophy?* New York: Columbia University Press, 1994.
Derrida, Jacques. "On the 'Priceless' or the 'Going Rate' of the Transaction." In *Negotiations: Interventions and Interviews, 1971–2001*, edited and translated by Elizabeth Rottenburg, 315–28. Stanford: Stanford University Press, 2002.
Goicoechea, David. *Zarathustra's Love Beyond Wisdom*. Binghamton: Global Publications, 2002.
Ingham, Mary Beth. "Re-Situating Scotist Thought." *Modern Theology* 21:4 (October 2005) 609–18.
Janz, Paul D. "Radical Orthodoxy and the New Culture of Obscurantism." *Modern Theology* 20:3 (July 2004) 363–405.
Kierkegaard, Søren. *Works of Love*. Translated by Howard Hong and Edna Hong. New York: Harper, 1962.
Luther, Martin. "Disputation Against Scholastic Theology."
Marty, Martin. "Nominalism." *Christian Century* (October 24–31, 2001) 39.
May, Todd. "Philosophy as a Spiritual Exercise in Foucault and Deleuze." *Angelaki* 5:2 (August 2000) 223–29.
McGrath, Sean J. "Heidegger and Duns Scotus on Truth and Language." *The Review of Metaphysics* 57 (December 2003) 339–58.
———. "The Forgetting of *Haecceitas*: Heidegger's 1915–1916 *Habilitationsschrift*." In *Between the Human and the Divine: Philosophical and Theological Hermeneutics*, edited by Andrzej Wiercinski, 355–77. Guernsey: Hermeneutic, 2002.
Milbank, John. Rachael Kohn, 7/11/1999, *Radio National*.
———. "The Last of the Last: Theology, Authority and Democracy." *Revista Portuguesa de Filosofia* 58 (2002) 271–98.
Nietzsche, Frederick. *The Anti-Christ*. Translated by H. L. Mencken. Tucson: Sharp, 1999.

Peirce, Charles Sanders. *Collected Papers.* Edited by Charles Hartshorne and Paul Weiss. Vol. 1. Cambridge: Harvard University Press, 1993.

Pickstock, Catharine. "Postmodernism." In *The Blackwell Companion to Political Theology*, edited by Peter Scott. Oxford: Blackwell, 2004.

Secomb, Linnell. "Amorous Politics: Between Derrida and Nancy." *Social Semiotics* 16:3 (2006) 449–60.

Scotus. *De anima* XXII.

———. *Questions on Metaphysics*, Book 7.

Sluhovsky, Moshe. "Discernment of Difference, the Introspective Subject, and the Birth of Modernity." *Journal of Medieval and Early Modern Studies* 36:1 (2006) 169–99.

Smith, James K. A. *Introducing Radical Orthodoxy: Mapping a Post-Secular Theology.* Grand Rapids: Baker Academic, 2004.

Tillich, Paul. *The Courage To Be.* New Haven: Yale University Press, 1952.

Tonner, Philip. "Duns Scotus' Concept of the Univocity of Being: Another Look." *Pli* 18 (2007) 129–46.

Watts, Melanie. *Scaredy Squirrel.* Toronto: Kids Can Press, 2006.

Wolter, Allan B. *The Philosophical Theology of John Duns Scotus.* Edited by Marilyn McCord Adams. Ithaca: Cornell University Press, 1990.

Zlomislić, Marko. "The Child's New Love." In *Joyful Wisdom: Zarathustra's Annunciations Of . . .* St. Catharines: Thought House, 2002.

———. *Franciscan Postmodernity* (forthcoming).

———. *Jacques Derrida's Aporetic Ethics.* New York: Lexington, 2006.

11

The Eucharist *Is* Drive

Marcus Pound

This is how we should approach the topic of the Eucharist: what exactly do we eat when we eat the body of Christ? We eat the partial object, the undead substance which redeems us and guarantees that we are raised above mortality, that while still alive here on earth, we already participate in the eternal divine Life. Does this not mean that the Eucharist is like the undead substance of the indestructible eternal life that invades the body in a horror movie? Are we not, through Eucharist, terrorized by an alien monster which invades our body? . . . Consequently, is not the "theological" dimension without which, Benjamin, revolution cannot win, the very dimension of the excess of drive, of its "too muchness"? In other words, is not our task—the properly *Christological* one—to change the modality of our being-stuck in a mode that allows, solicits even, the activity of sublimation?[1]

The above quote, taken from the concluding pages of Žižek's chapter "Building Blocks for a Materialist Theology" constitutes a Lacanian reading of the Eucharist. Žižek's reading is, I suggest, an original reading, breaking with previous attempts to treat theology from a Lacanian perspective to the extent it takes the drive [*Trieb*] rather than desire [*désir*] as the interpretive basis for understanding the Eucharist. Prior theological engagement with

1. Žižek, *The Parallax View*, 122–23.

The Poverty of Radical Orthodoxy

Lacan has tended to focus on desire[2] where desire is defined in terms of lack [*manqué*]. As Lacan says, "it is lack which causes desire to arise."[3] From the perspective of psychoanalysis, theological recourse to metaphysics, transcendence, or participation betrays desire: they are an attempt to say what cannot be said, a chase for the intrinsically lost object. Accordingly, theological responses to Lacan have tended to correct their standpoint. For example, Charles Winquist claims "[T]heology in the wake of Lacan will be a theology of desire . . . the form of interrogation, that instantiates a loss, constitutes knowledge of a lack, and fissures the completeness of symbolic expression: Theology . . . has no access to a hidden order of things . . . We will still be reading a text but the text will be marked and sometimes re-marked by fissured wrought by limiting questions, poetic indirections, and figures of brokenness."[4]

The problem arises because focusing on desire in this way leads theology down a broadly Kantian route: limiting knowledge to make room for faith; it is not so much what we can say, as what we cannot. And to this extent this approach colludes with the Kantian observance of the private/social split. Religion remains private for the sake of peace in the social sphere.[5]

Part of the problem lies in the way the texts of Lacan are appropriated with inadequate insight into the sheer breadth and complexity of his work. Simply put, these writers do not even consider drive.[6]

My task in what follows is to critically develop Žižek's suggestion and highlight the significance of this shift in psychoanalytic and theological terms. Briefly put, my argument is two-fold. First, Žižek's emphasis on the drive offers a defense of the Eucharist in advance of the critique of desire. The Eucharist is less a betrayal of inviting desire in a spurious transcendent in the realm of the everyday, rather it is the positive attempt to make

---

2. See for example the various contributors to Wyshodgrod, Crownfield, and Raschke (eds.), *Lacan and Theological Discourse*; Winquist, "Lacan and Theology" in *Post-Secular Theology*; Braungardt, "Theology After Lacan? A Psychoanalytic Approach to Theological Discourse"; see especially in regard to the liturgical elemen Pound, *Theology, Psychoanalysis, Trauma*, and Schneider, "The Transformation of Eros." The exception is Davis, "Subtractive Liturgy." Davis however does not explicitly invoke the terminology of the drive, but rather the language of Alain Badiou.

3. Lacan, *Le Séminar*, 139.

4. Winquist, "Lacan and Theology," 313–15.

5. Kant, "What is Enlightenment?" 4.

6. Schneider makes tacit reference to the drive, but the reference is left hanging. See "The Transformation of Eros," 280.

manifest precisely that element of occlusion, and in doing so reach a path of enjoyment [*jouissance*]. The significance of this reading is, I suggest, not simply in the shift from desire to enjoyment, but also whether we view the Eucharist in fundamentally conservative or transgressive terms: is the Eucharist a social form of "obsessional neurosis" [*Zwangsneurose*] (i.e., the ritual renunciation of constitutional instincts *a la* Freud)?[7] Or does it, as Žižek suggests, through the invocation of the drive, constitute ritual move beyond the symbolic into a realm of transgressive enjoyment.

Second, by bringing the liturgical context of the Eucharist into critical consideration theology is best placed to treat the drive and transgression because, while it invites transgressive enjoyment it—unlike its "undead" counterparts in the movies to which Žižek refers—refuses to let the undead run amok. Instead, the Eucharist offers the redemptive process as the true moment of transgressive horror.

In developing Žižek's work I take my orientation from Freud and Lacan. In section 1, I treat the developmental relationship of and between the two concepts, and read the implications of the discussion back into Žižek's quote to illuminate its significance. In section 2, I explore specifically what "sublimation" might mean in the context of the drive and Eucharist. Relevant here is the role of the death drive. This compels ethical consideration, and helps us to make sense why Žižek considers this the "Christological task." In section 3, I develop a reading of the "Christological task" with reference to the scopic drive, manifest in the "gaze." In section 4, I draw all these threads together, by inviting comparison with Catherine Pickstock's liturgical critique of modernity. I argue that despite their differing agendas and approaches they articulate a shared set of conceptual concerns. In section 5, "Horror and the mass," I conclude by reflecting on the relation between the unbearable horror elicited by the drive and its object, and the mass. As I argue, it doesn't do to oppose Žižek's description to a more benign theology of joy; rather one should radicalize Žižek's suggestion. Christian joy is the true horror.

Over the course of this paper I draw extensively upon Lacan's *Seminar XI, The Four Fundamental Concepts of Psychoanalysis*. In doing so I seek also to develop a latent question: it is not simply a question of applying Lacanian theory to the Eucharist in the manner of Žižek, but raising the question of the degree to which theology shapes Lacan in the first place?

---

7. Freud, "Obsessive Actions and Religious Practices," 127. Hereafter referred to as SE.

I: Desire and Drive

Traditional theological appropriations of Lacan have tended to take desire as the basis for engagement and rightly so. Desire is at the center of Lacan's thought: it is *"the essence of man."*[8] Yet for Lacan desire arises from an inexpressible lack. In his initial work this was taken as the result of the gap which opens up between our imagined sense of wholeness or self-identity, over and against the fragmented and contingent bodies we inhabit (what he termed the "mirror stage").[9] With the introduction of language, desire is further compounded as lack: "Desire is the surplus produced from the articulation of need [i.e., a biological imperative such as hunger] in demand [e.g. the symbolic]."[10] In other words, for a need to be expressed it must pass through signification. A child's cry elicits a response of the mother (mOther), yet the very presence of the mother generates an importance in itself that goes beyond the mere satisfaction of a need. This surplus is what Lacan calls desire. Desire therefore is not the desire for an object as such (e.g. food, a source of warmth etc.); rather it arises in relation to the Other because no object satisfies the excess that arises between a need and its articulation. Desire is the presence of an absence which marks all speech, "an insatiable longing for 'something more,' through which the subject articulates itself indirectly, in the surplus-meaning of its speech."[11] Hence, "the moment in which desire becomes human is also that in which the child is born into language."[12] And because desire is related to language in this fashion, desire is an inter-subjective phenomenon: "man's desire is the desire of the Other"; i.e., we desire from the perspective of the Other.[13]

Accordingly, Lacan's early work centered the direction of treatment on desire. For example, where desire becomes confused with the locus of the mOther, the aim is to distance oneself in this regard; i.e., castration—repositioning oneself "with respect to the Other as desire."[14] Or, in *Seminar VII*, Lacan develops an ethics of pure desire drawn from his reading of

---

8. Lacan, *The Seminar of Jacques Lacan, Vol. XI*, 275. Significantly, of the four fundamentals of psychoanalysis listed by Lacan, desire is not credited whilst drive is.

9. Ibid., "The Mirror Stage as Formative of the *I* Function as Revealed in Psychoanalytic Experience."

10. Ibid., *Écrits*, 689.

11. Braungardt, "Theology After Lacan?"

12. Lacan, *Écrits*, 262.

13. Ibid., *Seminar XI*, 35.

14. Schneider, "Eros Reconfigured," 279.

Greek tragedy. His argument is that traditional forms of moral thought, as highlighted by analytical practice, allow guilt to eclipse desire. This pushes the moral basis towards a utilitarian ethics in service of goods.[15] By contrast, in Lacan's work the analyzed is admonished not to "cede on one's desire."[16]

Yet as Christoph Schneider points out, because there is no such thing as the subject's 'own desire' that would lead away from or beyond that of the Other, Lacan's tack changes in his later work to focus instead on the subject's satisfaction in the partial object of the drive.[17]

Desire and drive are closely related in Lacan's work, both arising out of the differentiation between nature and culture. Freud, it will be recalled, initially described drives (as distinct from instincts) as "mythical entities, magnificent in their indefiniteness."[18] Drives were transcendentally deduced in the manner of Kant to account for the fact that, while sexuality was a biological function with the intent of reproduction of the species, clinical experience suggested otherwise: human sexuality exceeds the merely reproductive. Instincts are biological; drives exist in the realm of the symbolic. Instincts imply "a hereditary pattern peculiar to an animal species, varying little from one member of this species;[19] the drive conversely is on the side of singularity, it says something specific about that individual's process of subjectization."[20] Both desire and drive are then, as Dylan Evans suggests, on the side of the subject; the distinction pertains to "the partial aspect in which desire is realized. Desire is one and undivided, whereas the drives are partial manifestations of desire."[21]

Freud established four movements of the drive: 1) pressure; 2) source; 3) aim; and 4) satisfaction.[22] Drive involves a *pressure* which arises from a *source*, [*Quelle*], which in turn directs the organism to an *aim*—to eliminate the state of tension obtaining in the source—directed toward a specific *object*; it is in the *object* that the *aim* achieves its satisfaction.

---

15. Cognitive behavior therapy is one such example where the expediency of its methods aims to help the subject manage anxiety in such a way as to allow a productive life. In short, it treats the symptom, but not the initial question of desire.
16. Lacan, *The Seminar of Jacques Lacan, Vol. VII*, 319.
17. Schneider, "Eros Reconfigured," 280.
18. Lacan, *The Seminar of Jacques Lacan, XX*, 94.
19. Laplanche and Pontalis, *The Language of Psychoanalysis*, 214.
20. Harari, *Lacan's Four Fundamental Concepts*, 202.
21. Evans, *An Introductory Dictionary of Lacanian Psychoanalysis*, 49.
22. Freud, "Instincts and their Vicissitudes," 122.

Lacan modifies Freud in the following way: both instincts and drive involve a *pressure*, but "drive is not *Drang*, the absolute pressure of need,"[23] but that which exceeds it; i.e., the pressure of drive arises "precisely because no object of any need can satisfy the drive." For example: "Even when you stuff your mouth—the mouth that opens in the register of the drive—it is not the food that satisfies it, it is, as one says, the pleasure of the mouth. That is why, in the analytic experience, the oral drive is encountered at the final term, in a situation in which it does no more than order the menu."[24]

Where the *source* of pressure in the case of biological instincts result from the internal organs (e.g. hunger arises from stomach contractions) drive arises at the erogenous openings (i.e., mouth, anus, genitalia, eye, and ear). Maria Jannus calls these openings "vanishing points where the inside meets the outside."[25]

Where the *aim* of the instinct is met in an object (e.g. food), the aim of the drive is not an object as such, but a particular type of *object*, the object *a* [*objet petit a*]: the partial object.

What then is the partial object which Žižek cites as an instance of the Eucharist; i.e., that which gives rise to drive? Simply put, in the process of becoming, a subject assumes a principle moment of sacrifice: something must be ceded as condition of entry into social life, which forever manifests itself negativity in the felt experience of a primal loss; i.e., castration—both a physical castration from the body of the mother, and the castration that language brings to bare upon the subject.[26] Situated at the level of the body, although never wholly identified with the body, the loss in separation produces an object—*object a*—the paradoxical object which has no substance. The *object a* is "[i]nvisible and inaudible, it nonetheless gazes at us, or speaks inside us from the outside, arousing anxiety. It is the archaic object, annihilating or enticing us from the outside of our being with imminent non-being or the promise of fulfilment."[27]

Nowhere is the drama of the drive and its object more evidenced than in Freud's celebrated example of *fort-da*. A child throws a cotton reel on a piece of sting outside his cot uttering o-o-o-o, which Freud links to *fort*

---

23. Lacan, *Seminar XI*, 162.
24. Ibid., 167.
25. Jannus, "The *Démontage* of the Drive," 120.
26. Lacan expresses this in his dictum adapted from Kojève: "the symbol first manifests itself as the killing of the thing." *Écrits*, 262.
27. Jannus, "The *Démontage* of the Drive," 125.

[gone]. Pulling back the reel the child cries *da* [there]. Freud stresses the role of the pleasure principle in this game: it is the attempt to master the mother's absence. For Freud the reel stands for the mother, and the game, a form of mastery. By contrast, Lacan states:

> This reel is not the mother . . . it is a small part of the subject that detaches itself from him while still remaining his, still retained . . . If it is true that the signifier is the first mark, how can we fail to recognise here—from the very fact that this game is accompanied by one of the first oppositions to appear—that it is in the object to which the opposition is applied in the act, the reel, that we must designate the subject. This object we will later give the name it bears in the Lacanian algebra—the *petit a*.[28]

Lacan identifies the reel not with the mother, but the subject, the child himself from who "the object falls. That fall is primal."[29] So what is repeated in the game is "the mother's departure as cause of a *Spaltung* [the splitting of the subject] . . . It is aimed at what, essentially, is not there, *qua* represented."[30]

And because the object is prelinguistic and prespecular, it can never be spoken, only lived: "The essence of the drive . . . is the trace of the act."[31] This is Lacan's existential moment.

Why then is the object partial? The object is partial, not in the manner of a part constitutive of the whole; any more than it is the remainder of castration, it is "literally, the *product* of the cut of castration, the *surplus* generated by it;"[32] i.e., it is produced out of the very split, hence it is partial because *all* objects are partial: there is no whole to start with, only fragmentary pieces; or to put it in expressly Lacanian terms: its status falls within the ontology of the *non-all*.

Returning to Žižek's initial quote, "How to approach the topic Eucharist?" Put simply, the Eucharist, and more specifically the Eucharistic host, is a particular type of object: a partial object, an object of the drive. It is located within the body of the church, yet speaks from an external position; an archaic object more intimate to the church than the church because it

---

28. Lacan, *Seminar XI*, 162.
29. Ibid., *Television*, 85.
30. Ibid., *Seminar XI*, 63.
31. Ibid., 170.
32. Žižek et al., *The Neighbor*, 174.

arises from the loss in Christ's sacrifice. And its status draws attention to the specific subjectivity of the Church.

One can clarify the paradoxical status of the object with reference to Žižek's description of it as "undead." As Žižek explains, to say that someone is undead is not the same as saying he is alive. Where the latter (he is not dead) is merely a negative judgment, the former (he is *un*dead) implies the positive predication *of a* non-predicate: he is unhuman. So where the latter judgment implies that life is *external* to death (he is not dead), the former, whilst negating our understanding of death, nonetheless leaves it *inherent* within what it is to be alive: he is undead. In Žižek's metapsychology this is the mark of the inherent and excessive core from which humanity springs.[33] Similarly, to say the host is undead is to evoke Christ's death, not in terms of the negation of his life, but the negative excess from which the church springs.

Žižek's use of undead invites immediate comparison with the genre of horror to which he refers. I shall return to this question towards the end.

II: Sublimation and the Drive

Before turning to the implications of Žižek's reading, we should allow ourselves to be guided by the concluding sentences to Žižek's quote: "Consequently, is not the 'theological' dimension without which . . . revolution cannot win, the very dimension of the excess of the drive, of its 'too-muchness?' In other words, is not our task—the properly *Christological* one—to change the modality of our being-stuck into a mode that allows, solicits even, the activity of sublimation?"[34]

In Freud's work, the act of sublimation implies the redirection of the sexual drive towards a different object: "the component drive of sexuality, as well the sexual current which is composed of them, exhibit a large capacity for changing their object . . . the sexual trend abandoning its aim of obtaining a component or reproductive pleasure and taking another which is related genetically to the abandoned one is itself no longer sexual and must be described as social . . . we call this process sublimation."[35]

Sublimation accounted in Freud's work for artistic creativity and the basis of sociality, thereby lending it a conservative function. For Lacan by

---

33. Žižek, *The Parallax View*, 22.
34. Ibid., 123, 176.
35. Freud, *Introductory Lectures on Psychoanalysis*, 345.

contrast, sublimation involved not the change of the object (i.e., the substitution of one object for another), but rather the modification of the object itself: "[Sublimation] brings to the *Trieb* a different satisfaction of its aim—this always defined as the natural aim—is precisely what reveals the proper nature of the *Treib* insofar as it is not purely instinct but has a relation with *das Ding* [the Thing] as such, with the Thing insofar as it is distinct form the object.' In sublimation one elevates the object to the dignity of the Thing."[36]

We might understand the Thing [*das Ding*] along the lines of the *object a*, only more fundamental. The Thing is modeled specifically on mother incest.[37] To this extent the Thing has "a primordial function which is located at the level of the initial establishment of the gravitation of the unconscious."[38] The Thing is the impossible and unmapable real, which the primal repression of language has separated from the subject.

In sublimation, we accept then as a possibility that which by definition is excluded from the symbolic; sublimation makes space for the object which has no place in the symbolic. That is not to say in sublimation we directly access the Thing; the Thing is only accessed through the object raised to its status. In other words, it is not the Thing as much as the act of sublimation which satisfies the drive. Hence, the aim is not simply to resign oneself to the inevitable lack within the symbolic (the conservative line), but rather, to manifest that sublime lack in its primacy through the elevation of an object.

So, returning to the Eucharist, according to Žižek the Eucharist is an instance of sublimation, in which the host is elevated to the status of the Thing, the object of the drive, the impossible real—which is less an obscurity of the Truth than the negative excess—which, through sublimation, becomes constitutive of the social body: the church. So where Freud tended to see in religious rituals in terms of a social form of neurosis (albeit it a socially useful one), and hence symptomatic, Žižek reserves a more constitutive role to the Eucharist: sublimation makes space for the paradoxical object, which has no place in the symbolic yet says something specific about that social constitution.

What then of the "Christological task" Žižek attributes to sublimation? Or more particularly: what is the ethical status of sublimation? Here we need to make recourse to the pleasure principle, posited by Freud in

36. Lacan, *Seminar VII*, 111–12.
37. Ibid., 66.
38. Ibid., 62.

his meta-psychological writings. As Lacan explains, the pleasure principle acts in a manner akin to a "homeostatic device."[39] The aim of the pleasure principle is to maintain the psychic functioning of the subject at the lowest level of excitement. For example, in the case of a biological instinct such as hunger, once satisfied the provoked tension dies down. Hunger is satiated by eating well. In this sense, the pleasure principle admits a moment of Aristotelian moderation—one tries to eat neither too little, nor too much.

Yet faced with clinical data, Freud also posited the death drive as a negative counterpart to account for the compulsively reprised dreams or actions which appeared to run counter to the human imperative for self-preservation; i.e., the repetition compulsion. Where the pleasure principle acts in moderation, the drive is transgressive. The drive "has no day or night, no spring or autumn, no rise and fall. It is a constant force."[40]

This excessive quality of excitement at which the death drive aims is what Lacan calls *jouissance*. The pleasure principle is essentially prohibitive, setting limits to enjoyment, and hence is operative on the side of the symbolic (i.e., law), maintaining the status quo; *jouissance* by contrast is on the side of the real, that which is produced as the negative excess of the symbolic.

Returning then the ethical status of sublimation, the elevation of an object to the status of the Thing approaches precisely the transgressive moment which, in contrast to Aristotelian moderation, finds satisfaction in the excessive pleasure of the drive: *jouissance*.

In affirming the death drive in this principle way Lacan was not meaning to posit the death drive as standing alone, over and above all other drives within the series; rather, his point is that it serves as a fundamental component of all partial drives. How specifically does death relate to the partial drive? In the next section I wish to deepen the analysis of the "Christological task" with reference to the scopic drive and its partial object, the gaze.

III: Eucharist and Gaze

Freud initially identified two partial drives (oral, anal) related to the psycho-sexual stages of development; Lacan adds two more: invocatory and scopic; where the oral drive relates to the breast, the anal drive faeces, the invocatory drive relates to the voice, and the scopic drive relates to the gaze. The gaze functions as *object a* in relation to visual perception.

39. Ibid., *Seminar II*, 79–80.
40. Ibid., *Seminar XI*, 165.

For Lacan, it is not simply the case that one is either looking or being looked at; rather, to account for visual perception one must invoke a third element: the gaze. That is to say the act of seeing involves: 1) The subject, the one who sees; 2) the object, the other who is seen or sees; 3) the gaze, the locus that fails to coincide with the visual other. Or, to put it in terms of Oedipal developed in the manner of Boothby: the gaze arises not at the point at which the mother presents an image to the child, "but is seen to be looking for something herself; the suspicion dawns that the mother's desire is directed beyond the child itself to a third position (the Other)."[41] In short, Lacan introduces the *object a* into the theory of vision whose "presence-by-absence serves to produce 'the ambiguity that affects anything inscribed in the register of the scopic drive.'"[42] The *object a* "symbolizes what in the sphere of the signifier is always what presents itself as lost, as what is lost to signification;[43] 'the remainder of the constitution of the subject at the locus of the Other in so far as it has to constitute itself as a speaking [or seeing] subject, as barred subject."[44] The *object a* is "what is lacking, is non-specular, it is not graspable in the image'[45] and hence "it cannot occupy the positional focus of attention. Nonetheless, "it remains active in the invisible framing that produces all positional awareness . . . the *object a* is dispositional object."[46] So, whereas for Sartre "the revelation of the other's look threatens an extinction of my consciousness, for Lacan the gaze is the very condition of consciousness. The gaze is the horizon within which the realm of the visible is established."[47] It is in this sense that the gaze becomes constitutive of vision.

What then does it mean to practically identify with the gaze? It means to identify with what can be termed in the field of speech as the reflexive middle voice; not 'to see [active] or be seen [passive]; [but] to *make oneself seen*.[48] But seen to what?

Lacan's early reference to Roger Callious offers a striking example of what is at stake in the scopic drive and by extension the death drive, not

41. Boothby, *Freud as Philosopher*, 260.
42. Ibid.; Lacan, *Seminar XI*, 83.
43. Lacan, *Anxiety*.
44. Ibid.
45. Ibid.
46. Boothby, *Freud as Philosopher*, 260.
47. Ibid., 258.
48. Lacan, *Seminar XI*, 194–95.

least because it draws upon a heady mix of behavioral science, literature, anthropology, mythography, psychology, and social theory. In "Mimicry and Legendary Psychasthenia,"[49] to which Lacan refers in his early work on the mirror stage,[50] Caillois undertook an exploration of the mimetic functions of insects, in particular the morphological and behavioral adaptation of some species, so as to resemble and simulate their environment. Lacan wants to develop this for a structuralist account of the various forms of psychological behavior related to the eye, and mimicry such as voyeurism or transvestism.

Contrary to the common assumption that an animal's mimicry of its surrounding is a means of defense by way of concealment or camouflage, Caillois highlights the lack of rational connection between camouflage and survival, arguing instead for anti-utilitarian instincts of insects. For example, some inedible species with nothing to fear are also mimetic.[51] Moreover, mimesis "would only apply to carnivores that hunt by sight and not by smell as is often the case."[52] And "predators are not at all fooled by homomorphy or homochromy: they eat crickets that mingle with the foliage of oak trees or weevils that resemble small stones, completely invisible to man."[53] Caillois's own explanations highlight how mimesis is a "a dangerous luxury,"[54] for there are cases in which mimicry causes the creature to go from bad to worse. In the case of the Phyllia: "they browse among themselves, taking each other for real leaves, in such a way that one might accept the idea of a sort of collective masochism leading to mutual homophagy, the simulation of the leaf being a provocation to cannibalism in this kind of totem feast . . . It therefore seems that one ought to conclude with Cuénot that this [mimesis] is an 'epiphenomenon' whose 'defensive utility appears to be null.'"[55]

Caillois's own explanations make recourse to sympathetic magic according to which like produces like. "Mimicry would thus be accurately defined as an incantation fixed at its culminating point and having caught the

---

49. Caillois, "Mimicry and Legendary Psychasthenia."
50. Lacan, *Écrits*, 77.
51. Caillois, "Mimicry and Legendary Psychasthenia", 97.
52. Ibid., 96.
53. Ibid.
54. Ibid., 97.
55. Ibid.

sorcerer in his own trap."[56] Caillois point is two-fold. In the first instance, mimicry "is thus a real temptation by space."[57] In the second instance, it is with represented space that the drama becomes specific, since the living creature, the organism, is no longer the origin of the coordinates, but one point among others; it is dispossessed of its privilege and literally no longer knows where to place itself.[58] In short, the act of camouflage involves an act of renunciation of self (the dangerous luxury). It was this second point that allowed Caillois to make an intriguing connection between the animal mimicry and accounts of schizophrenia derived from psychologist Pierre Janet's writing.

> To these dispossessed souls, space seems to be a devouring force. Space pursues them, encircles them, digests them in a gigantic phagocytosis. It ends by replacing them. Then the body separates itself from thought, the individual breaks the boundary of his skin and occupies the other side of his senses. He tries to look at himself from any point whatever in space. He feels himself becoming space, dark space where things cannot be put. He is similar, not similar to something, but just similar. And he invents spaces of which he is "the convulsive possession." All these expressions shed light on a single process: depersonalization by assimilation to space, i.e., what mimicry achieves morphologically in certain animal species.[59]

As Lacan suggests, Caillois's conclusions are Freudian: "alongside the instinct of self-preservation, which in some way orients the creature towards life, there is generally speaking a sort of instinct of renunciation that orients it toward a mode of reduced existence." The "attraction by space" leads to a thanatophilic movement blurring the frontier between the organism and their milieu. In short, as Frank has puts it, Lacan uses "the terms legendary psychasthenia to classify morphological mimicry as an obsession with space in its derealizing effect."[60]

Lacan further developed this notion of the spatial or material mysticism founded in "Mimicry and Legendary Psychasthenia" in his review of Minkowski's *Le Temps vecu*, describing, "another space besides geometrical

---

56. Ibid.
57. Ibid., 99.
58. Ibid.
59. Ibid., 100.
60. Lacan, *Écrits*, 77.

space, namely the dark space of groping hallucination and music, which is the opposite of clear space, the framework of objectivity. We think we can safely say that this takes us into the 'night of the senses' that is, the 'obscure night' of the mystic."[61]

Lacan's reference to the mystical neatly returns us to the theological dimension. In *Seminar XI*, when he muses over the function of painting—a form of mimicry—he links the frame of a painting to a conservative function along the imaginary access to the extent it pacifies the viewers gaze. By contrast, he links the gaze to the icon. The icon breaks the imaginary function of a picture: at the level of icon, "the artist is operating on the sacrificial plane."[62] In short, Lacan's distinction between the icon and the painting (what Jean Luc Marion might term "idol"), corresponds to Callious's distinction between the conservative theory of mimesis and Legendary Psychasthenia; i.e., a conservative theory of mimicry or a transgressive de-realising of space through an act of renunciation.

Again, to read this into the Eucharist—the icon *par excellence*—one might say that as an object of the gaze—the partial object of the scopic drive—it functions less according to a conservative theory of ritual repetition (a further form of mimicry) than one which invites a derealization of the autonomous subject, all the more so because it is the constitutive moment of the church's subjective body; the Eucharist invites a moment of transgressive renunciation (the death drive) as the celebrant identifies with the object which alludes all clear identification, and the aim is not to merely reconcile one to the lack within the object; rather, by raising the host to the status of the thing actively constitute that lack in a way which awards the primacy of life.

One can put this point more specifically in terms of "repetition," the third of Lacan's *Four Fundamental Concepts of Psychoanalysis* (alongside the unconscious, transference, and drive). Where desire mistakenly looks for its satisfaction in object (the always already lost object), the drive finds satisfaction in precisely the repetitive circling of the object (i.e., the *object a*). Hence, sublimation does not concern rerouting libidinal economy through an alternative object, but raising the object to the status of *das ding* through a repeated loop, circulating round a positive but non-fetishizable *arrival*.

The point here is the repetition is not to be treated in terms of offering the "mythical goal of self-satisfaction" *a la* desire; rather, *a la* drive,

---

61. Ibid., 90.

62. Lacan, *Seminar XI*, 113.

repetition is the means by which the celebrants return to the circularity of the mass and its constant repetition—what Lacan considered the real path of enjoyment [*jouissance*]; the enjoyment that arises from the sheer circularity around the partial object of the drive.

And herein lies the key to Žižek's reading of the Eucharist: we return to the mass not for the sake of a social crutch, but the *jouissance* of the mass itself, which is animated by the centrality awarded a specific object: the *object a*, the partial object of the drive. And the ethical status of the mass in this regard transgresses or surpasses any utilitarian goods as its ends. The ethical status is found in the act of repetition itself. Eucharist is drive.

By way of highlighting this metapsychological account and its theological correlate, one can turn to the work of G. K. Chesterton, whose account of repetition serves in advance of Lacan, and captures fully the spirit the drive within the theological register:

> Now, to put the matter in a popular phrase, it might be true that the sun rises regularly because he never gets tired of rising. His routine might be due, not to a lifelessness, but to a rush of life. The thing I mean can be seen, for instance, in children, when they find some game or joke that they specially enjoy. A child kicks his legs rhythmically through excess, not absence, of life. Because children have abounding vitality, because they are in spirit fierce and free, therefore they want things repeated and unchanged. They always say, "Do it again"; and the grown-up person does it again until he is nearly dead. For grown-up people are not strong enough to exult in monotony. But perhaps God is strong enough to exult in monotony. It is possible that God says every morning, "Do it again" to the sun; and every evening, "Do it again" to the moon. It may not be automatic necessity that makes all daisies alike; it may be that God makes every daisy separately, but has never got tired of making them. It may be that He has the eternal appetite of infancy; for we have sinned and grown old, and our Father is younger than we. The repetition in Nature may not be a mere recurrence; it may be a theatrical ENCORE.[63]

The childlike playfulness Chesterton attributes to God's repetition in creation invites a comparison with Freud's *fort-da* game. Creation is God's *fort-da*. What is at stake for God in creation is not the constant mastery of it, any more than the repetition of the mass is aimed at the mastery of its

---

63. Chesterton, *Orthodoxy*, 92. I thank Marika Rose for highlighting this link and the passage quoted and for her critical comments on this text.

mysteries. That would be to live a life resigned to the absence of Christ's incarnation here on earth. Rather, it is the joy of the constitutive moment of the Church itself, which cannot be exhausted through the playful joy and wonder of childish monotony.

Moreover, given the way Lacan positions his argument in terms of the distinction painting/icon, and the theological resonances of repetition that Lacan derives from Kierkegaard,[64] one might say, not simply as Adrian Johnston does, that "the constant, repetitious iteration of a brute demand for enjoyment is a sufficient conception of the drive-source,"[65] but that the Eucharist is *the* sufficient conception of the drive-source par excellence?[66]

IV: The Liturgical Drive

By way of critical evaluation I wish to draw some comparisons between Catherine Pickstock's critique of the Eucharist in the light of the liturgical reforms of Vatican II,[67] and Žižek's account. According to Pickstock, modern liturgy, while trying to render the language clear and simple with a view to assisting in worship, has tended to corrupt the integrity of the syntax in ways which profoundly re-shape doxology and religious sentiment. In particular, the dominant trend of asyndeton; i.e., the omission of conjunctions from grammatical constructions such that independent clauses can appear separated out, thereby presenting belief as a series of independent articles of faith. As Pickstock explains, the liturgical reformers "ironed out liturgical stammer and constant re-beginning; they simplified the narrative and generic strategy of liturgy in conformity with recognizably secular structures, and rendered simple, constant and self-present the identity of the worshipper."[68] "The insanity of the Cross, the non-sense of sacrifice, gift, and excess, express a wisdom which is obscured in the rationalized exchanges of instrumentalized transactions of the mundane world."[69] As such, "The reader's gaze provokes an individualistic endeavour of self-satisfaction within an area of reduced garnish stimulus, via the supply of missing nutrients of

---

64. For a sustained treatment of Lacan, Kierkegaard, and repetition, see Pound, "Lacan, Kierkegaard and Repetition."

65. Johnston, *Time Driven*, 273.

66. Ibid.

67. Pickstock, *After Writing* and "Thomas Aquinas and the Quest for the Eucharist."

68. Pickstock, *After Writing*, 176.

69. Ibid., 227.

cognition, casting the consummation of subjectivity as epistemological, in contrast to the interpersonal and ontological gaze of Socratic *erōs*."[70]

Similarly, where the older Roman Rite employed syntax of continuous text, thereby mirroring the processional and temporal nature of salvation history, the modern employment of asyndeton presents time as series of discrete and unrelated moments, all in the name of clarity.[71]

For Pickstock, liturgy is not merely the external counterpart to a more primary internal honoring of God, "Rather, it is the most important initial way in which we come to know God and the path to which we must constantly return." Why? Because, as Pickstock puts it: "human beings are mixed creatures, part beast, part angel . . . we combine in our persons every level of the created order from the inorganic, through the organic, through animally psychic to the angelically intellectual."[72]

Hence, her favor for the "middle voice" found in earlier liturgy: a grammatical category, known in the Indo-European languages, and employed to denote a verb which is neither active nor passive. As she points out, some evidence points to its use "not simply to cast an action as either reciprocal or reflexive, but to express the mediation of divine by human action."[73]

Applied more directly to the Eucharistic host, her argument is that the traditional Catholic focus on transubstantiation or the real presence of Christ within the Eucharist yields an problematic dichotomy: either one retreats into the nostalgia for determinacy, such that the Eucharist is accounted for by the literal presence of God—a discrete and miraculous occurrence at the level of substance—or the Eucharist is a "non-essential illustrative symbol."[74] By contrast, her aim is to outwit the duality of presence and absence with recourse to a more contextual and existential account of the mass. Briefly: "the key to the transcending of the dichotomy . . . in the Eucharist lies in the 'logic' . . . of *mystery* which . . . implies a positive but not fetishizable *arrival* in which signs essentially participate, but which they cannot exhaust, for that mystery arrives by virtue of a transcendent plenitude which perfectly integrates absence and presence. Thus a more positive account of the sign is suggested, for the sign here is neither emptily

---

70. Ibid., 98.
71. Bates, "Sinful Asyndeton?"
72. Pickstock, "Liturgy and the Senses," in *Paul's New Moment*, 125.
73. Ibid., *After Writing*, 35.
74. Ibid., "Truth and Language," 93.

'left behind' through postponement, nor is it the instrumental Ramist sign which secures the real in an artificial exactitude."[75]

One may summarize the contours of her argument in the following way. For Pickstock, it is not that liturgy is man-made, but that it is both man-made and makes man, forming the celebrant subject. And the instrumentalism of modern liturgical reforms contributes to the modern autonomous individual, rendering belief is a matter of private faith. Her defense of the old Roman Rite and its complex syntax concerns the way it upsets the modern subject, in particular through its invocation of the middle voice. The middle voice resists simple binary oppositions (e.g. life/death) and helps mediate the divine. Hence, the Eucharist is not to be taken as an instance of dramatic intervention, but a procession which one repeats endlessly around an object whose arrival, like the subject, cannot be reified.

It is significant in this regard that Pickstock links the gaze to the middle voice, in the manner of Lacan. To gaze on the Host is not to provoke "satisfaction" but as Lacan suggests, an instance of the icon *par excellence*: Christ. Such identification cannot be drawn along the imaginary axis, but instead the symbolic and real; it is also an existential moment, an act of sublimation which transgresses the reduction of the mass to a homeostatic principle, i.e., a social neurosis, suggesting something instead of the order of *jouissance*. And with that identification comes risk, the dangerous luxury of self-renunciation, and the derealization of secular space in favor of liturgically shaped spaces.

V: The Horror of the Mass

What then is the relationship between horror and joy in these two approaches, psychoanalysis and theology? In the first place, one might ask what happens when we reduce them to the same in the manner of Žižek; i.e., we read the drive and the Eucharist through the genre of horror such that one amounts to the other? Here we can turn to Tina Pippen who uses zombie literature as a template for biblical interpretation. Taking Lazarus and Christ as her examples, she invites their comparison to zombies, the former being the undead precursor to the revenant Christ—"the King of the living dead"—whose undead substance is then taken up through the Eucharist.[76] In particular, she draws attention to the link between zombies and

---

75. Ibid.

76. Pippin, "Behold, I Stand at the Door and Knock."

the apocalyptic imagination: "zombies emerge out of Empire, from imperial injustices, economic inequities, environmental destruction (nuclear, viral), and despair about the future," which she matches by the biblical *parousia*. Indeed, Žižek's own apocalyptic soundings and fascination with the undead implicitly makes this connection.[77] Commenting on Žižek's reference with which we began—the linking of the Eucharist to the undead—she suggest in the first instance that we eat it out of a desire for eternal life; a life not quite with us. Dying to this world but not yet born to the next, Christians are Zombies, "the heaven-bound that got tired of waiting" (thus constituting a reading along the imaginary axis to the extent that the desire for eternal life amounts to a defense in the face of apocalyptic anxiety). But she also cautions the reader. The possibility of eternal life—a life between life and death—invokes the possibility of running amok infecting all those whom this narrative touches; translated politically, we might say transgression without progression.

In the second place, one could treat the wider contestation between their frameworks of thought: dialectics or participation.[78] As Jon Mills explains, there is a necessary determination to negation in dialectics because it springs from the primacy of the abyss. Dialectic proceeds *through* negation, the experience of which is death, and in the surpassing of that form, new life. Hence dialectics tends to oscillate between the two.[79] The problem arises when this is translated politically. A political act must traverse the abyss in the hope that the event gives rise to a situation the outcome of which cannot be determined. In short, if we are to speak of the drive in regard of political action, it also quickly turns into a politics of transgression without progression. By contrast, locating the depositional object of the drive liturgically invites the moment of transgression yet with progression, the processional body of Christ, a social theory in itself.

In the third place, one could assert a case of what Žižek calls the "parallax gap, the confrontation of two closely linked perspectives between which no neutral common ground is possible."[80] As incompatible as Žižek's dialectical ontology is with a Christian metaphysics of participation, their perspectives on the Eucharist are closely linked though their descriptions

---

77. Žižek, *Living in the End Times*.

78. For a sustained treatment of this aspect see Davis, Žižek, and Milbank, *The Monstrosity of Christ*.

79. Mills, *The Unconscious Abyss*, 13.

80. Žižek, *The Parallax View*, 4.

of a dispositional object (the *object a*; the Eucharist), and the shift from one position to the other is simply a shift of perspective (in this sense the parallax is variant of Jastrow's duck/rabbit). Žižek's work, and principally his introduction of the death drive, functions to assert that the distance a church places between itself and a culture of impurity is inherent to the church itself. Indeed, does not the gospel narrative of the parable of the Leaven make precisely this point? Christ identifies the kingdom of heaven with a form of mold that relishes dank-dark conditions. And while this may be a rhetorical dig at the pharisaic model—i.e., its not that this is a positive description of the kingdom but a means to challenge the existing structure—one must also contend with the greatest of paradoxes in which God is directly identified with humanity in the incarnation.

Hence, if horror films are to provide a template for theology, then one does well to radicalize the link between horror and Christianity: it is not so much the chaos and destruction wrought by individuals that is the most horrific moment of the film, but the very opposite. What is frightening about Lazarus and Christ, more specifically, is not that they are undead, but the very possibility that they signify in God the death of death and hence the excess of life and love.

In short, rather than reduce one to the other such that both amount to the same (i.e., the genre of horror), or oppose one reading to the other (i.e., analogy verses dialectics) one should explore the possibility that one side radicalizes the inner position of the former precisely by virtue of its opposition. Or, put another way, rather than see horror as the path that Christianity must take to radicalize its message of love *a la* Žižek, one can posit Christian love *as* the true horror.

By way of example, consider the climactic scenes of David Fincher's *Se7en*. As John Doe (Kevin Spacey), Detective Mills (Brad Pitt), and Detective Somerset (Morgan Freeman) "drive" out to the "drop" point, Doe tells Mills that following the sequence of events about to be played out, Mills will be remembered forever. In a calculated move Doe has decapitated Mill's wife (the sin of envy—Doe was jealous of Mill's normal life) in the expectation that upon discovering her severed head Mill himself will act out the final sin in the series: wrath, i.e., killing Doe in a moment of retributive rage. Yet the implication is not that Mill's will be remembered for playing out the hand given by Doe, but the possibility that he may resist the sin of wrath and thereby break the cycle, the very thing Doe was trying to do. This is the true horror that Mill is unable to confront: the love of forgiveness.

For this reason, one does well to read Žižek with Lacan and Pickstock in mind. From the perspective of the Lacanian drive, identification with the partial object repeats the constitutive moment of loss, and in doing so raises the object—the host—to the dignity of the Thing, around which celebrants endlessly process rather than run amok. The Eucharist is an act constituting lack in a way that awards the primacy to the path of enjoyment, the negative excess of joy upon which God's church—a social body—is constituted; a moment that takes us back to an infancy in which we may ask for more, for no other reason than the joy of worship, for joy may be the true redemptive horror offered in the Mass.

Bibliography

Bates, J. Barrington. "Sinful Asyndeton?: Problematic Syntax in Contemporary Liturgical Texts." *Theology Today* 58:403. No pages. Online: http://ttj.sagepub.com/content/58/3/399.

Boothby, Richard. *Freud as Philosopher: Metapsychology after Lacan*. New York: Routledge, 2001.

Braungardt, Jürgen. "Theology After Lacan? A Psychoanalytic Approach to Theological Discourse." *Other Voices* 1:3 (1999). No pages. Online: http://www.othervoices.org/1.3/jbraungardt/theology.html.

Caillois, Roger. "Mimicry and Legendary Psychasthenia." In *The Edge of Surrealism: A Roger Caillois Reader*, edited by Claudine Frank, 89–106. Durham: Duke University Press, 2003.

Chesterton, G. K. *Orthodoxy*. Chicago: Moody Bible Institute, 2009.

Davis, Creston. "Subtractive Liturgy." In *Paul's New Moment: Continental Philosophy and the Future of Christian Theology*, edited by John Milbank, Slavoj Žižek, and Creston Davis, 146–68. Grand Rapids: Brazos, 2010.

Evans, Dylan. *An Introductory Dictionary of Lacanian Psychoanalysis*. New York: Routledge, 1996.

Freud, Sigmund. "Obsessive Actions and Religious Practices." In *The Standard Edition of the Complete Works of Sigmund Freud*, edited and translated by J. Strachey, vol. 9. London: Hogarth, 1959.

———. "Instincts and their Vicissitudes." In *The Standard Edition of the Complete Works of Sigmund Freud*, edited and translated by J. Strachey, vol. 14. London: Hogarth, 1959.

Harari, Roberto. *Lacan's Four Fundamental Concepts of Psychoanalysis: An Introduction*. Translated by Judith Filc. New York: Other, 2004.

Jannus, Maire. "The *Démontage* of the Drive." In *Reading Seminar XI: Lacan's Four Fundamental Concepts of Psychoanalysis*, edited by Richard Feldstein et al. Albany, NY: SUNY, 1995.

Johnston, Adrian. *Time Driven: Metapsychology and the Splitting of the Drive*. Evanston, IL: Northwestern University Press, 2005.

Kant, Immanuel. "What is Enlightenment?" In *The Portable Enlightenment Reader*. Edited by Issac Kramnick. London: Penguin, 1995.

Lacan, J. *Anxiety*. Translated by C. Gallagher. Unpublished paper, the seminar of March 13 1963.

———. "The Mirror Stage as Formative of the *I* Function as Revealed in Psychoanalytic Experience." In *Écrits: The First Complete Edition in English*, translated by B. Fink, 75–81. New York: Norton, 2006.

———. *Seminar II: The Ego in Freud's Theory and in the Technique of Psychoanalysis, 1954–1955*. Edited by J-A. Miller. Translated by S. Tomaselli. New York: Norton, 1994.

———. *The Seminar of Jacques Lacan, Vol. VII: The Ethics of Psychoanalysis (1959–60)*. Translated by D. Porter. New York: Routledge, 1992.

———. *Le Séminar. Livre VIII. Le transfert, 1960–61*. Edited by J-A. Miller. Paris: Seuil, 1991.

———. *The Seminar of Jacques Lacan, Vol. XI: The Four Fundamental Concepts of Psychoanalysis*. Edited by J-A. Miller. Translated by A. Sheridan. London: Verso, 1998.

———. *The Seminar of Jacques Lacan, XX: On Feminine Sexuality: the Limits of Love and Knowledge (1972–1973)*. Edited by J-A Miller. Translated by B. Fink. New York: Norton, 1998.

———. *Television*. Translated by D. Hollier et al., New York: W. W. Norton, 1990.

Laplanche, Jean, and J.-B. Pontalis. *The Language of Psychoanalysis*. London: Karnac, 1988.

Milbank, John, and Slavoj Žižek. *The Monstrosity of Christ: Paradox or Dialectic*. Edited by Creston Davis. Cambridge: MIT, 2009.

Mills, Jon. *The Unconscious Abyss: Hegel's Anticipation of Psychoanalysis*. Albany, NY: SUNY, 2002.

Pickstock, Catherine. *After Writing: On the Liturgical Consumption of Philosophy*. Oxford: Blackwell, 1998.

———. "Liturgy and the Senses." In *Paul's New Moment: Continental Philosophy and the Future of Christian Theology*, edited by John Milbank, Slavoj Žižek, and Creston Davis. Grand Rapids: Brazos, 2010.

———. "Thomas Aquinas and the Quest for the Eucharist." In *The Radical Orthodoxy Reader*, edited by John Milbank and S. Oliver. London: Routledge, 2009.

———. "Truth and Language." In *Truth in Aquinas*, edited by J. Milbank and C. Pickstock, New York and London: Routledge, 2001.

Pippin, T. "Behold, I Stand at the Door and Knock: The living dead and apocalyptic dystopia." *Relegere* 6:3 (2010). No pages. Online: http://www.relegere.org/index.php/relegere/search/advanced.

Pound, M. "Lacan, Kierkegaard and Repetition." *Quodlibet Journal* 7:2 (2005)

———. *Theology, Psychoanalysis, Trauma*. London: SCM, 2007.

———. "The Transformation of Eros: Reflections on Desire in Jacques Lacan." In *Encounter Between Eastern Orthodoxy and Radical Orthodoxy: Transfiguring the World Through the Word*, edited by Adrian Pabst and Christoph Schneider, 271–290. Aldershot: Ashgate, 2009.

Winquist, C. "Lacan and Theology." In *Post-Secular Theology: Between Philosophy and Theology*, edited by Philip Blond, 305–17. London: Routledge, 1998.

Wyshodgrod, E. et al. *Lacan and Theological Discourse*. Albany, NY: SUNY, 1989.

Žižek, Slavoj. *Living in the End Times*. London, Verso, 2010.
———. *The Parallax View*. Cambridge: MIT, 2006.
Žižek, Slavoj, et al., *The Neighbor: Three Enquiries into Political Theology*. Chicago: University of Chicago Press, 2005.

www.ingramcontent.com/pod-product-compliance
Lightning Source LLC
Chambersburg PA
CBHW051054230426
43667CB00013B/2292